COUNTY COLLEGE OF MORRIS LIBRARY

Gone to Wear the Victor's Crown

Morris County, New Jersey and the Civil War
A Documentary Account

Compiled and Edited by David Mitros

A Publication of the Morris County
Heritage Commission

D0900406

Gone to Wear the Victor's Crown

Morris County, New Jersey and the Civil War
A Documentary Account

A collection of letters, newspaper articles, personal accounts, and other archival sources relating to Morris County's involvement in the Civil War — with an appendix listing Civil War veteran grave sites throughout Morris County.

Compiled and Edited by David Mitros

Foreword by G. Kurt Piehler, Ph.D.
Appendix Compiled by Nick DeRose

Published by the Morris County Heritage Commission with funding provided by a grant from the New Jersey Historical Commission. Additional funding provided by the Morris County Board of Chosen Freeholders.

Copyright 1998, Morris County Heritage Commission
All rights reserved

Library of Congress Catalog Card Number: 98-91477
ISBN: 0-9664119-0-0

Graphic design by Gene Cass
Printing by Redmond Press, Denville, NJ

Manufactured in the United States of America

Cover illustration: Etching, *A Rally Around the Flag* by Edwin Forbes, from *Thirty Years After: An Artist's Story of the Great War*.

Illustrations not otherwise attributed are taken from *Battles and Leaders of the Civil War*.

This book is printed on acid free paper.

F
142
Mf
56
1998

17|14|98

Foreword

Even before the guns had fallen silent, Americans strived to make sense of the Civil War. On a warm autumn day in 1864, Abraham Lincoln dedicated the Gettysburg Cemetery with a brief address that pondered whether a nation "conceived in Liberty, and dedicated to the proposition that all men were created equal" could survive the test of a long civil war. In speaking of the brave men "living and dead" who struggled the year before in the most decisive battle of the war, Lincoln declared that they helped ensure that the nation would "experience a new birth of freedom."

The Civil War forged a new nation and settled great constitutional issues that had divided Americans since the founding of the republic. Decades before Confederates attacked Fort Sumter in 1861, there were sharp sectional differences over the questions of federal supremacy and whether states should retain the right to leave the Union. Beginning in the 1820s, a growing number of white Southerners believed that the "right" of secession could be exercised by their respective state governments if the laws enacted in Washington threatened the institution of slavery. Robert E. Lee's surrender at Appomattox in 1865 settled this issue and ended Southern nationalism and the doctrine of secession. Most white Southerners mourned the "lost cause" of the Confederacy, but accepted federal supremacy even as they challenged the terms of postwar settlement under Reconstruction.

The Civil War put to rest the question of slavery, an issue that had torn asunder the fabric of American society for over eighty years. In 1775 all thirteen of the original colonies permitted human bondage. In the era of the Revolution, a growing number of Americans, most notably Thomas Jefferson, recognized the inconsistency between slavery and republican ideals expressed in the Declaration of Independence. In many regions, farmers found free labor more profitable to use than enslaved workers and, consequently, either freed or sold their slaves. These political and economic forces helped encourage an abolitionist movement that met with increasing success above the Mason-Dixon line. By the early 1820s, most Northern states had abolished slavery and liberated all but a small number of slaves.

Unfortunately, the invention of the cotton gin in 1793 breathed new life into the economic viability of slavery in the South. As a result, white Southerners and some Northern sympathizers began to develop a doctrine that proclaimed this institution as a necessary evil, even a positive good for maintaining white equality. A small group of abolitionists passionately challenged this view and insisted that holding fellow human beings in bondage was morally reprehensible. Most Northerners did not support abolition, but over the course of the 1840s and 1850s, a growing number feared that slavery posed a threat to a republican society because of the inexorable march of this institution into the western territories. The Republican Party of Abraham Lincoln maintained that the expansion of slavery must be halted to preserve opportunities for free white labor in the West. Lincoln had no plan nor desire for immediate abolition, but his election provoked South Carolina and a wave of Southern states to leave the Union for fear that his incoming administration would place restrictions on slavery in the territories. In this pivotal year, most Northerners and Southerners agreed on one point: that slavery needed new territories to thrive, otherwise the institution would eventually decay and die.

When Northerners went to war in 1861, most fought to preserve the Union, not free the slaves. But in the end, the Lincoln Administration, in 1862, embraced abolition as a way to strike at the economic and social fabric of Southern society. The Emancipation Proclamation did not end slavery in the United States; freedom was granted only to slaves held by disloyal Southerners. To a large degree, this proclamation recognized and responded to the enslaved and their quest for freedom. In the disorder of war, many African Americans fled their masters for what they hoped would be the safety of the Union lines. When given the opportunity to serve in the military, tens of thousands of free blacks from the North and recent slaves flocked to join the ranks of the Union army and navy. The black soldier and sailor doomed the institution of slavery and paved the way for the complete abolition of slavery in 1865 under the Thirteenth Amendment to the Constitution.

National unity and the abolition of slavery came at a terrible cost in lives. Advances in military technology, especially the use of the minié ball, vastly increased the "killing range," and led to staggering casualties on both sides. Medical care remained primitive by modern standards and if a soldier was not killed in battle, he often died of infection or faced the loss of a limb from an amputation. Until the twentieth century, most soldiers died not from an enemy's bullet but from disease, and the Civil War was no different. All told, over a million Americans on both sides were killed or wounded in this conflict.

When the fighting began in the Spring of 1861, both the amateur warrior and the seasoned graduate of West Point expected a brief and relatively bloodless war. In the first years of the war, the generals on both sides tried to follow the "lessons" of Napoleonic warfare that they had faithfully learned at the U.S. Military Academy at West Point by struggling for victory in a single climactic battle that would defeat the opposing side. In the end, the war would neither be won nor lost in one single battle, but in long and costly sieges during campaigns launched by Ulysses S. Grant against Lee's army in 1864 and 1865. In his march to the sea through Georgia and a succeeding campaign in South Carolina, William T. Sherman targeted civilian property for destruction as a way to undercut popular support for the Confederate war effort.

The story of the Civil War must include strategic plans of generals and the clash of great armies on the battlefield. Politicians in Washington and Richmond debated great and insignificant issues. To many Southern towns and cities, and even a number of Northern ones, the conflict brought devastation and destruction. Many communities, especially those in the line of Sherman's march in 1864 and 1865, took decades to recover from the war.

The Civil War had a profound impact on Morris County, New Jersey. Scores of residents answered Lincoln's call for troops in 1861; and some, like William Van Fleet of Parsippany, never again saw their families. Those who remained at home, especially women, supported the U.S. Sanitary Commission and other organizations designed to improve the medical care offered to wounded soldiers. As in other northern communities, the Emancipation Proclamation and the Lincoln Administration's conduct of the war generated intense debate. In the Election of 1864, Lincoln failed to win the support of the majority of the county's voters. But a few months later, residents of Morris County greeted the news of Lee's surrender in April 1865 with both exhilaration and relief. Like other loyal Americans, they grieved deeply at the word of Lincoln's assassination a few days later.

Residents of Morris County struggled for years after the fighting ended over the Civil War's legacy. They debated, as did the country, the degree to which the federal government should reorder Southern society and protect the rights of African Americans. And they remembered the fallen. Only six years after Appomattox, hundreds gathered on the Morristown Green and dedicated a memorial to those from Morris County who died in the service of a cause that preserved the Union and forever ended slavery in the United States.

The Morris County Heritage Commission and David Mitros have produced a volume that allows the participants in the Civil War to speak for themselves. By including the voices of both political leaders and officers as well as those of average soldiers and citizens, they have created an enduring work. It will inspire scholars and students to probe more deeply into the impact of the Civil War on Morris County. Above all, the average reader will come away from this book with a greater appreciation of the heroic sacrifices made by soldiers and citizens of Morris County in their struggle to ensure "that government of the people, by the people, for the people, shall not perish from the earth."

G. Kurt Piehler, Ph.D.

Preface

When the Public Television series "The Civil War," produced by Ken Burns, first aired in 1992, it stimulated renewed interest in America's greatest military conflict. This fine production featured archival photographs accompanied by a narrative that included readings of letters and other archival texts. The popularity of "The Civil War" shows that people welcome the opportunity to learn history through accurate firsthand accounts — as an alternative to learning it through fictionalized interpretations commonly found in literature and film. Moreover, the series made people aware of the value of letters, diaries, and other archival sources in bringing history to life.

This volume attempts to further our understanding of the issues surrounding the Civil War through the writings of people living in Morris County, New Jersey. It is intended for researchers and general readers alike. The documents that comprise this work include newspaper articles, letters, and a diary, all organized chronologically according to theme. Most were transcribed from original archival sources. Others had been previously transcribed and used with permission; the latter include the letters of James C. Vail — originally transcribed by Joanne Catlett of Historic Speedwell — and the letters of Josiah Quincy Grimes — originally prepared as a pamphlet by Norman V. Grimes, then later transcribed and deposited in the Rutgers Special Collections and University Archives, Rutgers University Library. Some of these writings and excerpts thereof have appeared elsewhere. For instance, Charles F. Hopkins' account of the Underground Railroad in Morris County originally appeared in the 1910 publication, *Boonton, Gem of the Mountain*, while his account of Andersonville Prison is the subject of a popular book edited by William B. Styple and John J. Fitzpatrick. Likewise, Edmund D. Halsey's Civil War diary has drawn the attention of several historians including Joseph G. Bilby, Marjorie Kaschewski (whose series of articles on Halsey appeared in Morris County's *Daily Record* in 1973), and most recently, Bruce Chadwick. (See the Select Bibliography for book titles.)

In addition to these writings, an extensive list of Civil War Veteran grave sites appears in the appendix. This list was compiled by Nick DeRose over a two-year period, then entered into a computer database by the editor.

All supplementary text has been written by the editor.

These archival writings have been carefully edited to make them more readable without violating the author's intent or stylistic integrity. Spelling and punctuation were modernized if necessary; long paragraphs were sometimes broken up. In some instances phrases, sentences, or paragraphs were eliminated. Ellipses were used to indicate deletions within a given paragraph or, in several cases, to join parts of two paragraphs to form a new paragraph. Ellipses were *not* used to indicate deletions of entire paragraphs. All annotations immediately follow the documents to which they relate.

This collection is by no means complete. Those seriously interested in further pursuing the subject are encouraged to visit Morris County's archives to research the sources from which these materials were compiled. They are also encouraged to use other sources not found in this collection. Some of these are listed in the "Select Bibliography." In addition, they should visit other archival depositories throughout the county that contain Civil War document collections. These include the Willows at Fosterfields Living Historic Farm, Macculloch Hall Historical Museum, Historic Speedwell, and the Joint Free Library of Morristown and Morris Township.

Acknowledgments

For assistance rendered, I wish to express my grateful appreciation —
To the Local History and Genealogy Department of the Joint Free Library of Morristown and Morris Township, Rutgers Special Collections and University Archives — Rutgers University Library, the Parsippany Historical and Preservation Society, Historic Speedwell, the Rockaway Borough Library, the Holmes Library in Boonton, and the Hunterdon County Historical Society. All provided access to primary source materials.

To Daniel J. Morris, great grandson of Edmund D. Halsey, for granting permission to publish sections of the Halsey diary; to Gerald Hopkins, grandson of Charles Hopkins, for granting permission to publish excerpts of Charles Hopkins' wartime diary.

To Peter Meany, O.S.B. of St. Mary's Abbey in Morristown, Bill Monroe and Mary Robinson of the Rockaway Historical Society, Joseph G. Bilby (author of *Three Rousing Cheers*), Bruce Chadwick (Edmund D. Halsey scholar), Jim Woodruff, Fran Kaminski, Pat Winship of the Newark Public Library Humanities Division, and the Reference Department staff of the Morris County Library. All these people provided information necessary for completing the book.

To G. Kurt Piehler, Ph.D., Department of History, Rutgers University, and author of *Remembering War the American Way* — for writing the foreword, reading the initial draft of the manuscript, and offering critical comments and many helpful suggestions. To Margaret Smith Crocco, Ph.D., Department of Social Studies, Columbia University, who also read the initial draft and offered helpful suggestions.

To Nick DeRose, Historical Society of the Rockaways — who generously provided his invaluable list of Civil War Veteran burial sites for inclusion in the appendix.

To Mary DeRose for providing information on Joseph Warren Revere and for offering useful comments and suggestions regarding the section of the manuscript devoted to Revere.

To Susan Lorenzo who helped transcribe articles from the *True Democratic Banner* and *Jerseyman*.

To all the members of the Morris County Heritage Commission. They have enthusiastically supported this project since its inception.

To Knute Seebohm, Jim DelGiudice, and Tom Waldron, for having generously volunteered their time to proofread the text.

Special acknowledgment goes to the New Jersey Historical Commission and the Morris County Board of Chosen Freeholders for having provided the funding that made this publication possible.

Contents

Introduction

Historian John T. Cunningham has often referred to New Jersey as the northernmost of the border states. The reason is partially geographic. New Jersey's southernmost boundary falls below the Mason-Dixon Line. More important than geography is the fact that New Jersey's pre-Civil War economy relied heavily (though not exclusively) on trade with the South. Southerners purchased large quantities of cereals and cider from Jersey farmers. They also bought a variety of goods manufactured in New Jersey's cities. For example, Newark, one of the largest leather producers in the country, found a very profitable market in the South for products that included saddlery, harnesses, and slave shoes.

Before the Civil War, many Jerseyans, like their Southern counterparts, ardently defended states' rights. Not surprisingly, they defended the rights of Southerners to keep slaves. Their pro-slavery stance stemmed, in part, from the fear that freed slaves from the South would migrate to New Jersey and compete for jobs. New Jersey's Democrats sent pro-slavery senators to Congress. Some New Jersey Democrats were secessionists who favored a Northern confederacy. Others, including former New Jersey Governor Rodman M. Price, advocated secession to the Southern Confederacy, hoping this would benefit the state's economy. Though pro-Southern, pro-slavery attitudes in New Jersey strongly influenced state politics, Jerseyans avoided the violent factional conflict normally associated with the politics of genuine border states.

Although one-third of New Jersey's voting population during the war consisted of well-organized Southern sympathizers known as "Copperheads," another third consisted of Democrats who remained loyal to the Union while opposing Lincoln; they advocated a negotiated settlement to the war. The remaining third, comprising Republicans and "War Democrats," supported the Administration, though the latter did not agree with the abolitionist views advocated by the Republican Party. At no point during the war did the Copperheads come close to controlling the state legislature.

During the election of 1860, Abraham Lincoln carried only ten counties in New Jersey, mostly from the central or southern part of the state. This region, with its substantial Quaker population, had traditionally been less tolerant of slavery. In the northern part of the state, where many people had owned slaves well into the nineteenth century, Lincoln carried only two counties — Morris and Passaic. But even in Morris County, substantial opposition to Lincoln arose among Morris County's Democrats. Still, when Fort Sumter fell, most of the County's residents,

1

Republicans and Democrats alike, united to support the Union cause, despite their differences on the slavery issue.

With the onset of war, an atmosphere of celebration prevailed. At public gatherings in Morris County and throughout the entire state, people expressed their patriotism by raising liberty poles and flags accompanied by colorful parades of local militias and military bands. Many greeted the war as if something wonderful were about to happen. Such enthusiasm was motivated by the highest of ideals, especially among Republicans who viewed the war not only as a struggle to save the Union, but also, as a holy war against slavery and the forces of oppression.

The conflict that followed resulted in a horrendous loss of life on both sides. Expectations of early Union victory gave way to disappointment when Gen. George McClellan failed to take Richmond early in the war. When it became evident that the war would be a prolonged and costly endeavor, volunteers grew fewer. Eventually the government imposed a draft, which many tried to escape, either legally, through hiring substitutes, or illegally, by "skedaddling." Although Lincoln was reelected in 1864, he failed to carry Kentucky, Delaware, and New Jersey. General McClellan, running as the Democratic candidate, defeated Lincoln by 396 votes in Morris County. The only townships carried by Lincoln in Morris County were Pequannock (by a margin of 352 votes), Hanover (by a margin of 72 votes), and Mendham (by a margin of four votes). Throughout the war, debate continued over the administration's policies, but the majority of both parties in Morris County and throughout the state remained staunchly pro-Union.

Morris County contributed significantly to the Union cause. Many Morris County men fought in the 11th and 15th New Jersey Regiments, both seeing heavy action in many major battles throughout the duration of the conflict. By the end of the war, Morris County had lost over 380 men. The nation, including both North and South, sustained casualties of over a million men killed or wounded, far more than in any other American war. At an enormous cost, the federal government succeeded in reuniting the nation and abolishing slavery.

For the families of the slain soldiers in Morris County and throughout the North, the sense of loss surely outweighed the triumph of victory, but many found consolation in the conviction that their fallen husbands, sons, and fathers had died for a just and noble cause.

Chapter 1

Prelude to the Civil War: Slavery, Abolitionism, and the Mexican War

Originally, the North fought the South to preserve the Union, not to free the slaves. But it was the slavery issue that caused the split between North and South that eventually led to war.

From our nation's inception, the federal government tried to regulate slavery. In 1785 Congress passed the Northwest Ordinance, which forbade the expansion of slavery into the region that now comprises Ohio, Indiana, and Illinois. Most states at that time wanted to shut off the African slave trade. But South Carolina and Georgia required slave labor in their rice paddies and malaria infested swamps. By way of compromise, Congress voted for the continuance of the slave trade until 1807.

Though slavery had declined during the eighteenth century, it experienced a resurgence after Eli Whitney invented the cotton gin in 1793. Whitney's new device removed seeds from cotton at an unprecedented rate, making large scale cotton production more feasible. This led to a greater demand for slaves by wealthy plantation owners who believed that white people could not labor under the hot sun without ruining their health. Throughout the nineteenth century, the cultivation of cotton through slave labor sustained the South's agrarian economy.

By contrast, the North based its economy on industrial production. As the Northern economy expanded, its population increased through an influx of European immigrants. Consequently, the balance of power in the House of Representatives favored the North. The South, however, maintained political equilibrium in the Senate. But in 1819 Congress threatened the balance of power when the House of Representatives passed the Tallmage Act in an attempt to prevent the admission of Missouri as a slave state. The Tallmage Act stipulated that no one could bring slaves into Missouri. It also provided for the gradual emancipation of children born to slave parents already living there.

During the ensuing debate, Southerners expressed their fear that Congress might ban slavery in other newly admitted states, or worse, that it might even try to abolish slavery in the older southern states. A small but vocal group of Northern abolitionists reinforced Southern fears by using the opportunity to condemn the evils of slavery, proclaiming their desire to stop it from spreading.

Despite abolitionist pleas, Congress agreed to admit Missouri as a slave state. But to maintain the balance of power in the Senate, Congress also admitted Maine, formerly part of Massachusetts, as a free state. In so doing, it maintained the balance of power in the Senate—12 free versus 12 slave states. In addition, Congress attempted to curb the expansion of slavery by restricting its spread south of the line 36° 30'—Missouri's southern boundary. The Missouri Compromise displeased many on both sides of the slavery debate, but it helped avoid a more serious split between Northern and Southern factions.

Slavery remained a prominent national issue, which became an international issue when American settlers introduced slaves to the Mexican territory of Texas in violation of the Mexican constitution. Though Mexico tolerated the Americans' presence, friction increased between Mexicans and Americans over slavery, immigration, and states rights. When the autocratic Mexican dictator Santa Anna assumed power in 1823, he disregarded many of the rights guaranteed to Texans by the Mexican Constitution. The Texans revolted. Santa Anna sent his numerically superior army against them. His soldiers killed 200 Americans defending the Alamo and slaughtered 400 more at Goliad after they had surrendered. A Texan force under Sam Houston retaliated by capturing Santa Anna and his army at San Jacinto. Houston made Santa Anna sign a treaty granting Texans the territory north of the Rio Grande River. When released, Santa Anna repudiated the agreement, maintaining, correctly, that Houston extorted it under duress. President Andrew Jackson, concerned about American neutrality, did not recognize Texas until his last day in office.

But Mexico still regarded Texas as Mexican territory and threatened war with the United States if it tried to annex Texas. Texas, vastly outnumbered by their Mexican foe, openly negotiated with England and France in the hope of securing protectorate status. Such a prospect especially attracted the British, eager to make Texas into a puppet state that would keep American expansionism in check.

Responding to the British threat, the lame-duck President John Tyler, in 1844, arranged to annex Texas by a joint resolution of Congress. Though antislavery forces opposed the annexation of the slave territory, the resolution passed early in 1845.

Following the annexation, Texans immediately wanted to extend the southern boundaries from the Nueces River to the Rio Grande. They were supported by President James K. Polk and encouraged by the popular Doctrine of Manifest Destiny, which viewed American expansionism as an expression of God's will that democracy should spread throughout the Western Hemisphere with the help of American intervention. The Mexicans, understandably, saw the Americans as arrogant bullies.

They still viewed Texas as a province in revolt. When President Polk's administration offered to purchase California from Mexico for 25 million dollars, the Mexicans would not permit American Ambassador John Slidell to present such an "insulting" proposition. Responding to this rebuff, President Polk, on January 13, 1846, ordered 4,000 troops under Gen. Zachary Taylor to the Rio Grande River to deliberately provoke a conflict with Mexican forces. When no conflict came, Polk, on May 9, informed his cabinet that he planned to propose to Congress a declaration of war on the tenuous basis of (a) unpaid claims against Mexico for damage to American property during the Texas rebellion, and (b) Ambassador Slidell's rejection. Two members of Polk's cabinet suggested that he should wait for the Mexicans to fire the first shot—which they did that very evening when a Mexican force crossed the Rio Grande and attacked the Americans, killing 16 of Gen. Taylor's men. Polk easily convinced Congress to declare war on Mexico for having shed American blood on "American soil."

Hotheaded Southwestern expansionists, desirous of additional Mexican territory, welcomed the war. So did Mexicans, eager to teach the "gringos" to the north a lesson by defeating its armies and freeing its Negro slaves.

Unfortunately for Mexico, the Americans had better generals. The Mexicans lost the war. With it they lost enormous territories extending to the west coast, including California. The United States partially compensated the Mexicans for their loss. According to the terms of the treaty, Mexico received $18,250,000. Supporters of the war maintained that the Americans offered the money in the "Anglo-Saxon spirit of fair play." Critics suggested that they offered it out of guilt.

Though most Americans supported the Mexican War, many Northern abolitionists saw it as a plot by the Southern "slavocracy" to expand slavery. The abolitionists took a strongly pacifist position. They also tried to prevent the formation of new slave territories. In 1846, shortly after the war began, David Wilmont of Pennsylvania introduced a bill that would have outlawed slavery in Texas or any other territory wrested from Mexico during the Mexican War. The bill passed in the House twice but not in the Senate where it met strong Southern opposition. Although the Wilmont Proviso failed to become law, antislavery men in the North continued to invoke it as they struggled against the expansion of slavery. By the 1848 election, abolitionists formed the Free Soil Party in response to the Whigs who preferred to avoid conflict over the slavery issue. Though their candidate lost to Whig Zachary Taylor, the Free-Soil Party remained an influential force.

By the time California applied for admission to the Union, it already had an antislavery state constitution. New Mexico and Utah also agitated for admission as non-slave states. This worried the South, which felt threatened by the shifting balance to power toward the North. In addition, the success of abolitionists in organizing and operating the clandestine Underground Railroad infuriated Southerners.

Responding to Southern fears, Congress, taking Daniel Webster's advice, worked out a compromise in 1850, forgoing legislation on the issue of slavery in the territories. This left the matter entirely to the state legislatures. Congress also passed a more stringent fugitive slave law. According to the law's provisions, escaping slaves could not testify in their own behalf and were denied trial by jury. The law caused much friction between North and South since many Northerners, believing the law unjust, deliberately ignored it. Massachusetts even legislated against its enforcement.

The most significant threat to the future of the Union came when Senator Stephen A. Douglas of Illinois successfully orchestrated and rammed through Congress the Kansas Nebraska Act, which repealed the Missouri Compromise of 1820, thus allowing slavery in Kansas, north of the 36° 30' line. Douglas did this to elicit Southern support for opening up the Kansas and Nebraska territory to railroad interests in which he had invested money. Historians consider this action one of the greatest blunders in American history. Northern abolitionists considered the legislation as an act of bad faith. Southerners became angry at subsequent attempts of Union Free-Soilers to control Kansas.

Kansas became a battleground between Free-Soilers and slaveowners. At one point during the conflict, Free-Soilers established their own extralegal regime in Topeka after pro-slavery forces gained power by allowing pro-slavery activists from Missouri to vote in Kansas' election for state legislatures. Matters worsened when a gang of pro-slavery raiders burned part of the free-soil town of Lawrence.

When Kansas finally applied for annexation, the pro-slavery forces in control of power devised a document known as the Lecompton Constitution, which forbade people from voting for the state constitution unless they accepted it with slavery. Many Free-Soilers boycotted the election, and Kansas adopted the pro-slavery constitution. The Democratic Party split over the issue. President James Buchanan backed the Lecompton Constitution while Stephen Douglas opposed it. Though the Kansas conflict severely weakened the Democratic party, it led to the birth to the Republican Party. Formed of disgruntled Whigs, Democrats, and Free-Soilers, the Republican Party quickly became the second major political party.

Hopes for compromise between North and South ended with the Dred

Scott Decision in 1857. Dred Scott, a Negro slave, lived with his master in Illinois and Wisconsin Territory. Backed by abolitionists, he sued for his freedom on the basis of his long residence on free soil. The pro-Southern Supreme Court ruled that Dred Scott was not a citizen but a slave who could not sue in a federal court. The Court further ruled that blacks were inferior beings with no rights that whites were bound to respect. It also ruled that the repealed Missouri Compromise, which had forbidden slavery north of 36° 30', had always been unconstitutional. Southerners rejoiced over the decision. Henceforth slavery could not be barred in any of the territories despite majority wishes to the contrary. But the Court's action appalled pro-sovereignty Northern Democrats including Senator Douglas. Northern and Southern Democrats split into two completely separate factions. Republicans totally disregarded the legality of the Dred Scott Decision, calling it the opinion of a "Southern debating society." This Republican defiance inflamed the Southerners even more.

The point of no return on the path to war came when the abolitionist fanatic John Brown and his followers seized a federal arsenal at Harper's Ferry, Virginia, in an attempt to instigate a slave rebellion. His followers killed seven innocent people in the process, including a free black man. Brown, though insane, maintained his dignity and composure in the court room. When sentenced to death for his crime, he instantly attained martyr status among abolitionists. This further infuriated Southerners, many of whom came to view all Northerners as murderous abolitionist fanatics. A year later the South voted for secession.

During the period leading up to the Civil War, Northern Abolitionists constituted perhaps the most important organized force for social and political change. Since the early 1800s, antislavery societies proliferated throughout the country. In 1826 there were 103 antislavery societies in the South and 40 in the North. Most advocated gradual freeing of the slaves with compensation to the slaveowner. But during the 1830s and 40s, radical abolitionists in the North increased in number. Inspired by successful efforts of British antislavery societies aimed at banning slavery within the British Empire, they believed in immediate unconditional emancipation. Radicals, such as William Lloyd Garrison, vilified Southern slaveowners as sinners worse than criminals, whose slaves should be freed without any compensation. Garrison refused to commit the "sinful act" of voting under such a system and advocated secession of the North from the South. He burnt a copy of the Constitution, which upheld slavery, calling it "a covenant with death and hell."

Garrison and other radicals helped foment disunion by alienating Southerners. Their anti-Southern stance completely undermined the efforts of the moderate Southern antislavery societies. Still, the radical abolitionists did hasten the freeing of the slaves. This happened at a tremendous cost of a million men killed or disabled, plus 20 billion dollars in war costs. If a plan of gradual, compensated emancipation could have been implemented, it would have cost 2 billion dollars and lives would have been saved. But at a time when other nations of the western world had already recognized the immorality of slavery, the idea of prolonging such an evil seemed evermore untenable in the minds of reformers.

In Morris County, New Jersey, the abolitionist movement centered in Madison, Florham Park, Randolph, and Boonton. Madison abolitionists included such prominent citizens as Alfred M. Treadwell and Francis Stebbins Lathrop, both of whom helped establish Madison's Grace Episcopal Church. In nearby Florham Park, tradition has it that Baxter Sayre and Methodist minister Henry Hedges actively participated in the Underground Railroad. And in Randolph, Jacob Lundy Brotherton, with the support of his fellow Quakers, helped found the New Jersey Anti-Slavery Society.

One of the most important New Jersey abolitionists, Dr. John Grimes of Boonton, edited the Boonton-based abolitionist newspaper, the *New Jersey Freeman*. He also served as secretary of the New Jersey Anti-Slavery Society, which for a time, had its headquarters in Boonton. Grimes' antislavery activities went beyond editorializing. He and other Boonton abolitionists including Charles Hopkins (who later won the Congressional Medal of Honor during the Civil War) organized a branch of the Underground Railroad that went through Boonton.

In his writings, Hopkins identified Dr. Grimes' house on the corner of Main and Liberty Streets in Boonton as the most important station along the railroad. Confirmation of Hopkins' story comes from Josiah Quincy Grimes, nephew of John, who wrote about his uncle's many trips "on rough roads after dark." Another important station was the Powerville Hotel, owned by Hopkins' father Nathan, and located in nearby Boonton Township along the Morris Canal at lock number 11. Canal historians believe that abolitionists used the Morris Canal to transport fugitives on boats from Easton, Pennsylvania, through Morris County to Jersey City, a major underground station.

In addition to their antislavery activities, abolitionists frequently involved themselves in other causes. Throughout the pages of the *New Jersey Freeman*, Grimes, inspired by a religious humanitarianism, espoused women's rights, prohibition, and socialism. He also opposed capital punishment and practiced vegetarianism. During the Mexican War, Grimes, like most abolitionists, advocated pacifism. He modified his strict pacifist stance after the Civil War began, as did other abolition-

Dr. John Grimes, Physician and Abolitionist (Courtesy of Rutgers Special Collections and University Archives, Rutgers University Library).

ists, who welcomed the conflict as a war of liberation on behalf of the slaves. Grimes joined the army, where he served in the 13th Regiment, New Jersey Volunteers as a lieutenant-colonel.

Although Grimes viewed radical abolitionists, including William Lloyd Garrison, as headstrong, abusive, and "pharisaical," he still praised them for their "reckless daring" and "unflagging perseverance to so great an enterprise." He also agreed with the radicals that the abolition of slavery should be immediate, total, and unconditional.

In 1844 Grimes supported James G. Birney, presidential candidate of the abolitionist Liberty Party. When the anti-slavery Free-Soil Party formed in 1848, Grimes did not embrace the new party since it would not support some of the less popular abolitionist objectives including full equality for blacks.

Grimes believed in equality for all people. He consistently supported the faction of the Liberty Party that advocated broad social reform on behalf of the poor and oppressed classes throughout the world. He spoke out against despotism and economic oppression everywhere. In his last published issue of the *New Jersey Freeman*, he advocated socialism, calling for "a total reconstruction of our systems of industry and property [as] the only effective remedy for existing evils."

The following writings include several editorials by Grimes, and some poems relating to the injustice of slavery and the immorality of war; also a Democratic response to the abolitionists in the pages of Morristown's *True Democratic Banner*. These are followed by an account of the activities of the Underground Railroad in Boonton by Charles Hopkins; and the text of an 1844 resolution by the New Jersey Anti-Slavery Society regarding the practice of slavery in New Jersey, which was not completely abolished until 1846.

Selections From John Grimes' *New Jersey Freeman*

New Jersey Freeman   *October 26, 1844*

THE SLAVE BOY

Mother the fields are bright and green
And gay with flowers you see;
The sun sheds joy and light around,
But all is gloom to me.

My fetters they are fast and strong,
I am a poor slave boy,

The voice of gladness never hear
Or aught of hope or joy.

I never see my mother smile,
I only trace the tear,
Is it for me that you weep?
Speak, mother let me hear.

Oh shall we never see the light,
Of freedom's dawning day?
Is slavery then one endless night?
Oh mother, mother say.

There is my boy, a God above,
He marks our anguish wild,
He sees our sorrows, hears our groans,
And pities us, poor child.

And to a band of mobbed men,
Strong hearted, free and brave,
He's given a heart of pitying love,
They labor for the slave.

And in their happy freeman's home,
They think of thee and me,
They'll break the bonds that fetter us,
We will, we shall be free.

J.

New Jersey Freeman   *October 24, 1846*

THE MEXICAN WAR

Our readers no doubt all know that this war is progressing and that a severe battle has just been fought at Monterey at which something like ONE THOUSAND of our fellow men have been slaughtered. The Slaughter of so many of our race is horrible to think of under any circumstances, but when we reflect that this war is one of unprovoked aggression on our part, infamously unjust toward Mexico, and carried on for the sole purpose of perpetuating the Slavery of the human race, we are unable to think of it with composure, and are led to enquire, "who are the authors

11

of this war?" We cannot lay it to [Senator Henry] Clay, Polk, or Tyler any more than we can to any other slaveholder. The wicked scheme of Texan annexation concocted among the slaveholders twenty years ago has been pursued ever since with a steady and single eye to its final accomplishment. In order to bring it about, it was necessary that a slaveholding and pro-slavery public sentiment should be infused into the heart of this nation.

Each of the individuals above named has given his influence in his own particular sphere towards making and securing this public sentiment. They have all advocated Texas in their own way, according to the circumstances in which they have been placed; and the respective parties to which they belong have always regarded the interest of party far above that of every other interest, and have always yielded a hearty acquiescence to the demands of slaveholders in reference to this and every other matter. The claims of the Whigs to a different position are unfounded. When prominent Texas men and slaveholders have been proposed to fill the Cabinet offices to represent us abroad, to officer our Army and Navy etc., a Whig Senate has always been ready to sanction their propositions. When the interests of the Slaveholders demanded the repeal of the Tariff [which protected Northern manufacturers from foreign competition but penalized cotton growers whose exports were subjected to counter-tariffs in retaliation], Whig votes were needed to accomplish it; they had all they wanted, and so they always will have until the party sees that its own dissolution is inevitable [through lack of support from antislavery factions]. The slaveholders have always been united in the determination to extend the area of slavery and they have thus far always succeeded, and this gives them the confidence to believe they will be successful in the future, hence their continued efforts to secure California and Mexico. The South never could have accomplished this without the aid of the North. They have made the political parties at the North bow the knee, they have, by their bullying threats, frightened some, and by their sophistry, deceived others. By getting up Texas script and selling it to northern people, and threatening to withdraw their patronage from northern merchants and manufactories, they have secured the influence of those who always carry their souls in their pockets. They have secured the influence of the church South, and the silence of the church North with few exceptions. The Political and religious press of the North have bowed down in humble and obedient servility to the slaveholders. They secured the public sentiment referred to, and have brought into actual service the great majority of the people of the north, and made them their willing slaves. Under the influence they got Texas, and are now at the point of the bayonet, wresting California and Mexico from its rightful possessors, and almost the whole north, Whigs and Democrats, are setting on the dogs, and exulting over the infamous butcheries which our troops are perpetuating in Mexico. Polk is only the willing instrument, which slavery is using for the accomplishment of its base purposes. He issues his infamous proclamations full of lies, and calls for troops to go into Mexico, and Whig governors and Democrat governors promptly and heartily respond to the call, and preeminent Whigs as well as Democrats are found volunteering to go and fight the battles of slavery; and when a bill is before the senate providing that all territory acquired by treaty shall be free territory, we find a Whig senate from Massachusetts defending the Bill.

Third Day of the Siege of Monterey (from Pictorial Life of General Taylor*)*

Yes, more than twenty years have been spent in pro-slavery maneuvering with an eye on the final consummation of this wicked work, and none but the abolitionists have labored to prevent it, none but these have lifted up their warning voice before this nation. They have been faithful in their opposition to this Texas scheme, of which this Mexican war is a part, through persecution and abuse of every sort. Whigs and Democrats have done everything to oppose them that the interest of the party required. They have voted our petitions under foot, sustained gags, stifled free discussion and cast all the odium they could on the oppressors of Texas annexation. The Whigs can claim no credit for what some of them have said against Texas, for they never said anything of the kind until they thought the interest of their party demanded it.

New Jersey Freeman   *September 4, 1847*

WHAT HAS THE NORTH TO DO WITH SLAVERY?

The *Washington Union* of July contains an Advertisement for the sale of two Negro women by Alexander Hunter, U.S. Marshall for the District of Columbia, to take place on the 13 [of] July. This sale actually took place, and our government pocketed $530 as the avails of this sale, which will probably be paid over to Gen. [Winfield] Scott[1] or [Zachary] Taylor, or some other of the robbers of Mexico for the extension of slavery. The Government traffics in slaves, and then uses the profits of the trade in procuring more slave territory; and we of the North have nothing to do with it, have we? Does the government belong exclusively to the slaveholders? Are we their slaves?

Sales like the above are no new things in this land of liberty. Our national officers are continually dealing in slaves, catching fugitives and returning them to their masters, and in various other ways giving their countenance and aid, directly and indirectly in favor of slavery, and that too with the sanction and approval of the government. We of the North, cannot shake the guilt of slavery from our skirts, until we give all the influence we have towards forming a northern public antislavery sentiment that will sweep slavery out of this nation. Let the people of the north unite in their efforts for this purpose, and slavery must fall. Nothing short of this will accomplish this work.

[1] General Winfield Scott played a key role in the Mexican War. Despite inadequate numbers of troops, he successfully took Mexico City in what many have called one of the most brilliant campaigns in American military history. He ran as the Whig candidate for president in 1852 but lost to Franklin Pierce.

New Jersey Freeman   *October 2, 1847*

WHAT IS WAR?

What is the chief business of war? It is to destroy life; to mangle the limbs; to gash and hew the body; to plunge the sword into the heart of a fellow creature; to strew the earth with bleeding frames, and to trample them under foot with horses hoofs. It is to batter down and burn cities; to turn fruitful fields into deserts; to level the cottage of the peasant, and the magnificent abode of opulence; to scourge nations with famine, to multiply widows and orphans. Are these honorable deeds? Were we called to name exploits worthy of demons, would we not naturally select such as these? We have thought that it was honorable to heal, to save, to mitigate pain, to snatch the sick and sinking from the jaws of death. We have placed among the benefactors of the human race, the discoverers of arts which alleviate human sufferings, which prolong, adorn, and cheer human life; and if these arts are honorable, where is the glory of multiplying and aggravating tortures and death?

The following verse typifies many of the poems that frequently appeared in the New Jersey Freeman. *These poems were usually taken from other publications.*

New Jersey Freeman   *October 2, 1847*

PEACE AND WAR
BY AN UNLETTERED YOUTH

War

Town deserted; burning village;
Murder; rape; destruction; pillage;
Man compelled man's blood to shed;
Weeping; wailing; want of bread;
Commerce checked grave citizens
Armed with sword instead of pens;
Harvests trampled; homesteads burned;
That is war, why is't not spurned?

Peace

Busy town and happy village;
Fruitful fields by careful tillage;
Smiling wife and children gay;
Labor singing through the day;
Bounteous harvests; busy farms;
Rusty swords; disused firearms;

War's vain glory set at nought;
This is Peace! Why is't not sought?

The following lines, by [18th century Scottish poet John] Scott, of Amwell are cut from an old magazine. They tell a homely truth, we should do well to heed. Would that all eyes were as clear to see the fact of war through its outside glitter. *Penn. Freeman*

ODE

I hate that drum's discordant sound,
Parading round and round and round;
To thoughtless youth it pleasure yields,
And lures from cities and from fields,
To sell their liberty for charms
Of tawdry lace and glittering arms;
And when Ambition's voice commands,
To march, and fight, and fall, in foreign lands.

I hate that drum's discordant sound,
Parading round and round and round,
To me it talks of ravaged plains,
And burning towns and ruined swains,
And mangled limbs, and dying groans,
And widow's tears, and orphan's moans,
And all that Misery's hand bestows,
To fill the catalogue of human woes.

A Democratic Response to the Abolitionists

The following True Democratic Banner *editorial focuses on the Wilmont Proviso, a bill originally introduced by David Wilmont of Pennsylvania in 1846 that would have outlawed slavery in Texas or any other territory wrested from Mexico during the Mexican War. The bill passed in the House twice but not in the Senate where it met strong Southern opposition. Although the Wilmont Proviso failed to become law, antislavery men in the North continued to invoke it as they struggled against the expansion of slavery. The pro-slavery author of the editorial blames the North for polarizing the nation over the slavery issue. He cites the Constitution and the Bible to support his view that Southerners have a right to own slaves. He maintains that those who oppose slavery threaten the Union and sin against God through their actions.*

True Democratic Banner   *October 2, 1850*

THE WILMONT PROVISO – THE FEDERAL UNION

As was anticipated by many, the regulation and disposition of the new territory acquired from Mexico has involved us in a formidable difficulty. The slavery question, which has hung over this Union for more than thirty years, like a dark and deadly specter, is now again presented in a form more destructive and dreadful than ever before.

When the bill providing for the purchase of the new territory was before the House of Representatives, Mr. David Wilmont, a member from Pennsylvania, offered an amendment to the bill, the tenor and purport of which, was, that in no part of the territory to be acquired from Mexico, should slavery or involuntary servitude be allowed to exist, except as a punishment for crime, whereof the party shall first be duly convicted. The bill for purchasing this territory was finally passed without Mr. Wilmont's amendment, or proviso, as it is called; but ever since, when-ever any attempt has been made to legislate with reference to that terri-tory, he and his coadjutors have insisted upon the application of the 'proviso,' with unyielding tenacity. The object of this measure, as is very apparent, is to exclude Negro slavery from all of the newly acquired domain. The South, of course, resists the measure. The advocates of this 'proviso' have declared that they will dissolve the Union, rather than yield its provisions. The South, on the other hand, unanimously declares that if it be passed, they will secede. The arrival of the controversy at this important and fearful crisis, must arouse every patriotic citizen – every lover of our glorious confederacy[1] – to consider the merits of the ques-tion at issue.

And now what are they – which party is in the wrong, the North or the South? Undoubtedly the agitators on both sides have gone to ex-tremes. But, in my apprehension, the North has, in this instance, pro-posed and insisted upon a measure fraught with the grossest injustice. Look at the owners of the territory to which this proviso is intended to apply. Who are they? The North and South, as tenants in common. The South has contributed, or is willing to, and if she continues in the Union, *must* contribute her full proportion of the purchase money; of the blood and labor expended to bring about that purchase, her citizens furnished more than their proportion. According to the first and clearest principles of natural justice, the South has the same rights to that territory that the North has. If a Northern man has a right to remove thither, to take with him his property, and to be protected in the enjoyment of that property when there, why has not a Southern man precisely the same rights? If a

17

Northern citizen may say to one from the South, "If you take your slave into that territory, your property in that state shall be taken away from you," would it not be quite as just for a Southern citizen to say to one from the North, "If you bring your horse into that territory, your property in the horse shall be taken away from you?" It is no answer to this position, to say that "man cannot have property in man" — the assertion is not true. The Constitution of the United States directly and repeatedly acknowledges that slaves are property — God himself by prescribing laws which recognize and sanction slavery has declared that man can have property in man.

Those who hold the dogma that man cannot hold property in man without contravening the principles of right and sinning against God, are in a dilemma. Their assertion implies one or the other of two things — either that God committed a wrong in sanctioning slavery in the Jewish Theocracy, or that the immutable principles of Right have undergone a change in modern times.

It is very clear that the North has no more right to prescribe to the South, by Congressional enactments, what property they may remove to and hold in those territories, than the South has the right to make a similar prescription for the North. *Neither one has any such right,* and any project of either side, to exercise such power over the other is unjust and tyrannical. The object, open and avowed, of this 'Wilmont Proviso' is, to limit, if not to prohibit the South in the enjoyment of their equal rights in that territory, by destroying their title to their slaves, in case they bring those slaves into territories which they have shed the blood of their noblest sons and expended their money to obtain. Suppose the South, having a majority in Congress, should enact a law that no man should have a right to own horses in those new territories, would not we of the North, who might wish to own horses there, conclude that we would be wronged in being prohibited from holding and using our property on our own soil. (I would not equalize horses and negroes, but in one respect there is an exact analogy — both of them are, and always have been, subjects of property.)

If the North, by a majority in Congress, may prohibit Southerners from holding one species of property in those territories, they may prohibit another species, and so extend the application of principle as to prohibit them from the holding of any property whatsoever. Because, if we admit that Congress has such power, we can place no limit to its exercise.

As might be expected, this measure has produced great alarm and excitement at the South. There can be no doubt but that if this proviso or anything like it be passed, the South will secede from the Union. Her course is marked out and her people, much as they love the Union, will unanimously pursue it. If this proviso be dropped and Congress shall resolve to take no action either for or against slavery in the territories, the South will be content. If the people who settle those territories shall form proper State governments and prohibit slavery therein, the South will abide in their decision; because the institution will then be prohibited in a legitimate way. The people of a State have powers over this subject of slavery while Congress has not. It is the assumption by Congress of a power which they do not possess by the Constitution, dangerous in principle and tendencies, and working rank injustice, to which the South objects.

The North ought then to leave the question of slavery in those territories to be settled at once. The South will be satisfied with what the North can yield without injury to herself — And since we can yield enough to perpetuate and strengthen the Union, without self-injury — since such concession will be just and magnanimous — it is the climax of folly and madness to refuse it. Every lover of the Union, who can wield a pen, would at once speak out through the press. Public meetings should at once be held and sentiments of compromise and determination to support the Union, should be expressed for the guidance of our Congressmen.

[1] Democrats, believing strongly in states' rights, frequently referred to the United States of America as a confederacy.

Morris Abolitionists Fight Slavery in New Jersey

Like other abolitionist organizations, the New Jersey Anti-Slavery Society opposed Southern slavery and its expansion to the West. They considered invalid all laws and legal contracts that did not recognize racial equality. They also acknowledged that slavery was not confined to the South — that it still existed within New Jersey — despite the passage in 1804 of "An Act for the Gradual Abolition of Slavery." The law freed children of slaves born after July 4, 1804 — at age 21 for women and 25 for men. Consequently, free black New Jerseyans (12,460) outnumbered those still in bondage (7,557) by 1820. But militant abolitionists wanted slavery completely abolished. Throughout the 1830s and into the 1840s, they submitted numerous anti-slavery petitions to the state legislature in the hope of attaining their goal. In 1844 they grew hopeful when the state adopted a new constitution containing a "Bill of Rights," which they interpreted as an antislavery document. The New Jersey Supreme Court did not agree with their argument, ruling it "a doubtful construction of an indefinite abstract political proposition." The justices maintained that the framers of the state constitution had not in-

tended to apply the doctrine of equal rights "to man in his private, individual or domestic capacity; or to define his individual rights or interfere with his domestic relations, or his individual condition." But by 1846, abolitionists finally met with success. In that year a second emancipation law formally abolished slavery by freeing all black children born after its passage. It reclassified remaining slaves as "apprentices for life." This gave them some limited rights including the right to sue for their freedom if their masters abused them. A 1860 Federal census listed 18 of these "apprentices for life" as "slaves." In 1865 the 13th Amendment to the United States Constitution ended all involuntary servitude in New Jersey.

The following minutes of a 1844 meeting of the New Jersey Anti-Slavery Society in Madison contain a resolution on the slavery issue based on the Society's antislavery interpretation of the recently adopted New Jersey Constitution. The resolution was reprinted in the New Jersey Freeman.

New Jersey Freeman   *September, 1844*

MEETING OF THE NEW JERSEY
ANTISLAVERY SOCIETY IN MADISON

The semiannual meeting of the New Jersey Anti-Slavery Society was held in Mr. [Henry] Keep's long room in Madison, according to a previous notice, Aug. 22nd, 1844.

The meeting was called to order by the President at 11 o'clock A.M., and prayer was offered by Mr. Cochran of New York.

The Chairman of the business committee reported the following resolutions, which were accepted.

1. *Resolved*, That the law of God is supreme; and therefore, all constitutions, compacts, and statutory enactments whatever, are valid and obligatory, just in so far forth, as they embody and apply its grand principle, and no farther; consequently, all contracts & laws, constituting ties between the North and the South, which in any way compromise this principle, are so far, of no force or obligation whatever and should be abolished.

2. *Resolved*, That Slavery or the holding of human beings as property is a sin under all circumstances and therefore ought to be immediately, and unconditionally abandoned.

3. *Resolved*, That to deprive a man of the elective franchise on account of his color, is not only an act of injustice toward the individual, but an insult to his Maker.

4. Whereas the bill of rights contained in the constitution recently formed for this State teaches the doctrine of natural and universal liberty, and Whereas, the dictation of this new constitution is clearly at variance with all the existing laws of this State, which favor the maintenance and continuance of Slavery, therefore, *Resolved* that a committee be appointed to bring the matter before the proper Courts, that a decision may be obtained, which shall settle the question of the existence of slavery under the new Constitution, and that this committee be authorized to make an immediate appeal for funds to the friends of liberty, and to proceed as early as the receipt of funds will warrant.

5. *Resolved*, That peace, kindly feeling, and harmonious action, as between the members of a religious society, is a great and ever to be desired good—but though a good, it is not the ultimate good. When the condition of peace is, that the minister of Christ must cease to preach the whole truth, thus obeying man rather than God, cease to rebuke sin under its widest and most hideous forms, in deference to the narrow selfish prejudices of the human heart, on the plea that said sin is not in our State, and that it is authorized by law; then peace in such terms costs too much.

6. *Resolved*, that the argument urged by some, that anti-slavery men, who do not vote for the Whig candidate [William Henry Harrison], do virtually vote for the contrary candidate and [the annexation of] Texas too; is an absurd and ridiculous sophistry.[1]

7. *Resolved*, That a Slaveholder is not more qualified to preside in a Democratic Government, than a practical Atheist is to preach the Gospel.

8. *Resolved*, That a Committee of three be appointed to take up Collection, and secure pledges for means to pay arrearages and continue the operations of the society on behalf of the Slave.

---

[1] Though the Whig party dodged troublesome issues including slavery, many abolitionists considered it the lesser of two evils when compared to the pro-slavery Democratic Party. Others felt they could not support the Whig party with its lack of total commitment to abolitionism. In 1840 the Whig party put ex-Democrat John Tyler on the Whig ticket as running mate to William Henry Harrison in an attempt to unify the party. Tyler unexpectedly became president after Harrison contracted pneumonia and died only four weeks after his inauguration. Tyler's views, particularly on economic issues, tended toward the Democratic position. A caucus of Whig congressmen formally expelled him from the Whig party for opposing their efforts to create a centralized bank. By the 1844 election, voters focused on the annexation of Texas as a major issue. Many Whigs opposed the annexation of Texas to placate the abolitionists who opposed add-

ing slave territory to the Union. When the Democrat presidential nominee James K. Polk triumphed over Whig Henry Clay, lame-duck President Tyler saw this as a mandate to acquire Texas, which he then annexed through a joint resolution of Congress.

The Underground Railroad in Morris County

Few episodes in American history have more popular appeal than the Underground Railroad. This informal network of people and places assisted fugitive slaves fleeing from the South to freedom in Canada. The individuals involved in the "railroad," called "agents" or "conductors," provided stops or "stations" along the way where fugitive slaves hid from authorities.

Although some slaves escaped from the South in the eighteenth century, the underground movement did not develop until the 1830s, when antislavery leaders launched a crusade to abolish slavery. From that time on, the controversy over slavery became the most divisive issue in the nation. Railroad activity reached its peak after Congress passed the Fugitive Slave Act of 1850. The law made it possible for federal officials to issue warrants for the arrest of escaped slaves. Citizens who refused to cooperate with the law risked fines or imprisonment. Abolitionists and their sympathizers expressed indignation at the law by extending even greater assistance to fugitive slaves, hiding their illicit activities from the watchful eyes of local law officials.

In Morris County, stories about the Underground Railroad abound. Unfortunately many of these stories are unsubstantiated, frequently based on misconceptions of how the railroad worked — misconceptions that have even led some to believe that the railroad literally travelled underground. Legends have arisen that link the railroad to the discovery of brick-lined tunnels found beneath the ground in several municipalities. In fact, 18th and 19th century engineers designed these tunnels to carry the towns' water supply. The real Underground Railroad carried slaves overland, travelling by carriage, sleigh, and foot.

The best documentation of the Underground Railroad comes from the pen of Charles Hopkins. Hopkins, a Boonton resident, is best known for having won the Congressional Medal of Honor for acts of heroism during the Civil War. Raised by abolitionist parents, he viewed the conflict as a war of liberation to free the slaves. Even as a young man, he helped his father Nathan Hopkins transport slaves. Nathan owned the Powerville Hotel (still standing) located along the Morris Canal at lock number 11. Some canal historians believe that conductors used the Morris Canal to transport fugitives on barges from Easton, Pennsylvania, through Morris County to Jersey City, known to be a major underground station. Nathan and Charles Hopkins were part of a ring of Boonton abolitionists. These prominent citizens included Dr. John Grimes, John Hill, William G. Lathrop, Charles B. Norris, Thomas C. Willis, and Philip Wooton.

In the following account written later in his life, Charles Hopkins relates an incident that occurred during the operation of Boonton's Underground Railroad.

THE UNDERGROUND RAILROAD
BY CHARLES F. HOPKINS

Few if any of the principals are alive today that were active in the conduct of slaves on the road to Canada after escaping the "nigger catchers" of the South and reaching a free State of the North, i.e., above Mason and Dixon's line.

The writer's knowledge thereof begins in 1856, when but past fourteen years of age, my father being one of the conductors of that road, and a very strong antislavery advocate. All such men were steady readers of the *New York Tribune*, and admirers of Horace Greeley. Among the promoters and active workers and financiers of this "underground" line, were Dr. John Grimes, William G. Lathrop, John Hill, Philip Wooton, Thomas C. Willis, Nathan Hopkins, George Ely, Charles B. Norris, Frederick Stone, James Grimes, William Coates, and others that do not readily come to mind. Headquarters in Boonton was the house of Dr. Grimes on the corner of Liberty and Main streets, where the slave who had gone beyond the loud baying of the bloodhound of the South and escaped the terrors of recapture within the lines of the slave states, and had tasted the hope of freedom, and breathed the air of a free people, reached a haven of comfort, shelter, advice, and aid such as he needed. The nearest station to Boonton was the Hotel at Powerville. There were stations at Rockaway, Dover, Pompton Plains, Newfoundland, Canisteer, Stockholm, and Charlottenburg, all known to the writer, but his experience was in the main confined to Boonton, Stockholm, and Canisteer.

There was always the price upon the head of the runaway slave, from $50 to $300 and $500; depending on the value of the slave as a chattel, as the horse or other animal.

Much to the credit of local constables, they would rather aid the slave to escape if not caught in the act, than arrest him. The love of freedom to mankind was stronger than the love of gold that brought misery worse than death to the recaptured slave.

One constable in Morris County known to the writer lacked every attribute of manhood or principle, was devoid of human feelings for all but himself, and would have sold his best friend for a price. He is dead and gone to the keeping of his former master in crime. He was the only officer to the knowledge of the writer that spent his time to obtain the rewards, if possible, by the arrest of the runaway. He was a fit companion of a [Simon] Legree, with none of Legree's cunning. As I never knew him to earn a single reward, he may have been rewarded some other way by his employers.

The game of hunting may have been for the excitement, from which he may have felt compensated, but game he never potted on the road to freedom via the Boonton route.

This officer closely watched the Boonton-Powerville route. A slave would reach the haven of Dr. Grimes. Word was mysteriously sent to Powerville; time and place was set where the slave would be found, for transfer to Powerville, Canisteer or Stockholm. My orders from father were: "Keep your eyes open, ears also, and never spare horseflesh, take all chances yourself, but save your charge from recapture at all hazards." This, to a fourteen-year-old boy, was rather stiff orders, but being young and a strong enthusiast in the cause, and not knowing the possible risks and results, I comforted my mind with the idea that the worst possible thing was failure to save a recapture, as that would have been mortifying in the extreme, both to my parent and my own ambition to succeed. We had a gray mare that was superior to any in this section on the run and for a long and hard drive, and a two-wheeled conveyance called a "sulky," made for the occasion, we judge by the six foot wheel, and built so strong in every way, which was always used when a single person beside the driver was to be taken over the "underground" road.

With the constable hanging about watching my father's every move, I was used as a blind and sent to Boonton in the sulky, the constable following, of course. I went to D. C. Norris' store and got some goods, and from Frederick Stone obtained the information as to the place the slave would be, came back, and hitched a good black mare we had to a Rockaway wagon (a closed affair used in those days), opened the barn doors in south end (towards Boonton) and tied her, when father gave me instructions what to do in case the constable followed him to Boonton, which he was sure to do. Father, moving in mysterious manner towards the barn, excited the officer, and when he saw the "Rockaway" move out of rear of barn when he expected something from the front, he gave chase after a horse that was in much higher class than his; I followed them, keeping out of site of the officer until he passed beyond Marble Cottage Hill, when I turned in the Whitehead lane (now a road leading up in the woods near the house of 7's homestead), made my way to the junction of the wood road near the swamp (now Hillery's Lake), and found my man, and at the simple word "yes" spoken by him, he got on the seat under me. Not another word was spoken until hours after, we following the rough road that led to Splitrock and from the head of the pond to Charlottenburg, as it was then called, passing through the dark woods of what was then a very lonesome and very rough road, when I heard a voice, halted, and asked my charge to get into the woods until we knew what was doing. He spryly did so, and I drew as far into the side of the road as possible, and was compelled to hail the oncomer, for two could not pass and one keep all the road. I hailed, "Hold up there," and coming close, was surprised to know that I was to meet William Earles on his way home at a late hour. After some questioning as to why I was up in those woods at that hour of the night, and not getting any good reason, after expressing himself that it was "damn funny," passed on. We signalled, the passenger mounted again, and the road was clear to our destination, until within the sight of the signal of a light in the upper window of a house, when two forms stepped in the road in front of us. I pulled the whip which was never needed on this animal, intending to make a run, but a light was instantly shown by a swing to the right, and my very much disturbed heart felt better. I could feel the constrained stiffness of the man under me relax, as he was ready to leave the sulky if I rose up. The password "yes" and the slave got down and went to the house, and I was instructed to return to Newfoundland and put out until morning. I slept a little, and as Billings says, rolled over a good deal, thinking of the past five hours and its probabilities.

So far the boy of fourteen was a success and enjoyed the idea that he was part of the system. A number of times this was repeated, but not all exciting. However, upon one occasion, I was chased fourteen miles by this constable while I had a slave, his wife, and a child, but I beat him to a place of shelter at Pompton Plains and unloaded before he saw where, and passed beyond some distance, then deliberately turned about, and passed him at a run and outdistanced him to a private crossroad where I kept out of his way on his flight after me, he having two "nigger catchers" with him, thus handicapping him some, though he was not in it when the gray was on her mettle. After he passed where I was, I returned to the shelter and took up my passengers and safely delivered them at Stockholm.

In all these lonely night drives, talk was forbidden except when actually necessary. When I think of those night rides on the roads through rocks, roots, mud, and brush, scarcely able to see a yard ahead, often in stormy weather, no one to talk to, heart up to the throat at every sound, imaginary forms looming up out of the gloom, and a fear of nonsuccess, yet none of personal harm, I have thought since, that it was well worth the trouble and worry.

Chapter 2

Morris County Prepares for War — A Newspaper Account

During the Civil War, newspapers functioned primarily as editorial mouthpieces for the political parties whom they represented. Republican papers such as Morristown's *Jerseyman* supported the war with patriotic enthusiasm. At the war's onset it called upon women "to buckle on the sword and send their husbands, fathers, and sons out to fight for God and their native land." At the other extreme, Democrat Copperhead papers including Newark's *Daily Journal* condemned the war as unjust. It denounced Lincoln as a "corrupt tyrant" and "wicked usurper."

Following the fall of Fort Sumter, moderate Democrat papers including Morristown's *True Democratic Banner* joined their Republican adversaries in supporting the Union cause. But like its Copperhead counterparts, the *Banner* firmly opposed abolitionism, labeling its opponents "black republican disunionists" and "anti-constitution-slavery intermeddlers and fanatics." It portrayed slaves as racially inferior savages who would start a race war if freed. The *Jerseyman* countered by questioning the patriotism of the Democratic party, which often opposed federal policies. It also ran stories about Southern atrocities committed against blacks. Such politically partisan papers cannot always be relied upon for accuracy in reporting. But despite their inaccuracies, they are worth reading because they inform us about people's attitudes toward the war. The following articles excerpted from these papers include descriptions of local patriotic celebrations and meetings, personal accounts of war-related events, editorial commentaries, and other writings.

The People Express Their Patriotism

Jerseyman   *April 20, 1861*

Hoisting the National Flag — Like the people of every other place at the North, the citizens of Morristown have been intensely excited by the stirring events of the past weeks, and the patriotic fires which burnt so brightly and so steadily in the breasts of their Fathers have been rekindled in the sons. On Monday evening last, an informal meeting of a number of our leading citizens of all parties was held at the office of V. Dalrymple, Esq., at which it was resolved to hold a Public Meeting to sustain the

Government at an early day. On Tuesday, it was determined to hoist the National Flag from the Liberty Pole[1] on the Square and there keep it flying daily; but some objection being made by two or three persons to the wearing out of the flag already belonging to the town, it was thought proper to purchase one for the purpose. Accordingly, a subscription was started, the money soon subscribed, a gentleman sent to New York to purchase one, and, it being known that it would be ready to raise on Thursday evening, Gen. [Joseph Warren] Revere[2] ordered out our military companies to add to the interest of the occasion.

The Companies came out about half past eight, and after a short parade, took up their position near the Liberty Pole. A large number of persons were now collected there. The Band played a national air, and after prayer by Rev. Mr. [M. E.] Ellison [pastor of the Methodist Church of Morristown], in which he invoked the blessing of the God of Battles upon the Flag and the Arms of our country, the Flag was raised by Capt. [William] Duncan. The Band played "The Star Spangled Banner," and a salute of 34 guns was fired by the Ringgold Artillery.[3] Some delay was occasioned by the rope getting twisted, but it is now all right, and the Flag floats proudly to the breeze. After the salute was fired, patriotic and spirit stirring addresses were made by Vancleve Dalrymple, Esq., Rev. G. Douglas Brewerton [pastor of the Morristown Baptist Church], and H. C. Pitney, Esq. [leading Morristown lawyer and trustee of the First Presbyterian Church, Morristown]. Mr. Brewerton, in the course of his remarks, said that, although a Baptist minister, he had not yet forgotten his old trade, and could do something in the service of his country without going out of Town, and that was to drill the men who would volunteer, if they desired it. Mr. B. was for seven years an officer in the U.S. Army, and this announcement was received with cheers.

In the evening, the Morris Greys' Capt. Duncan, met at their Armory, and, by a unanimous vote, resolved to tender their services to the Governor to take up the four Regiments called for from this State. Sixteen new members were enrolled, which makes the whole number of the Company forty-five. The National Guards, [and] Capt. [Edwin K.] Bishop, of Boonton, we learn, have also volunteered, and filled their ranks to upwards of 70.[4]

---

[1] Used as a symbol of liberty during the American and French revolutions, a liberty pole was a tall flagstaff surmounted by a flag or liberty cap—a close fitting conical cap that symbolized freedom.

[2] Considered a hero by many prior to the war, Joseph Warren Revere, grandson of Paul Revere, is often remembered for the controversial actions he took at the Battle of Chancellorsville, which led to his court-martial. Lincoln later revoked the court-martial. (See Chapter 10.)

[3] The Ringgold Artillery, the Morris Greys (named after the color of their uniforms), and the National Guards were local militias. Their presence must have surprised many since the militia system had already become obsolete. In fact, these local militias permanently disbanded soon after the war began. But they still served the war effort by drawing many volunteers commanded by local leaders who eventually organized them into companies of soldiers. For instance, Capt. William Duncan of the Morris Greys tried but failed in his attempt to get his militia accepted into a New Jersey regiment. He nonetheless succeeded in raising a company of soldiers for the District of Columbia. This company, made up of men from Boonton and Morristown, formed part of the President's Guard. Companies from neighboring towns formed regiments with a strong sense of state identity. Friends and relatives often fought in the same company or regiment. Volunteer regiments functioned as community organizations in which enlisted men elected many of their own officers—a practice the Union Army ended in 1863. The war would prove particularly calamitous to those towns whose regiments suffered heavy losses.

[4] The four regiments referred to are the New Jersey 7th, 11th, 15th, and 27th.

Mass Meeting at Rockaway

True Democratic Banner   *May 2, 1861*

The citizens of Rockaway Township assembled on Saturday afternoon last, in the square in front of C. A. McCarty's Hotel, to raise a Liberty Pole, display the stars and stripes, and manifest their loyalty to the Union. The meeting was extraordinarily large, over one thousand persons being present. A salute of 34 guns was fired, and the greatest enthusiasm prevailed. The pole is over 75 feet in height, and as fine a one as there is in the Country.

The meeting was called to order by Henry D. Tuttle, and the following officers nominated and duly elected:

President—Hubbard S. Stickle

Vice Presidents—Samuel B. Halsey, John W. Jackson, Samuel S. Bassett, Jacob L. Fichter, Freeman Wood, Stephen J. Jackson, Barnabas K. Stickle, John Cox, Columbus Beach, Col. N. Mott, Charles A. McCarty, Alex Norris, Jacob P. Stickle, John Garrigus, Mahlon Hoagland, Isaac N. Beach, George Richards, John M. McCarty, Charles C. De Hart, Francis Peer, Samuel S. Beach, Joseph H. Bruen, John Mott, Michael Galligan, Joseph J. Ayers.

Secretaries—John M. Pollard, John F. Stickle, George W. Lee, Edmund D. Halsey, Thomas B. McGrath, William Boyd, John G. Mott.

The President, on taking the chair, denounced succession in strong language, and showed the necessity of putting it down, and maintaining the integrity of the Union at all hazards.

William J. Wood, Esq., then introduced the following resolutions, prefacing them with a few remarks:

Whereas, An armed, powerful and well organized rebellion menaces the Capital and threatens either the division or overthrow of the Government.

And whereas, The President, who has been constitutionally elected by the people, has called on the Governors of loyal States for the proper quota of troops from each to suppress such re-rebellion and restore order and quiet;

Therefore, be it

Resolved, That our country is the whole United States.

Resolved, That by the Constitution we are one nation, indissoluble by the action of any State or section . . . that the Union of the States is what the Fathers designed, perpetual and of deathless immortality.

Resolved, that the Constitution and the Union have made us what we are — great and powerful at home, honored and respected abroad.

Resolved that secession is treason, and that we utterly execrate and abhor the promoters of, and the leaders in this foul and black-hearted rebellion, as enemies of all good, as perjured and apostate, traitors, false to their country, their oaths, and their honor.

Resolved, that the Capital, founded by Washington, is the sacred home and stand point of the Government, and should be guarded and held at all hazards and through every extremity, though it costs millions of treasure and rivers of blood.

Resolved, That the great highways of travel to the Capital of the nation should, and of right, ought to be kept open, free and unobstructed, and to this end it is that duty of the Federal authorities to annihilate any and all opposition.

Resolved, That we heartily approve, without equivocation or reservation, of the call, recently made by the President, for troops to put down causeless, wanton and cold-blooded insurrection and rebellion, and if more troops are wanted for that purpose they should, without delay, be called into the field, and the most active and vigorous measure and effective means, permitted by the law and the Constitution to the Federal Administration, should be adopted and used for the purpose of protecting the public property, executing the laws, and bringing to justice the traitors, who, for the accomplishment of selfish and wicked purposes, have plunged this great and glorious country into civil war.

Resolved, That New Jersey should, and we believe will, respond (now in the day of our nation's trial and peril) with alacrity and promptness to the requisition so made upon her by the President of the United States.

Resolved, That casting aside all political questions and ignoring all political division, we will stand by the Federal Government in its present efforts to defend the Constitution, execute the laws, and maintain the Union.

Resolved, That Major Robert Anderson, by his heroic defense of Fort Sumter, has won for himself a name of which the whole American people will be proud in all future times, and that the victory obtained over him and his 70 gallant men when reduced almost to a state of starvation by the Southern chivalry with their 17 batteries and 7,000 troops, is cause of humiliation to the victors and not the vanquished.[1]

Resolved, That the attempt to provision the starving garrison at Fort Sumter was only humane and was eminently right and proper and that an evacuation of that fort without such attempt would have entailed lasting disgrace upon the nation.

Resolved, That New Jersey, whose soil was moistened by the blood of the Revolution, should not, and will never under any circumstances or form of compromise, consent to join Jefferson Davis and his privateersmen in their Southern Confederacy, but will, in all time to come, stand fast by the Union as long as another State will stand with her, and if the time should ever come when she shall be deserted by all her sister States, she will stand alone, proud in her own integrity and love for freedom, and with the Constitution in one hand and weapons in the other, and the stars and stripes waving over her head, she will exterminate all traitors within and repel all invaders from without.

Resolved, That a committee, consisting of L. A. Chandler, George Richards, Charles A. McCarty, Columbus Beach, [and] W. J. Wood be appointed to raise and distribute all funds necessary to equip and put in the field all the volunteers who desire to go from this town, in answer to the call of the President, and that said committee be further charged with the raising of all funds necessary to support and provide for the families of such volunteers as will be left without ample means of support.

Resolved, That we recommend the formation of an association, which shall drill in the manual exercise of arms once a week, or oftener, as its members shall determine whose duty it shall be to exercise the utmost care that neither arms, ammunition, food, advice, or intelligence, so far as it can be prevented, be sent from this town or its vicinity to the traitors.

Eloquent speeches were made by Charles H. Kitchell, Esq., Hon. L. A. Chandler, Rev. C.C. Clark, S. O. Hatfield, and others. The meeting was interspersed with patriotic songs. Some twenty names were enrolled as volunteers and ample provision was made for their proper equipment and the support of their families during their absence. It was really gratifying to see the unanimity, with which partisan feeling was thrown aside and the ardent patriotism which inspired all, in the common cause to save our country.

¹ As the seceding states left the Union, they seized a number of federal properties including arsenals and mints. But Fort Sumter in Charleston Harbor remained under Federal control. With provisions in the fort running out, President Lincoln informed the South Carolinians that he would order an expedition to provision the 70-man garrison but not reinforce it. The South viewed this as an act of aggression. On April 12, 1861, the Carolinians began a bombardment of Sumter, which lasted 34 hours. The dazed Union garrison commanded by Maj. Robert Anderson surrendered. The fall of Fort Sumter united public sentiment in the North against the secessionist states. Soon thereafter, Lincoln issued a call for 75,000 militiamen in preparation for war.

Raising a Morris County Regiment

Jerseyman   *May 11, 1861*

A MORRIS COUNTY REGIMENT—We understand that an effort is being made to raise a regiment in Morris County. This is as it should be. We had begun to fear that the spirit which animated our fathers in our country's dark days, had grown "small by degrees," until her citizens now, when the services of strong hands and willing hearts are required, had become too ease-loving to move without a draft." Thank God, we were mistaken. Morris, if a little slow, seems disposed, when she does a thing, to do it thoroughly.

We have abundant material in this County to turn out as fine a regiment as there is in the field. Our hills are filled with one of the most important elements of warfare [i.e., iron ore], and our soil, though not perhaps so fruitful in cereals, as that of some counties, is fruitful in men able, and we have no doubt, willing, to do their country service as our fathers were in the days when every man here was a soldier, and when Morris County was an ark of refuge to patriots who elsewhere within our borders hardly found rest for the soles of their feet. Now, as then, our women are ready to buckle on the sword and send their husbands, fathers, and sons out to fight for God and their native land. With this the case, we can hardly be backward, and we look to see the ranks of the forming regiment speedily filled with the youth and hope of the Country; and we look as confidently, too, to see them win honor for themselves and their birthplace, if they shall ever meet their country's enemies in the fight.

It is the purpose we understand, to raise the regiment under the state law, and when complete, offer it to the General Government.

Patriotism in Boonton

Jerseyman   *May 25, 1861*

PATRIOTISM AT BOONTON — The Editor of the *Paterson Guardian* who spent a short time at Boonton, the other day, thus discourseth:

The fires of heroism burn brightly at Boonton. The captain of the military company there, has aroused "Old Pequannoc;" and at least two hundred of as hardy, stalwart men as ever dashed into a bayonet charge, could be raised in a week's time. They are hungering and thirsting after a chance to meet our aristocratic foes. Shall they not have it! The uniformed company is a splendid one, and what a mine of true gold is in the spirits and muscle of the undrilled athletes of that village.

The Nail factory now presents an animated and pleasing appearance. Some two hundred of those savage iron eating machines have small flags of the stars and stripes pattern affixed to their moving parts, and as they keep bobbing up and down in ceaseless movement, help, no doubt, to fan the flame of love for country, for home, and for honor.

A subscription paper for a large flag for this particular factory happened to be going around as we visited this department, and a few quarters from our part, brought such a shout from those stentorian throats, as made the noisy rattle of those hammering monsters of the iron maws like a maiden's whisper in comparison.

Why don't our City Blues fraternize with the Boonton and Morristown companies, and, with the remaining companies at Newark, form an independent Regiment![1]

[1] The "companies" of soldiers referred to are local militias.

Letter From Soldier Awaiting Battle

Jerseyman   *June 15, 1861*

Mr. A. A. Vance:

Dear Sir — I am induced to crave a small space in your column by the belief that anything concerning the patriotic boys from your town will be welcome news to your readers. We are very pleasantly situated in a large sandy field, some two miles from Trenton, and are enjoying excellent health. We are waiting rather impatiently for orders to leave the consecrated ground on which was decided the great struggle of American Independence and march to meet the foe that dare assail our glorious flag — that emblem of Liberty which we have pledged our lives to defend and protect. Our names are enrolled in our country's defense, and we go forth at our country's call to defend her from every foe. May the God of Battles lead us on to victory; and when the places that now know us shall know us no more, then may our memories be enshrined in the hearts of our countrymen, as worthy sons of patriotic sires.

I am constrained to offer, in behalf of the boys from Morristown and Madison, and also those from old Sussex [County], heartfelt thanks to the ladies of the above named places for the interest they have taken in our well being. Imagine our joy if you can, when the Expressman called at our tent to deliver a large box marked "C. H. Carrel, care of Capt. H. O. Ryerson," etc. The donors would have felt themselves amply paid by gratitude could they at that moment have looked in upon us as C. H. Carrol and Charles Stevens proceeded to divest the box of its lid, and sort over the good things therein contained, deposited by fair hands with palpitating hearts and eyes glistening with tears as they thought of those whose comfort they were then ministering to. But I will not attempt to trace the gratitude which cannot be expressed. We can never cease to remember with grateful hearts those who have so kindly thought of us. May God in his wisdom and mercy bless and protect you all. May His richest blessing be showered upon you, and happiness and prosperity attend you through life. If we should never meet again on earth, may God grant us a reunion for eternity at His right hand in Heaven.

> Farewell, dear friends.
> R. J. W.

Pro-Union Minister Hissed While Delivering Sermon

Jerseyman   *June 29, 1861*

Rev. S. Armstrong, formerly pastor of the Methodist Episcopal Church in Mendham, now at Newark, was hissed in his pulpit last Sunday evening, during the delivery of a Sermon on "peace." In the course of the Sermon, he spoke rather disparagingly of those who, under the rallying cry of Peace, seek to swell the rebellious hosts who now clamor for the blood of our soldiers and the destruction of our Government, and those who, like the wicked, "flee when no man pursueth," which was taken home by one or two traitors who happened to be present and retaliated by hissing. They narrowly escaped severe handling—the congregation being deterred from inflicting summary justice upon them at the earnest request of the Minister.

Pole and Flag Raising at Boonton

Jerseyman   *July 20, 1861*

The Brewerton Zouaves[1] of Morristown honor the occasion with their presence.

Mr. Editor: Saturday last was a gala day for our quiet little village. About 10 o'clock A. M., the place was thrown into no little excitement by the announcement that the "Zouaves" were coming; and with their "havelocks"[2] over their caps they presented a formidable appearance as the long procession came into the village. They proceeded to Liberty Hall, where they were alighted from their carriages, and then, under the command of Captain Miller, formed into line, and were escorted to Union Hall, where they were drilled by Rev. Mr. [G. D.] Brewerton. At 1 o'clock they dined at Liberty Hall, and at 2 o'clock turned out for full dress parade; and led by the Washington Corner Band, in full uniform, they paraded through the principal streets of the village to the foot of Liberty Street, where the new Pole of 110 feet high was raised, and a splendid Star Spangled Banner thrown to the breeze. A platform was erected on Liberty Street; and George Jenkins, Esq., appointed chairman, who upon taking the chair, made some very happy and appropriate remarks; and after some music by the Band, addresses were delivered by John Hill, Esq., Rev. G. D. Brewerton, and Mr. King of Morristown, and John Grimes. The address of Mr. Brewerton was received with the greatest enthusiasm; it was soul stirring and patriotic. After the addresses, the Zouaves went through with their drill to the great delight of all, and they elicited a great deal of praise and admiration from all present. At the conclusion of their maneuvering, they formed in line, and, with the Band, marched out of town to their carriages below the hill. We have witnessed many military companies and drills, but seldom have we seen any that did themselves more credit than these youthful Zouaves. Their gentlemanly appearance, good behavior, and orderly conduct, attracted the attention of every one and set an example for our boys we hope they will not soon forget. Already are our youth excited to form a Zouave Company. Our citizens were so well pleased with the young visitors, that we shall expect them soon to visit us again, when we hope to form a better acquaintance with them. The Pole raised on Saturday makes the tenth Pole and Flag raised in our village, besides numerous small ones. Boonton is loyal to the Union, and we all love and respect the Flag of our country — "The Star Spangled Banner, long may it wave, O'er the land of the free and the home of the brave."

[1] Zouaves were originally members of the infantry in the French North African army of Napoleon III composed of Algerians distinguished not only for their colorful uniforms but also for military excellence and bravery. During the American Civil War, Zouaves comprised elite volunteer military units whose soldiers wore uniforms similar to their French counterparts. Some of these units found that the red trousers and fez typical of most Zouave uniforms made them conspicuous targets and they later adopted standard-issue uniforms.

[2] Havelocks were coverings attached to a cap to protect the neck from sunlight or bad weather.

A Former Resident of Madison, N.J., Flees His Southern Residence and Returns North

Jerseyman   *July 20, 1861*

The following extract of a letter from Mr. William B. Smith formerly of this County, to his mother in Madison, is deemed to possess an interest wider than the family circle, and has been sent to us for publication:

Kekue, Iowa, May 25, 1861—

I was getting along very well in Memphis and should have stayed there had it not been for the political troubles. But knowing if I stayed there I would have to fight against my principals and my government, and swear allegiance to Jeff Davis, I resolved to leave at the sacrifice of everything.

Accordingly, I sold my house for one third of its value, and succeeded in getting my family and household goods on board a steamboat bound for St. Louis. I was followed to Columbus, Kentucky, and arrested on board the boat, on a false charge of obtaining money under false pretences, threatened with being taken back to Memphis and delivered up to the Vigilance Committee, there being persons there ready to swear that I was a Black Republican and Abolitionist, in which case nothing short of hanging me would have satisfied them. I had reasons to fear for my life at Columbus for the people were greatly excited on account of one of the citizens being held prisoner at Cairo for attempting to set fire to a railroad bridge above that place. When I was taken from the boat, the cry was raised that they had taken an Abolitionist from the boat and were going to hang him. Had it not been for the landlord of the hotel and one or two moderately disposed persons, I don't know what might have happened. My wife and the two children got off with me, but Laura went on to Cairo, 20 miles distant, and came back the next day. My wife was in a dreadful state of mind, and myself, not much better. Finally we compromised the matter by giving all the money we had, and my wife had to give up her watch to settle our hotel bill and get money to take us to St. Louis; we were detained there two days, and I assure you we were never so glad to get out of any place in our lives. If we had stayed in Memphis a little longer we would not have been allowed to leave at all. When we arrived in St. Louis we has just 70 cents left. I borrowed $5 [from] one of my wife's friends and left Laura at his house, and the rest of us came to this place.

Liberty Pole Raised in Chester

True Democratic Banner   *September 5, 1861*

MEETINGS AT CHESTER—On Thursday last, was raised the largest and most beautiful Liberty Pole to be found in our country. Men of all parties cooperated in procuring and erecting it. In the afternoon a large meeting of the substantial citizens of the village and surrounding country was convened . . . in the yard of the Chester Institute[1]. . . . Speeches were made by Jacob Vanatta and V. Dalrymple, Esqs.

That the stable citizens of Chester, without respect to party, will maintain the Union—and, by their words, acts, and contribution of their substance, aid in a vigorous prosecution of the war—cannot, we think, be doubted. We can see a thousand reasons why Chester is and should be theoretically and practically patriotic; we cannot see a single good reason why she should be otherwise.

[1] The Chester Institute was a private preparatory school, formerly a stage coach stop, presently a restaurant and inn known as the Publick House.

Call to Join a Morris County Company

Jerseyman   *September 21, 1861*

A Morris County Company is now forming for the War, to be commanded by Captain James M. Brown. It is already accepted, and will be attached to General Revere's Regiment. Headquarters on the Public Square. Now is the chance for all who wish to join a Morris Company. Let it be eagerly embraced.[1]

[1] On July 24, 1861, President Lincoln made a second call for three-year men. New Jersey had a quota of four regiments to fill. In response, Capt. James M. Brown raised Company K of the 7th New Jersey Regiment, the first distinctly Morris County company. Within a week 64 men enlisted. Company K soon had its full complement of men.

Republicans Advocate Creation of a Union Party

Jerseyman   *September 28, 1861*

A UNION MOVEMENT IN MORRIS COUNTY—At a meeting of the Republican Executive Committee of the County of Morris, held at the office of H. C. Pitney, Esq., on Tuesday, September 24, 1861—present A. A. Vance, Samuel Van Ness, Alfred B. Britten, S. S. Halsey, Alfred Mills, and H. C. Pitney—the following preamble and resolutions were unanimously adopted:

In view of the present condition of the country, true patriotism requires that party ties should be obliterated for the present, and that all loyal citizens, without regard to previous differences of opinion, should unite for the purpose of more effectively rendering the Government the material and moral support due to it from the whole people, and also preventing any divisions among its friends upon minute and unimportant issues—therefore

Resolved, That this Committee desires to bring about such results in the County of Morris, and that we believe this to be the wish of the Republicans of the County, it can be effected upon a fair and honorable basis.

Resolved, That we hereby invite the Democratic Committee of this County to meet with us at such time as may be convenient for them within a brief period, to cooperate with us in an effort to bring about this result.

Resolved, That H. C. Pitney and A. A. Vance be appointed to wait upon the Democratic Central Committee of this County, and make arrangements for such Joint meeting, if agreeable to them.

Resolved, That these resolutions be published in the *True Democratic Banner* and the *Jerseyman.*

A. A. Vance, Ch'n.
Alfred Mills, Sec'y.

The resolutions published above explain themselves. It is proper to say, however, in addition, that this action of the Committee has been taken in response to what they believed to be the almost unanimous wish of the party which they represent, and also of a large portion of the Democracy. The desire has been very generally expressed by prominent men of both parties, in view of what has been and is being done elsewhere, that some arrangements should be made here to avoid a partisan conflict this Fall, and through which all who are sincerely and honestly in favor of giving strength to the arm of the Federal Government, might testify the fact by the support of a single ticket. They have taken the initiative in the matter in good faith, seeking no party advantage. They have done so because they had been led to believe that they would be met by the representatives of the Democratic organization in a corresponding spirit. It is with some surprise, therefore, that they find a call for a Democratic County Convention in the *Banner* of this week; and the only reasonable explanation of the fact, under the circumstances, that they are able to give, is, that it was done by the Chairman of their last Convention without consultation with the loyal masses, or with the leading men in his own party who are in favor of supporting the Government by a vigorous prosecution of the War.

Democrats Respond to Republican Call For Creation of a Union Party

True Democratic Banner   *October 3, 1861*

It is a little singular that all of the dyed-in-the wool, most bitter, and, heretofore, most uncompromising members of the Black Republican Executive Committee present at its recent meeting, should now favor so unanimously a total obliteration of party ties, and advocate the forming of a union ticket. The members generally, it will be observed, are mere pop-guns of the party, put forward by the cunning old coons to be laughed at should their efforts to use us fail; and shows that the arch leaders of the opposition were not willing to expose themselves to the mortification of an almost certain failure of their miserable expedient to get the Democratic party to give strength to their waning fortunes. It is an insult to ask the Democracy to abandon party at this crisis—at the very time when it is putting forth all it strength, and doing more than its opponents to save the country from the impending dangers which now threaten it. In the State of New York, twenty-five thousand volunteers are yet wanted to make up its quota. While the Democratic city of New York has more than done its duty, it is a remarkable fact that the counties in the state which gave such heavy majorities for Mr. Lincoln, are those which particularly give the smallest number of volunteers to support his government—or, as it would be more correct to say, to support their country against those who are bent upon effecting its destruction under his administration. Are they cowardly or are they hypocritical? Are they really in favor of letting "the Union slide,"[1] as some of their partisan journals have it, or have they not the courage to fight in a quarrel they have done so much to institute?

While Democratic New Jersey has, and is still doing more than is required of her, it is highly probable that the cowardly wideawakes of New York State will be compelled by drafting to come out from their hiding places and face the troubles they have brought upon us. Let us hear no more of a union of parties. The Democracy have nobly done their duty, and don't want their record tarnished by alliances with Black Republicanism.

[1] Before the war some Republican newspaper editors called upon the federal government to let the Southern states secede in peace, regarding this as preferable to maintaining a union that tolerated slavery.

Farewell to Morris County Company K

Jerseyman   *Oct. 5, 1861*

The interest of this community in the company of Volunteers that has been gathering for a short time past, culminated on Tuesday evening (Oct. 1) in the First Presbyterian Church of this town, which was filled by the largest audience ever compressed within its walls, while hundreds left the doors of the building unable to obtain a foot of standing room.

A large number of patriotic and earnest youth had gone from our midst since the commencement of the war and attached themselves to companies formed in our own or adjoining States, yet no complete company organized and filled up by our own loyal citizens had gone to the seat of war—Capt. Brown, a highly respected gentleman of this Town, assisted by Henry C. Pitney, Esq., and others, determined to raise a company of one hundred men, to be connected with the 7th Regiment, commanded by our gallant townsman, Colonel Revere. The effort was in a few days crowned with success.

Others interested in the well-being of the volunteers, and desirous of enlisting the fullest sympathy of the community on their behalf, called a Farewell Meeting on the evening prior to their departure in the First Church. Long before the hour of services, the building was filled, except the place reserved for the Company, by a highly appreciative congregation, who were absorbed in all that was said and done. There were mothers with streaming eyes and swelling hearts, gazing, it might be for the last time, upon their noble boys; there were fathers with moistened cheeks, looking with manly pride upon the enthusiasm and patriotic bearing of the sons; wives, deeply moved, were present, commending their husbands to the preserving care and benignant smiles of a gracious Providence. Children looked upon the scene with variable feelings, knowing that on the morrow their fathers were to leave them; while not a few with peculiar emotions and the purist and strongest affections were scattered through the audience unable to restrain their feelings, check their thoughts or still their fears; and the hearts of all beat in harmony with the occasion, throbbing with mighty resolve and strong devotion to their country's flag, honor, and perpetuity.

The Company, as they marched in and took the assigned seats, were seen to be composed of material like the others that have gone to the war from the numerous towns and villages of the North. It had in it the hardy mechanic, the sturdy farmer, the young merchant, with not a few reared for other employment, drawn mainly from Morristown, Mendham, Boonton, and Madison. There was one without his coat, who hearing of the Company's departure, and fearing that he might be too late, left the place of his labor, and without bidding adieu to friends, started for the meeting. There is another who has near relatives in the South, sympathizing deeply with the rebels; a third has a brother in the Confederate army; a fourth was an only child; upon a fifth entered the hopes of a widowed mother; and each had a history peculiar to himself, and ties as strong to bind him to home and loved ones as the many who were present to bid him farewell. But love of country drowned every other consideration, and impelled them to rise above every obstacle that stood in their way, and go forth with the swelling hosts to maintain the honor of their country's flag, or die in its defense.

The services were opened with an appropriate prayer by Rev. Mr. Samuel L. Tuttle [pastor of the Presbyterian Church] of Madison, which was followed by the anthem "In God is our trust," sung by the choir. Addresses, able, thrilling, and in the fullest sympathy with the meeting, were made by Messrs. Little, Vanatta, and Hill, which were succeeded by others just as decided and earnest for the prosecution of the war and the integrity of the Union by the Reverend Messrs. Tuttle and Ellison.

A beautiful sword, sash, belt, and pistol were presented to Captain Brown by Alfred Mills., Esq. in a neat and suitable address. The articles were purchased by a few citizens of this Town and presented as a token of confidence in the officer. The Captain replied in a few pertinent and emphatic words, thanking the donors for their appreciative kindness, and in the name of his Company, thanking the gentlemen who had generously provided each member with an Indian rubber blanket [for protection from the rain when sleeping in the field].

The Reverend D. Irving, [pastor of the First Presbyterian Church, Morristown,] in the name of the Morris County Bible Society, presented to the Captain and each of the men, with a few appropriate words, a copy of the New Testament and Psalms.

The whole service was concluded by the choir and congregation singing the Army Hymn—"O Lord of Hosts, Almighty King, Behold the sacrifice we bring"—and then by the Benediction, pronounced by Rev. Mr. [C. S.] Vancleve [former pastor of the Methodist Church, Morristown].

Though a request was made by the pastor of the church that the audience would remember the solemnity of the occasion and the character of the house of worship, the pent feelings could not be repressed, but broke over all restraints. Never was the heart of the community more deeply stirred, and never was there a more united assembly for the furtherance of an object at any and all hazards.

The enthusiasm thus aroused was in no way stilled by the slumbers of the night. Early next morning the town was alive, and as the volunteers marched to the [railroad] cars, they were not only joined by new recruits, but were followed by hundreds to shake them by the hands, to speak a word of comfort, to bid the tearful farewell, and to give the parting benediction and the parting cheer.

A Young Girl's Patriotic Poem

Jerseyman   *November 2, 1861*

Within the past few weeks about a dozen volunteers have gone to the War from the vicinity of New Vernon in this County. The following piece of Poetry addressed to them was written by a young girl of that village, and has been sent to us for publication.

TO THE NEW VERNON VOLUNTEERS

Good Bye, ye gallant Volunteers,
New Vernon bids you go;
Go take your stand on the battle field,
And strike down every foe.

March bravely on, ye Volunteers,
And battle for the right;
For Liberty, Union, Blessed Peace,
An our glorious Union rights.

Go boldly on, ye Union band,
And bravely face the foe;
You are not forgotten by those at home—
They anxiously think of you.

They watch the daily news,
As by the post it comes.
And eager eyes do search the page
To see the news from you.

Stand bravely up, our boast and pride,
God give the victory to you,
And bring you back to loving friends,
And the laurels prepared for you.

Patriotic Meeting at Boonton

Jerseyman   *August 2, 1862*

A large and enthusiastic meeting was held at Boonton on Saturday evening last, and was addressed by H. C. Pitney and Theodore Little, Esqs., Col. S. F. Headley, and Hon. John Hill. Patriotic resolutions were passed, among them, one to raise $1,000 for bounty money[1] to be paid to the Volunteers who enlist from "Old Pequannoc," the most of which, we learn, has been raised, and a number of recruits obtained — Pequannoc is waking up to the importance of active and energetic measure in carrying on the war; and in the spirit of one of the resolutions, her patriotic citizens pledge their property and their lives, if necessary, to put down the rebellion and sustain the Government of the United States, and defend and keep flying the good old flag.

[1] Local communities frequently gave a cash gift to its volunteers.

Chapter 3

Secessionism

Though most Jerseyans supported the war, a large Copperhead minority remained active, especially in Newark and other cities that had strong economic ties to the South. Even in very strongly pro-Union counties such as Morris, Copperheads sometimes openly voiced their pro-Southern views. They advocated secessionism to the South or the formation of a separate central confederacy.

The following newspaper articles relate to secessionism in New Jersey and the response of Unionists to secessionist activities.

Secessionists in Morris County

Jerseyman   *May 25, 1861*

SECESSIONISTS IN MORRIS COUNTY—One would think that secession would not take root in the soil of New Jersey. Yet there are some here whose words and actions would more remind one of the attitude of South Carolina than of free and enlightened New Jersey. On Sunday last, while an aged minister was preaching in a school house near the outskirts of Parsippany, several persons stood outside, directly opposite the front windows of the building, annoying the congregation and openly avowing their sympathy with traitors; and because, on a former occasion, the minister had expressed himself in favor of the preservation of the Union, one of them made the remark in a loud tone of voice that he would like to see the old scoundrel hung. They also threatened other prominent citizens, Union men, with the same fate; and some were saying that the smallpox and yellow fever were doing a good work among the Northern troops at the South. This is but a specimen of their language, which more resembled that of South Carolina fire eaters[1] than that of Jerseymen. Is it not time that such actions were put a stop to! It is deserving of severe rebuke for any person, on common occasions, to express themselves in favor of treason; but when on the Sabbath they choose to disturb a religious meeting, and make threats against an aged minister, for no other reason than because he was a Union man, and make a parade of their sympathy with traitors, it is deserving of something more than rebuke. It is to be hoped that they will speedily learn that the freemen of New Jersey will not tolerate open avowed sympathy with traitors.

---

[1] *Fire eaters* refers to the militant political partisans from the South.

Secessionist Hung in Effigy

Jerseyman   *June 8, 1861*

We learn that a Littleton[1] Secessionist was hung in effigy and the effigy afterward burnt by the indignant citizens of that neighborhood on Tuesday night last.

---

[1] Littleton is now a part of Parsippany-Troy Hills.

The Secret Conspiracy

In contrast to Copperhead newspapers such as Newark's Daily Journal, *moderate Democrat papers supported the Union including Morristown's* True Democratic Banner. *The following* Banner *editorial attempts to uncover a secessionist conspiracy by a secret society, identified in a previous editorial (omitted here) as the Knights of the Golden Circle. This Southern secessionist organization, founded in 1855 by Virginian George Bickley, promoted the idea of a Southern empire consisting of a "golden circle" of slave states from the American South through Mexico and Central America to the rim of South America curving northward through the West Indies and onto Key West, Florida. Unionists frequently accused Northern chapters of the Knights of engaging in subversive activities.*

True Democratic Banner   *September 12, 1861*

THE SECRET CONSPIRACY — When we first alluded to an organized secret conspiracy in this State, having for its object the annexation of New Jersey to the Southern Confederacy, very few, but the initiated, believed in its existence. In that we were not disappointed. We expected just such incredulity. Our greater fear, in respect to the conspiracy, was that it would make its preparations and strike before its designs and purposes should be suspected and fully understood. The dangers to be apprehended from that secret conspiracy are not yet passed. It is true that every day discloses some new evidence as to its existence and purposes, and public attention is more generally directed to it. By that means it has received a check, but the only effect of that is to lead the conspirators to exercise greatest caution and to alter their mode of operations without, in any way, abandoning their purpose.

The scheme and purpose of the conspirators is Satanic— their means of operation are perfidious and devilish.

The main purpose of the arch-conspirators is, as we said, to precipitate New Jersey into revolution, and, in the confusion of a revolution, annex her to Jeff Davis' conspiracy — sometimes called the Southern Confederacy.

They have intended to employ the Democratic party as the main instrument in accomplishing this hellish purpose. They seek to rain and blast a glorious state and a glorious party at one and the same time.

The detail operators in this scheme of hideous crime and disaster, are men, some of whom, like Judas Iscariot, are impelled by love and hope of gain — others, by unhallowed ambition, and others, by a combination of these two incentives.

The work these conspirators are expected and which they desire to accomplish, is to elect a legislature favorable to Jeff Davis and secession. When this shall be done, some means will be devised to get rid of [New Jersey's] Governor [Charles S.] Olden and supply his place with a member of the conspiracy.

One means of getting a secession legislature is this; in counties where a sheriff, surrogate, or clerk is to be elected, the financial head (in this State) of the conspiracy assures a candidate that he will provide him with funds, enough to secure his election, provided he will insure the election of members of the legislature from his county who will support the schemes of the conspirators. We have reason to believe that not a few such bargains have been made. To operate the same end, mercenary agents have been employed in every county. Their business is to unite and organize men in opposition to the prosecution of the defensive war in which the Government is now engaged. Opposition to the Government in the prosecution, by it, of the defense, in the war now waged against it by the Davis conspiracy, is precisely the same thing as a declaration in favor of the Davis rebellion and the Southern Confederacy.

In selecting candidates in opposition to the war, the conspirators design to take such men as then can, by bribes, intimidations, and caucuses, and use them for any scheme they may seek to undertake. They will sail many of their candidates under the Union flag, but they will, in every case, be such men as can, in the hands of the conspirators, be moulded like dough in the hands of the baker.

It has been suggested that the lodges which have been established by the conspirators should be indicted by the Grand Jury of the United States courts as treasonable combinations.

That may, or may not be done, and it may or may not, if done, effectually crush the conspiracy. One thing, however, can be done. Every member of that conspiracy and every one of its tools can be defeated at the next election, and it should be done.

God has graciously provided that the conspiracy and its chief members shall be exposed by its own members. The names of the chief conspirators and their schemes and purposes have been and will be fully betrayed. Let the people see to it that not one of the members of tools of the conspiracy shall be elected to any office, no matter by whom or in what manner he may be nominated.

Unless we take that course we will be cursed with such a legislature as now disgraces and damns Maryland, and our State, like Missouri, before the 1st of April next, will be devastated with civil war.

The cabal in this State, to which we refer, is a branch of that society or league, the members of which, in Baltimore, arranged the assassination of the President elect of the United States[1] — burned the bridges and fired upon the troops.[2] And this branch of the same society in Missouri is now engaged in murdering and robbing Union men, driving them from their homes, burning their dwellings, firing into railroad trains filled with men, women and children, and in throwing trains loaded with passengers from bridges and embankments.[3]

Such a society should be closely watched and discouraged, opposed and reprobated in every legal way.

Very few men will or knowingly countenance the society or its schemes. The point to be guarded against, is to save men from being misled and inveigled into it by pretexts and artful devices.

[1] Prior to his inauguration, Lincoln made a rail tour on his way to Washington to greet the American people. Two days before his scheduled Baltimore stop, Pinkerton detectives informed him of an assassination plot, which he subsequently avoided by changing his schedule. This allowed him to pass through Baltimore in the middle of the night.

[2] This refers to a secessionist uprising that occurred when the 6th Massachusetts Regiment entered Baltimore on their way to Washington. When pro-secessionist rioters attacked the rear companies of the regiment with bricks, stones, and pistols, several soldiers opened fire, leaving 12 civilians dead and many more wounded. The city mayor and the chief of police ordered the destruction of bridges and roads entering from Philadelphia and Harrisburg to prevent more Union regiments from entering the state. They also had telegraph wires from Washington to Maryland torn down. These actions seriously threatened Washington itself, but the pro-Southern Maryland legislature preferred neutrality to hostility. Eventually Unionist factions prevailed in Maryland.

[3] This refers to Rebel led guerilla warfare that took place in Missouri in the spring of 1861 following the "mini Civil War" between forces led by Missouri's pro-slavery governor Claiborne Fox Jackson, and Capt. Nathaniel Lyon, commander of the soldiers stationed at the Federal arsenal in St. Louis. Jackson initiated the conflict by mobilizing the pro-Southern state militia and seizing a small U.S. arsenal at Liberty, near Kansas City. Lyon responded by mustering into service several regiments organized by the pro-Union German-American population. Lyon took St. Louis but not without inflicting 28 civilian casualties following mob violence by pro-Southern sympathizers who hurled rocks and brickbats (along with anti-German epithets) at Lyon's men. Jackson extended an olive branch, offering to disband his regiments if Lyon did the same. Lyon indignantly refused, stating that he would rather see Jackson plus "every man, woman, and child in

the State dead and buried." Lyon declared war against secessionist forces and success-fully drove them down to the southwest corner of the state within a month. Though he gained control of the state, he helped polarize it into two extreme camps. Violent con-flict between Confederate guerillas and Unionist counterinsurgency forces continued in this border state throughout the war, resulting in hatreds that continued long after the war.

Chapter 4

War

Newspaper articles providing information on Morris County men killed or wounded in battle, and letters of soldiers relating the experience of war, frequently appeared in the *Jerseyman* and *True Democratic Banner*. Examples of both appear in this chapter.

Soldiers' letters do not always provide a complete and accurate overview or analysis of military operations. But they do provide vivid descriptions of military activities with details of specific events during different stages of battle. Some of these subjective first-hand accounts present Union defeats in a positive light. For instance, the writer of "Report From Chancellorsville" includes praise for actions taken by the 7th N.J Regiment—and an expression of full confidence in Joseph Hooker, the Northern general most responsible for the Union defeat.

Sometimes soldiers expressed personal opinions that complemented the editorial position of the newspaper that printed their letters. This is evident in the account of the Battle of Williamsburg that appeared in the *True Democratic Banner*—written by a pro-Union Democrat who uses very strong language against Northern abolitionists.

Skirmish at Cloud's Mills, Virginia

Although Gen. George B. McClellan's Army of the Potomoc did not see major action prior to the Peninsular Campaign, Union soldiers engaged the Confederates during several skirmishes that resulted in casualties. The following are two successive accounts of one such incident in which a Morris County man lost his life.

Jerseyman   *September 7, 1861*

On Friday of last week, while Col. [George W.] Taylor's Regiment (3d New Jersey) was scouting near Cloud's Mills in Virginia, they fell into an ambush . . . and four men were wounded and two killed. Among the wounded was William Cole, of this Town, son of Mr. Henry Cole, who belonged to Capt. [Leonard H.] Regur's (Plainfield) Company. His thigh was perforated by a ball, and the wound is said to be a serious one.

Jerseyman   *September 14, 1861*

Death of a Morristown Volunteer—William Cole, formerly of this town, whom we noticed last week as having been wounded in a skirmish near Cloud's Mills, on Saturday, August 31st, died the following morning. He was taken in charge by two or three of the Morristown boys when he fell, who rendered him constant attention until he died, and afterwards buried the body—it being found impracticable to transport to his friends. We learn that Colonel Taylor and Captain Regur each bestowed their personal attention upon young Cole, and did everything in their power to make him comfortable in his last hours upon earth. Among his last words to his comrades, he said, "Boys, you may fight—fight bravely; but I must die."

General McClellan's Army Moves Against A Confederate Fortification Along the Potomac River

True Democratic Banner   *March 27, 1862*

Letter from a Morristown Volunteer—Messrs. Editors: On Sunday the 9th, I was strolling by the side of our beautiful river—the Potomac. The day was beautiful, the air as balmy as Spring, and, to make the picture still more lovely, the sweet notes of birds could be heard echoing from every dell. Not a sail was to be seen on the smooth glassy surface of the river, save one, a small gunboat, the *Anicosta*. She came steering close along the Virginia shore until almost abreast of Cock Pit battery. When bang went a gun, and shortly after, the report of the bursting shell was heard far up in the hills. She continued firing at long range until she seemed to be even more saucy, and went right in front of the rebel battery and let go two guns, but receiving no replay, she immediately put out launches, filled with men, who went ashore, tore down the secession rag, and raised the dear old Stars and Stripes. While this part of the great alactrum movus[1] was going on, a dense smoke was seen to rise from Shipping Point battery; it seemed to be trains of powder which had been laid by the rebels, and almost as sudden were flames seen to burst forth from the captured steamer *George Paige*, which, you remember, was taken from us in September last. This, at last, attracted the attention of our fleet up the river, which immediately steamed down and fired a few shots at the retreating cavalry. Our 1st Regiment, Massachusetts Volunteers, manned a large boat, carrying one company of one hundred, and landed on the Point, and then, over the deserted entrenchments, raised the gallant flag of our country. At this juncture, night threw her sable mantle over the earth, and we returned to our tents. The next morning, five hundred of the Massachusetts and five hundred of the New Jersey brigade crossed over for the purpose of securing the guns they had left behind, tents, commissary stores, etc. On landing, two companies were detailed for scouting duty, each being provided with side arms and rifles. They say it was one of the strongest fortified places they ever saw. Built on a peninsula extending into the river, it mounted ten guns of the heaviest caliber; two 64-pounders, two 120-pounders, and six 32-pounders. Others found proved to be nothing more than harmless pieces of wood, termed dummies. It was rather a dangerous place for us to be, as we thought it was undermined, and explosions were taking place all around us. Every gun was found to be loaded to the muzzle, and spiked.[2] We found five magazines filled with shot, shell, and, in fact, all the missiles of war. On opening these, which were carefully bolted and locked, they were found to be on fire, but nipping the fuse and throwing it out saved them. One magazine was lost, and the explosion was terrific, but no one was hurt. The camp was filthy, but we presume they must have lived well, for in one place an ox and a half was found freshly killed; [also] bags of flour, and such like articles, but no coffee—tobacco in quantities. They ran away so suddenly that on entering a house on the Point, a nicely burning fire was found, plates and cups on the table; on the fire swung the kettle boiling. On lifting the covers, a nicely boiled ham was found as well as other sundry brands, but they were not disturbed. On going into the interior, which our boys did, going six miles back, they came to the camp of the famous Texan Rangers but found here everything standing—tents as they left them, besides large quantities of forage which they had left in their hasty retreat. In this place they came across a sutler's shanty,[3] which could not have contained less than $4,000 worth of stuff, including silks and all other articles of ladies wear, for the wives of the soldiers. One incident will show you how the people are frightened into this war. One of the party sent got lost, and on making his way back to the river, came to a house in which he found rather a young girl, not sixteen. He made a few commonplace remarks to her after the usual greeting, taking a seat by the fire. She asked him if he was not afraid to stay, that all the soldiers had left, and that the Yankees were across the river. He told her he was not afraid of them, that they would not hurt anyone. He turned to leave; she pressed him to stay and take tea, but in came one of his mess mates and let out that they were Yankees; whereupon the girl gave a scream and rushed out of the house, since which time she has not been seen.

On Wednesday our gallant boys went over in the morning and continued there removing guns, etc., but on calling the roll at night, two lieutenants were missing, and it is feared they went outside the lines and were taken prisoners by rebel cavalry, of which there are quite a number about acting as scouts, and I suppose are on their way to Richmond. On Thursday some five hundred of our Jersey brigade went in as far as a place call Dumfries where they discovered a pile of stores for the army. Instead of taking it in charge and sending down for reinforcements, they set it on fire, and then beat a retreat, and did not stop until they reached camp, thereby, it is said, destroying $10,000 worth of useful articles.

We are under orders to be ready to march within twenty-four hours. Yours truly, R. G. L.

[1] alactrum movus: "a quick motion"; here this refers to a rapid advance of troops.

[2] A spiked cannon had a large spike driven into its vent, disabling it to prevent its use by the enemy.

[3] A sutler was a provisioner to an army post established in a shop sometimes called a sutler's shanty.

The Horror of War

A Morristown soldier graphically describes scenes from the battle for Williamsburg, which took place during General McClellan's unsuccessful Peninsular Campaign. This soldier, a Democrat, defends McClellan (a fellow Democrat) against Republican criticism. He also includes some strong words aimed at the abolitionist Republican editor of the Jerseyman. *Such anti-Republican sentiments were frequently expressed in the pages of the* True Democratic Banner.

True Democratic Banner   *May 22, 1862*

We make the following extracts from an interesting letter handed us, from a young volunteer in Captain [James H.] Brown's Company, to his father, in this town. The letter is dated the 14th inst., at Camp, 7th N.J. Volunteers, New Kent County, Virginia:

Dear Father: Since the fight on the 5th, and as we are now laying still for a few days, I though it a good opportunity to let you know of my whereabouts. After the fight we encamped in any place we could find room enough to lie down in, two or three in a place, but in the morning all came together, and we had quite a respectable company. In the afternoon we moved inside the rebel quarters in front of Williamsburg and sent out squads of men to bury the dead, Union men first, and rebels after. I took a stroll through the woods, and for the first time in my life witnessed the horrors of a battlefield. It was awful in the extreme. In some places where our grape and canister shot had found them, there were piled dead rebels in heaps of from four to ten in a place, and in one place I counted thirteen rebel haversacks in a place, not more than twenty yards square, that had been left there after the dead and wounded had been carried away. The most of them were shot through the head and from the expression of their faces must have died very hard. In one place we found one sitting against a tree just in the act of tearing a cartridge between his teeth, when the fatal bullet found him, and he died with the charge between his fingers. Some of the rebels treated our wounded with humanity, but others, especially the Louisiana Tigers,[1] ran bayonets through the dead and dying, and mutilated the bodies in a horrid manner. I hear that Captain Brown has gone home, and that his wound is not as dangerous as at first supposed; we will miss him very much, and hope he will soon recover. We left Joseph Watkins in Williamsburg; he was in good spirits, but I am afraid his health is not good enough to stand the shock, as the weather is quite warm. We are now quartered about fifteen miles from Williamsburg, but where we are going I cannot say at present. Lieutenant [Michael] Mullery received a *Jerseyman* four days ago in which Mr. [Alanson A.] Vance [the *Jerseyman*'s editor] seemed inclined to run down General McClellan for letting the rebels get away from Yorktown, without bagging them. Please tell Mr. Vance that if he knows more about General McClellan's business than he does himself, he had better supersede him; but if he does not and cannot find anything else to write about but to try to stir up dissatisfaction in the army that is perfectly satisfied with its leader, than he had better suspend the publication of his paper, as I for one hate an abolitionist as bad as a rebel, and if my old gun could talk, it would say that we together tried to make one less on the 5th of the present month, every time I brought it up to my shoulder.

---

[1] The Louisiana Tigers consisted of approximately 12,000 Louisiana infantrymen who served in the Confederate Army of Northern Virginia. Though known for their exceptional bravery in battle, they developed an unsavory reputation as drunken lawless renegades who often posed a greater threat to Southern civilians than the Union army. In fact, Louisiana probably had a higher percentage of criminals, drunkards, and deserters in their commands than any other Confederate state, according to Terry L. Jones, author of *Lee's Tigers*. The account of atrocities committed by the Louisiana Tigers as described in this letter is probably accurate.

Death by Disease

Jerseyman   *May 24, 1862*

Death of a Volunteer—George Wesley Peer, of Co. K, 7th New Jersey Volunteers, died at Yorktown Hospital, a few days since, of typhoid fever.[1] He was the youngest son of Jacob Peer, of Denville, Morris County, and aged 17 years. Young Peer was a noble fellow. A generous nature, warm affections, and remarkable amiability had secured for him the attachment of a large circle of friends. He was a good soldier, and much beloved by all his comrades. His career was brief, but the honors of a patriot soldier will ever cling to his memory. His remains will be brought to Denville for internment, as soon as possible—where the funeral services will be held immediately upon their arrival—probably the latter part of next week.

[1] During the Civil War, twice as many soldiers died from disease as were killed in action. This is low by nineteenth century standards. For instance, during the Mexican War, seven Americans died by disease for every one killed in action. The three main killers during the Civil War were diarrhea, dysentery, and typhoid.

The Death of Infantryman John M. Powers

True Democratic Banner   *October 2, 1862*

Camp Grover, Sept. 27—The following mention of the gallantry and worth of one of Morris County's sons, [John M. Powers,] we copy from a letter by Capt. J. R. Dobson, of the company to which young Powers belonged, written to the friends of deceased:

John M. Powers, formerly of Rockaway, N.J., a member of Company G, First Infantry regiment Pennsylvania R. V. C., was slain in the battle of South Mountain,[1] September 14, 1862, in the 21st year of his age.

The above simply records but feebly tells of all loss that has been felt by an entire company for one who was the embodiment of cheerfulness, gallantry, and bravery—ever cheerful in the camp, in the march, and on the battlefield, and always an unassuming example where duty was to be performed or danger met. In the numerous battles in which his regiment has been so conspicuously engaged, he has distinguished himself in each and all; and at South Mountain—where other regiments faltered and failed to advance before the dreadful fire of the enemy . . . the First Regiment was called upon to sustain the reputation of our corps, . . . [W]e charge[d] over fences, up the mountain's rugged side, until no living rebel's foot was left to press the blood-stained peak;

the brilliant encomiums of our general and the thinning of our brave ranks but too plainly speak. There our noble comrade met his death; a death he was never known to fear—and of all the Union troops who spent their life's blood there, none can be mourned more earnestly by his compatriots in arms than young Powers, and they feel that their relatives and friends in New Jersey will unite with them in this simple epitaph: "Requiescat in pace."[2]

[1] Following the Confederate victory at the Second Battle of Bull Run, Gen. Robert E. Lee moved his troops into Maryland. From there he planned to continue on to Harrisburg, Pennsylvania, cutting Washington's railroad lines to the west. But Lee delayed his move through Maryland, sending part of his army under Gen. Thomas J. (Stonewall) Jackson to Harper's Ferry, West Virginia, to eliminate a Union garrison that threatened his rear flank. In the meantime, two Union soldiers found a copy of Lee's battle plans wrapped around some cigars misplaced by a careless Southern officer. They sent the map on to General McClellan, whom Lincoln had recently reappointed as commander of the Army of the Potomac. With this information, McClellan planned to attack Lee's divided army piece by piece. But McClellan delayed the attack for 18 hours. As McClellan carefully planned his action, the Confederates obtained word of his strategy from a Maryland civilian sympathetic to the Confederacy. Lee concentrated his forces at the pass through South Mountain and blocked the Union advance for one day. Though a Union corps under Gen. William B. Franklin broke through at Crampton's Pass, they failed to save Harper's Ferry from Jackson's army. Lee remained undefeated. But although Lee saved his army from disaster, Union forces decisively stopped his invasion of Maryland at the Battle of Antietam that soon followed.

[2] Requiescat in pace: "Rest in peace."

Tragic Loss of Morris County Volunteers

The following incident involving members of the 27th New Jersey Regiment happened shortly before the regiment's tour expired.

True Democratic Banner   *May 14, 1863*

The 27th New Jersey Regiment, in recrossing the Cumberland River at St. Igail's ferry . . . on the 5th inst., had one of their boats upset, and thirty-three men were drowned, nineteen of them belonging to Rockaway Township. The following is a list of their names:

Company A—George Emery, George A. Sigaffus, Andrew Dickson, Cornelius Derrone. Company B—Captain John T. Alexander, First Sergeant Albert Wiggens, Erastas Bran. Company C—Corporal Charles Stephens, Amos G. Stephens, Benjamin Stoney, Edward Dalland, Joan B. McPeak, Andrew J. Willets, Andrew J. Young. Company L—Sergeant William H. Weaver, Gideon Bostido, Ralston Peer, James O'Neil, Wilson Pettigrew, James Shaw, Samuel H. Smith, John

McClusky, L. W. Shawger, J. Demouth, Lewis O. Green, William Ocobec, Thomas Odell, Ed Nichols, J. H. Fuller, R. K. Miller, L. Degraw, Eliakine Saners, Joseph Class.

Two ropes were stretched across the river and a boat used at each, and these men were in the upper boat and two-thirds across the stream, when the boatmen who were managing it, although experienced, from some mishap, allowed the rope to escape them, and the boat was carried down to the lower rope. Had they passed the rope over their heads, all would have been safe; but, unfortunately, some of them caught hold of it, and the boat was at once capsized. The remaining boat was at once despatched to the relief of the drowning men, and every available means used; yet, in spite of all efforts, thirty-three of the number were drowned.[1] This is a terrible blow, and falls with crushing force on the citizens of Rockaway.

[1] A soldier who observed this incident later wrote, "The men became panic stricken and rushed to the opposite end of the boat, which caused it to sink, and in less time than it has taken me to write this account, the whole boatload was swept by the lower rope into the rapid Cumberland. Those who could swim were seized by the death grasp of those who could not swim. It was an awful sight. May God spare me from being again a spectator of such a scene." (Munsell, *History of the County*, 91)

Report From Chancellorsville

True Democratic Banner   *May 21, 1863*

Lieutenant [William] Axtel of Capt. [Durastus B.] Logan's Company 11th regiment writes home, (Morristown) under date of May 7th, at Chancellorsville,[1] that the Captain was hit, but is now with the regiment: Lt. Ira Cory had one of his knuckles skinned by a passing ball, and he, (Lt. A.) was touched in the same way: George Stevens was shot in the cheek — not serious; there were four killed and ten wounded in the company; and 20 killed, 137 wounded and 9 missing in the regiment. He was at the hospital to see the boys, and found them getting along pretty well. He says, "I don't think that old Joe [Hooker] will give it up so; his men think as much of him as ever, and will fight for him again with just as much confidence as before. He was on the field himself; we gave three good cheers for him; then made a charge . . . with the 7th N.J., and took several prisoners. New Jersey needn't be ashamed of her troops; they say a Jersey boy don't know enough to stop fighting; it seemed so on Sunday, the way they fought, when everything else left the field.

[1] This refers to the Battle of Chancellorsville, which the North lost. Gen. Joseph Hooker's

plan to crush the Confederates between two Union forces failed when Lee divided his already smaller army in two, sending Gen. "Stonewall" Jackson to attack Hooker's front. Jackson took Hooker by surprise. Though numerical odds favored Hooker by two to one, Hooker miscalculated the true strength of Jackson's army and ordered a retreat, much to the astonishment and confusion of Union officers and soldiers. It was Lee's greatest victory though it cost the life of Jackson, who died in the conflict, mistakenly shot by one of his own men. (For more on the Battle of Chancellorsville see pages 105, 119 and 148).

Captain Edward Payson Berry Dies at Gettysburg

Jerseyman   *July 25, 1863*

Capt. Edward Payson Berry

The above named, an officer in the 5th Regiment N.J. Volunteers, a highly esteemed and promising young man, died at Gettysburg, on the 10th last, after peculiarly severe suffering, from a wound received in battle at that place, on the 2nd.

Captain Berry was a native and resident of Dover, in this county, and his loss is sincerely mourned by a large community. The arrival of his body at Dover, unannounced, and when all supposed him to be convalescent, caused a deep feeling of gloom throughout the town. A public meeting was held at Union Hall, where many addresses on the character of the deceased, and of others that have fallen in the army, were made, and resolutions passed.

On Friday of last week, during the funeral obsequies, all business was suspended and the stores and shops closed.

The following resolutions have been sent us for publication:

Resolution of Respect and Condolence to the memory of Capt. Edward Payson Berry, passed by the citizens of Dover, at a Public Meeting, July 16, 1863.

Whereas, in the afflictive providence of God, our esteemed fellow townsman, Capt. Edward Payson Berry, has been removed from among us by death, caused from the effects of a wound received in the late battle of Gettysburg, Pennsylvania—and Whereas, it is eminently fitting that distinguished worth and self-sacrificing devotion to our country in this, her great struggle for national existence and Constitutional freedom, should be publicly recognized—

Resolved,

1. That we, the citizens of Dover, lamenting the death of this faithful young officer, thus in the prime of life and usefulness, still rejoice to know that he died as he had ever lived, at the post of duty, nobly and bravely battling for the maintenance of right, truth and liberty,

and that his noble example survives him to guide and cheer those still struggling in defense of the flag under which he fought, and the Union for which he gave his life.

2. That, remembering our association with the deceased, in which we had daily revelations of his character, we desire to place on record our testimony of his exalted worth, illustrated in a life of perfect integrity, pure and exemplary habits, and of high and inflexible devotion to duty under all circumstances.

3. That his true worth and courage, as displayed in the many battles in which he participated previous to the one in which he gave up his life, his last offering to his country, were publicly appreciated by his several promotions from a private soldier, to those of Second and First Lieutenant, Quartermaster, Adjutant, and Captain.

4. That in his death, the citizens of Dover have lost a valued friend; one whose Christian virtues and heroic conduct have reflected honor upon his native town, and the country, one of its most devoted and promising officers.

5. That high-toned Christian patriotism is clearly exemplified, in the voluntary relinquishment of his studies, and early enlistment in his country's service.

6. That we deeply sympathize with the bereaved family of the deceased, and especially with his young and widowed companion in their irreparable loss, and begging to share with them the burden of their grief, commend them to the solacing care of "Him who doth all things well."

7. That a copy of the foregoing be signed by the President and Secretary of this meeting and forwarded to the family of the deceased, and that copies be furnished [to] the county papers.

> Henry McFarland,
> President
>
> M. H. Dickerson,
> Secretary

Chapter 5

The Draft

In August of 1862, Lincoln authorized Secretary of War Edwin M. Stanton to issue a call for a draft of 300,000 militia to serve for nine months. Stanton's August 4 order was not a draft in the modern sense. It gave states the option of raising their own volunteer regiments as before. The federal government promised that it would not draft additional volunteers if the states succeeded in enrolling their required quota of men by September 5.

To encourage volunteers, New Jersey's Governor Charles S. Olden announced that the state would pay a cash bounty of six dollars per month to each volunteer. In addition, cities and towns often added their own cash bounties. Consequently, New Jersey fulfilled its quota, though it did not meet the September 5 deadline.

By the following year, enlistment had slackened. Throughout the North, local towns and counties failed to meet the quota, which compelled Congress to pass the first federal conscription law in U.S. history. This time, local towns and counties were not as successful raising volunteers. Draft evasion, known as "skedaddling," became commonplace. Those able to afford it could legally hire substitutes to serve in their place. Many wealthier members of society, including the young John D. Rockefeller, purchased outright exemption for $300.

Conscripting an Army

The author of the following Jerseyman *editorial discusses some of the issues related to the problems of raising an army. First, he questions the wisdom of raising cash bounties through local taxes prior to the commencement of the draft. He also expresses concern that Morris County might have difficulty filling its quota since those who anticipate being drafted might prefer to earn more money enlisting in towns and cities offering higher bounties. Finally, he criticizes New Jersey's Democratic governor Joel Parker for not fully cooperating with Congress in the implementation of the draft. Though Parker was a Unionist, his ambivalence regarding the draft stemmed from his dislike of Lincoln and abolitionism. Parker preferred reconciliation with the South through compromise on the slavery issue.*

Jerseyman   **August 22, 1863**

Strong efforts are being made in various counties in this State to raise their quotas by volunteering by the 25th when the thirty days grace expires and the draft is to commence. Large bounties are offered, and meetings held to stir up the people and secure the object. Yet it is doubtful whether in a single instance complete success will be achieved, while complications, difficulties, and litigation will almost certainly ensue. In the County of Morris, the prevailing sentiment among all parties had been, and still is, to let the draft take its course; or, if money was raised at all to promote volunteering, it should be done by private subscription, and not by either the county or the townships. The wisdom of this latter course will be more apparent by and by, when the counties which have voted money, attempt to collect it by taxation. It is perfectly clear that neither a township nor a county have a legal right to levy a tax for any such purpose, and it is equally clear that they cannot collect the tax where payment is resisted in the Courts. We are not surprised, therefore, to learn that the loans thus authorized go to a begging in many places. The money cannot be had. Capitalists, who have their wits about them, are slow to invest their means in a such uncertain securities.

But there is likely to be another trouble growing out of this volunteering business in some Counties. Suppose a man is regularly enrolled in the township of Morris, where he resided at the time of the enrollment; his name is placed in the wheel, and he is drafted. When inquiry is made for him, it turns out that, tempted by the large bounties offered in Newark, Jersey City, Sussex County, or elsewhere, he had volunteered, and, at the time of the draft, was in the service. What then? He could not certainly be treated as a deserter, and would not be removed from the service; but he must necessarily, it seems to us, be counted upon the quota of Morris Township, and not upon that where he volunteered. So that, in case of another draft, the community who paid his bounty would simply get nothing for their money. This view of the matter would probably be opposed, but as it is founded in justice and common sense, would unquestionably be taken by the authorities to whom it was referred. Otherwise, a small township might be deprived of all the material from which a draft could be made, and left with a quota which it was utterly impossible to fill.

There are still other difficulties occurring to us, growing out of the unfortunate interference of Governor Parker with the regular operations of the law of Congress for placing men in the field, but we forbear comment upon them. It will prove in the end as fruitless, as, under the circumstances, it was unpatriotic and ill-timed.

Escaping the Draft

As the Civil War dragged on, Democratic opposition to its continuation grew — even among Unionist Democrats who had initially supported the war. Widespread draft evasion and lack of volunteers indicated public dissatisfaction with the continuing conflict. Not surprisingly, articles focusing on draft dodging appeared more frequently in Democratic newspapers including the True Democratic Banner. *The author of the article on the following page takes particular delight in attacking the hypocrisy of those Republicans who avoided the draft by hiring substitutes.*

Ads offering "professional" draft evasion assistance frequently appeared in the **True Democratic Banner.**

True Democratic Banner   *June 2, 1864*

THE DRAFT—As the draft has been the absorbing topic of the week, we make room for it to the exclusion of other matter. There has been much skedaddling, we learn, from the mines and iron works of Rockaway Township. One of our town wags[1] who happened in Hoboken as a train arrived with a party of skedaddlers on board with trunks, boxes, bags, etc., remarked in a loud voice to a friend—"Jim, Major Brown has fixed things alright at this ferry—No man crosses it without having his pass examined." The skedaddlers who were leaning towards the ferry, at once stopped, and then with alarmed looks, scattered in various directions, some going to the Jersey City Ferry.

Some of the wide-a-wakes who thought they were doing a big thing for their country when, with banner, torch, and cape, they paraded their fanaticism before the public, having been delightfully excited over the draft; and seem at a loss to find epithets and curses deep enough to express their change of sentiment with, while pulling the hard earned dollars out of their pockets to obtain exemption. They have paid pretty dear for participating as showmen to Abe Lincoln. . . .

Chatham and Pequannoc have by this time got the substitutes they contracted for to fill their quotas. Other townships are taking measures to obtain substitutes also, and a number of associations have been formed to pay the exemption fees of those of its members who are drafted.

Furnishing Substitutes—From an important circular from Provost Marshal General Fry in reference to furnishing substitutes, it appears that any person enrolled may furnish at any time, previous to a draft, an acceptable substitute; and further, that such persons may furnish substitutes at any place other than where they reside or are enrolled. This is important in many respects. For instance, a person enrolled may be absent from his district or place of enrollment. In whatever district or city he happens to be, he may, if he chooses, hire his substitute, take him before the Provost Marshal for acceptance, who will duly notify the Provost Marshal of the district where he stands enrolled, which fully exempts him the same as though he had not left his district or had there furnished his substitute.

---

[1] wag: "joker" or "prankster"

Chapter 6

The Slavery Debate

Throughout the war, a debate raged in New Jersey over the status of Southern blacks, especially after Lincoln issued the Emancipation Proclamation on January 1, 1863. Many Republican abolitionists hoped that blacks would rise up against their masters. Democrats, both Unionists and Copperheads alike, found this idea appalling. They feared that blacks, once liberated, would commit brutal acts of terrorism against the white population. Republicans responded by castigating Democrats for defending an economic system they viewed as oppressive and brutal. This chapter features writings that express opposing views regarding the slavery issue.

The White Man's Party

The following True Democratic Banner *editorial defines the Democratic Party as a "white man's party," whose purpose is to secure white men's personal liberty by defeating the "black man's party," i.e., the Republicans. The editorialist cites what he sees as negative economic consequences of the war. He then appeals to working class fears, asserting that freed Southern blacks would compete with whites for jobs and that wages would be reduced as a result of the black influx to the North.*

True Democratic Banner   *May 22, 1862*

Although this republic was founded by white men to secure to white men personal liberty, religious liberty, and the individual and collective prosperity which naturally flows from enlightened free institutions, we have now a Congress and many State Legislatures whose sole occupation seems to be exclusive legislation for the benefit of the blacks.

The imperative requirements of the war; the consequent necessities of the Treasury; the stagnation of commerce and manufacturers; the languishing condition of labor, which daily appeal to the hearts and heads of our legislators, are drowned in the mighty rush of zeal that inspires our Solons[1] with multitudinous expedients to blacken the records of Congressional legislation!

The resolutions and acts, the speeches of that national body might lead to the belief that the government was located in Timbuctoo,[2] were it not that the documentary evidence we daily receive of this African legislation are dated from Washington, in the District of Columbia.

White laborers already look with apprehension upon the numerous bands of runaway blacks who daily invade our soil, wending their way northward and westward, and there is no exaggeration in saying that, ere long, our white laborers will meet runaway blacks face to face in competition for employment. The inevitable consequences of this competition must and will be the degradation of labor, and the reduction of wages; they will then detect, when too late, the false pretences of the Republican party, whose laudations of "the dignity of labor" were but a cheat to lure them from the ranks of the Democratic party, which alone has, ever since the Revolution, honestly protected white labor against the constant encroachments of the aristocracy of wealth. The day is not far distant when the white citizens of the North will awaken, as if from an impressive dream, to the dreadful realities which surround them, and will join in mass the white man's party that is destined to hurl from power the black man's party—now hurrying the nation into anarchy and irretrievable ruin.

[1] Solons: lawgivers

[2] Timbuctoo: town in Mali (formerly French Sudan) near the Niger River in West Africa.

Chester Minister Praises Lincoln, Criticizes Abolitionists

In the following sermon, reprinted in the July 24, 1862, True Democratic Banner, *the pastor of the First Presbyterian Church in Chester, Rev. James F. Brewster, enthusiastically supports the war and the efforts of Lincoln to restore the Union. Although Brewster speaks highly of President Lincoln, he disagrees with those who would abolish slavery. According to him, this would "put the torch and the sword in the hands of an abject race...to let loose upon our misguided enemies...horrors whose very thought chills the heart and curdles the blood."*

A PATRIOTIC SERMON DELIVERED AT THE 1ST PRESBYTERIAN CHURCH, CHESTER, BY REV. JAMES F. BREWSTER, ON SUNDAY, JULY 13, 1862

"Be of good courage, and let us play the men for our people, and for the cities of our God; and the Lord do that which seemeth him good." — 2d Samuel 10:12.

Religion and Patriotism are twin sisters, and ever dwell together in the heart, which is regulated by the spirit of Heaven.

The man who loves his God will love the creations whom he has made; but this affection will entwine itself still more closely around those who are bound to him by the ties of a common country, common interests, and common institutions.

The blessing of peace and tranquility, of law and order, and good government, are among the most priceless that can be bestowed upon the human race, and when these blessings are lost, or imperilled, we feel that every other interest is secondary, and every other pursuit should, if necessary, be abandoned, until these are recovered or secured. Though our country be dear to us in the sunny days of peace — though we may exult with honest pride over all that is honorable in her history — over all that has been heroic in her struggles — over her increasing wealth and power — over her advancement in art, and learning, and refinement — yet we find that she lies still nearer to our hearts, and that we cling to her with a love still more intense in her days of sorrow, perplexity, and peril. A community of blessings and sympathies may furnish a strong love of union, but when men have suffered and prayed together, when they have freely poured forth their treasures and their blood in a common cause and for mutual interest, it rallies them together as with links of steel. It is strange what a power there is in danger and suffering to cement the hearts of those who have nobly borne it together. There is no bond of union so close as the bond of common sorrows. There is no brotherhood so deep and true as the brotherhood of calamity and misfortune. There is a subtle influence of pain and sorrow to knot fellow suffers heart to heart and soul to soul as no participation in joy and pleasure can ever unite them. The survivors of the wreck who can recall the days and hours of danger and exposure, of alternating hopes and despair which they bore together, the remnant of the forlorn hope, who stood side by side, while shot and shell were raining death around them; or the few brave and true hearts who together have struggled through the protracted and terrible siege, and whose friendship is cemented by a thousand associations of sympathy and endurance, cannot choose but feel for each other a deeper than common interest.

It is thus that as citizens of a common country, we are drawn more closely to each other and to it, now when its holiest interests are imperiled and we are enduring sacrifices and danger in its defense.

The highest motives of humanity and religion sometimes compel us to throw aside implements of peace, and, with a prayer in the God of justice, commit our cause to the decision of the sad and solemn field of battle.

Our duty to ourselves, to our county and to our God, all demand that we meet the responsibility and encounter the peril which we cannot avoid.

There are times when the call to armed resistance is the call of honor and of duty. The blessings of peace are dear, and to be cherished as our highest boon, and yet men have often been compelled to wade through blood in order to secure them. Nothing can be more agreeable to Heaven than that harmony prevail among his creatures; and he has laid down as one of the strongest obligations of our holy religion, "Follow peace with all men;" and Christ has crowned with benediction those who labor to secure it; "Blessed are the peacemakers, for they shall be called the children of God."

But in this disordered world where sin throws all things into confusion—when avarice would rob us of our property, and ambition would deprive us of our rights . . . then Heaven forbid that peace should be maintained at such fearful cost, and so long as we have the means to make resistance. Peace sometimes is disgraceful and unmanly. There are times when God bids us draw the sword, and the art of war becomes a part of our religion—then, blessed are they who offer themselves upon the alter of their country, and who faithfully discharge their duty.

In regard to private offences, individual wrongs, the law of God demands unlimited forgiveness and forbids retaliation; but this rule does not extend to public injuries, where acquaintances and meek submission would serve only to invite the aggressions of tyranny, and would be compelled soon to surrender every principle of humanity and religion.

The courage that is here demanded is a readiness to brave danger in the discharge of duty. It is widely different from the spirit of mad revenge and ferocious hate. It is not the fury of inflamed passion broke loose from reason, and acting only by the vagaries of a frenzied impulse; but it is a determination, calm, deliberate, and rational—the courage of a man and not of a tiger.

While on the one hand it is a sickly sentimentality, and not religious principle which refuses to draw the sword in necessary warfare, yet, on the other hand, it is the first duty of the Christian to guard against the vindictive and revengeful spirit, which is utterly inconsistent with the dictates of humanity and the law of God. Brute courage is not Christian heroism. My cheek pales when I hear men exulting in the terrible results of massacre and carnage, and see, sometimes, even gentle women, eager to put the torch and the sword in the hands of an abject race, not yet entirely freed from their native barbarism, and to let loose upon our misguided enemies, upon the wives, and the daughters, and the children of those who once were dear, horrors whose very thought chills the heart and curdles the blood.

It was one of the bitterest wrongs in our past wars, when the enemy let loose upon us the savage Indian, with his knife and tomahawk; and yet there are some around us eager to inaugurate a policy which may lead to results still more sad and terrible. Never until every other means have been tried and found unavailing should we think of adding the horrors of servile insurrection to the terror and distress of honorable warfare.

Compelled by a sad and awful necessity, we slay the enemies, but to exult over the work of death, to rejoice in its necessity, or do aught to magnify its torture, were monstrous. Our work is one of appalling solemnity. Our enemy, reckless in rebellion, have renounced their allegiance. They have defied our rulers and our government. They have aimed a fatal blow at the very foundation of constitutional liberty. They have torn down our starry flag and flung out an insulting banner. They have inaugurated butch cry and war. They have slain thousands of our brave men and imprecated upon themselves a heavy curse. To every unprejudiced mind the path of duty is clear. We must stand by our government and defend its honor. We must put down insurrection and maintain the authority of the Constitution and the laws, even though it cost millions of treasure and long years of struggle; though it take the last dollar from our pockets and the last man from our soil. But we want the spirit of earnest, determined, conscientious men—the spirit that enters upon stern deeds only from a sense of duty, and is therefore all the more determined and brave—the spirit of unselfish devotion which Heaven will bless and on which God will smile. An army of Christian soldiers is invincible, and we rejoice that there are so many in our ranks today—from the youthful general who commands our forces, and who, with a humble trust in God, is battling against a thousand difficulties—down through officers and men, so many who are soldiers of the Cross, and living in the fear of God. A belief in the righteousness of their cause nerves their arm with new power, while a sense of pardoned sin and a hope of Heaven on high, makes them bid defiance to danger and death in their most shocking forms.

We vainly imagined at the onset of this unnatural struggle, that our numbers, our wealth, our vast resources, would at once crush rebellion and give us victory, but the event has demonstrated this to be a fearful mistake.

After the first shock, which ran like electric fire through the country, the North rose up in its power and went forth with confidence. But in the first great battle, when we expected success [i.e., the First Battle of Bull Run], our forces were seized with panic, and fled in wild confusion from a field their valor had well nigh won.

Two weeks ago and the magnificent columns of our army had swept on from the Potomac and high hopes were thundering at the gates of Richmond. Today with ranks shattered and bleeding, they are resting miles from the rebel capital; our hospitals are filled with the mutilated and the dying, and our country is convulsed with grief.[1] Though not defeated, yet there is wide spread disappointment and sorrow. Jehovah can crush the highest hope and he can give success when least expected.

We have had a week of fearful battles, and in the solemn pause which now marks our history, we hear the groans of the dying and the distant wail of the bereaved. Like Egypt on that fatal night when God's curse hung over her, there is hardly a family in our land but is mourning its dead. From Maine to Missouri, from Virginia to Texas, there is sorrow, desolation and woe. God's hand is heavy on us. We of the North have not been innocent in regard to the causes of this war, and Jehovah is teaching us how terrible is its evil, and how "fearful is the guilt of those who have plunged the county into its horrid jaws." There is a disposition in some quarters, to lose sight of the first principals on which we sprung to arms—the defense of our Union and our Constitution, and the supremacy of law—and an effort to make this contest an instrument, if not of partisan scheme, at least to secure results which the thoughtful and dispassioned portion of our people regard as wild impracticable and undesirable. All this makes us anxious, but it should also make us vigilant, and active, and prayerful. God is humbling us, but he has not abandoned us. There is much for which we should be thankful, and take courage.

At the head of our government is a man of unpretending manners and great simplicity of character, but who, with wonderful prudence, has won and preserved the confidence of the great bulk of the nation. Of unbending firmness, yet mild and gentle, he seems to have studied honestly the public good. I cannot help believing that God has raised him up for this crisis, and if he shall act in the future as wisely and as well as he has acted in the past, than future generations will enroll his name among the benefactors of his country.

Again, we may take courage from the magnificent skill and bravery which has been displayed by our army and its leaders, who in that fearful week, whose record furnishes such a bloody page, fought like heroes against overwhelming numbers; and though scarred, and bleeding, and broken, have won laurels which shall never fade. Their courage, and determination, and fitness, and eagerness to meet the foe never were greater than they are today; and while we weep that our county has been drained so largely of her life-blood, yet we rejoice over the manifestation of such discipline and valor—such patient endurance and undaunted courage. From the banks of that river where the Anglo-Saxon first planted his colonies, still unflinching facing the enemy, those brave men are calling to you for assistance. There is no desire to turn their backs on the foe; but give the necessary aid and they are ready again to peril their lives in your defense.

That call should meet a prompt response. Now to withhold men and means would be suicidal. The cause of humanity demands that we should arouse more vigorously, and strike a blow which will end these scenes of horror, and bring back the blessings of peace. Unless we would have years of useless struggle, we must tax our energies far more than we have done before. . . . In response to a call so imperative as that which is now before us, let us yield up our best and our bravest, and let no one seek to dissuade those who are ready promptly to step forward into these broken ranks. Services now rendered never can be forgotten.

New Jersey will not, I trust, be the last to rally round the flag which our fathers carried through the battle fields of our own State and covered with imperishable glory. It has ever been her aim to avoid a policy which would lead to the horrors of war. She has never been foremost in sectional strife, but when her country's welfare really needs her treasure and her blood, she has never held them back.

In our Revolution, New Jersey bore the brunt and suffered most severely; and so now the field has been most bloody and the fight most deadly when the enemy have met the gallant regiments of our native State.

If our cause win the smile of God, let us not forget that He must be acknowledged in it and constantly entreated; and remember that the contribution to success are not only men and cannon, but there are contributions of sympathy and money, and prayers demanded from us all.

"Help us, O Lord our God, for we rest on Thee, and in Thy name we go against this multitude. O Lord, Thou art our God, let not man prevail against Thee!"

When our people and our rulers loyal to the Great White Throne shall pour forth their souls in such strains as King David used, "Thine O Lord is the kingdom and the power, and the glory, and the victory, and the majesty"; when they shall ascribe to Him the Kingdom; when they shall lay down the arms of spiritual rebellion and acknowledge that He ruleth over all — then instead of devastation and war we may look for the continued smile of Heaven, and all the blessings which have been procured and will be bestowed by the Prince of Peace.

---

[1] Here Reverend Brewster refers to General McClellan's attempt to take Richmond during the Seven Day Campaign, which resulted in a strategic victory for the Confederates, despite significantly higher Rebel casualties.

An Abolitionist Responds to Rev. James F. Brewster's Patriotic Sermon

The following letter to the editor is a response to Rev. James F. Brewster's patriotic sermon by an unidentified Unionist and abolitionist who agreed with Reverend Brewster's pro-Union sentiments but ridiculed his idea that blacks would indiscriminately brutalize and murder whites. To support his arguments, the anonymous writer quotes extensively from the pro-Union Virginian abolitionist, and political leader, Francis Harrison Pierpoint.

Jerseyman   *August 2, 1862*

PATRIOTISM IN CHESTER

Mr. Editor: Having lately read a couple of interesting productions on the recent state of the country, one a speech and the other a sermon, and both delivered in the neighboring village of Chester, I have felt moved to say something on this same subject. The speech was that of Jacob Vanatta, Esq., at a Fourth of July celebration, and the sermon was that of the Rev. James F. Brewster, pastor of the Presbyterian Church at Chester, preached on Sunday, July 13th. The speech is very patriotic, vigorous and appropriate. The sermon is very pious, and, if it had been delivered about twelve months ago, would have been well nigh up to the times. As matters now stand, and especially in view of the Confiscation Law recently passed, which authorizes the President to "organize and use as many persons of African decent so he may think proper, and in such manner as he may judge best for the public welfare," it is something like last year's almanac, a little out of date.

The views of the sermon in regard to the importance of crushing the rebellion itself are innately sound, but in regard to the importance of eradicating its cause, namely, Slavery, they have a decided leaning toward the South side of Mason's and Dixon's line. The method proposed is to dry up the stream and leave the fountain running, or in other words, to put an end to the rebellion, and, at the same time, to leave in full operation its malignant cause. Whether this method will commend itself to the patriotism and good sense of the people of Morris County, remains to be seen. Its popularity elsewhere in the loyal states, and among really loyal people, is about gone. When Governor Pierpoint of Virginia, and Gen. [Lovell Harrison] Rosseau[1] of Kentucky, himself a slaveholder, and the American Congress representing the loyalty of the nation, declare that slavery is the diabolical assassin whose knife is now at the throat of our Government, and that it ought therefore to be smitten down, it is a little too late in the day to proclaim, on the banks of the Black River, that Slavery is still divine, and ought still to be worshipped with reverence and holy fear.

The sermon charges upon "men" whom the preacher "hears," and "even gentle women" whom he "sees" that the former "exult in the terrible results of massacre and carnage" and that the latter are "eager to put the torch and the sword in the hands of an abject race, not yet entirely freed from their native barbarism, and let loose upon our misguided enemies, upon the wives and daughters, and the children of those who were once dear, horrors whose very thought chills the heart and curdles the blood." What can this mean? Is it true that there are in Chester, or anywhere in the loyal States, "men" and "even gentle women" who have become so fiendish as this statement would make us believe? Are there people in this good County of Morris so demonized as to exult in, and be eager to help on, these horrid enormities? Yes, it is even so. The preacher tells us that he "hears" and "sees" them, and his very "cheek pales" and puts on the ashy hue of death, at the frightful exhibition. Again we ask, is this true? Or is it the mere rhetorical seasoning of "massacre" and "carnage" of "horrors" and "curdled blood" thrown in to make the dish a little more savory? Don't be alarmed gentle reader; sleep on and take your rest; for these wicked furies here spoken of, are only "the dear little creatures of the imagination." All that any one proposes to do is to draw away the slaves of traitors from their masters by the promise of freedom, and to enlist them as orderly laborers and soldiers in the service of the Government. The passage quoted from the sermon, therefore, is mere bosh.

But how about these Negroes, members of "an abject race" born in the midst of Southern refinement and high religious culture, who are "not yet entirely freed from their native barbarism?" Is not slavery a great agency to promote civilization! Does it not exert a very refining influence! Is it not a great missionary institution to prepare men for civil society here and the joys of heaven hereafter! And yet these people who were born under its blessed way, and have always enjoyed its benefits, have not yet got rid of "their native barbarism." How ineffably barbarous they must have been when they were born! Who will say after this that it is not a great convenience to blow hot or blow cold, just as it happens to suit you! Condemn slavery as barbarous and brutalizing, and at once it is a means of grace and salvation. Talk of organizing the slaves into armies of free men to defend the national life against the murderous wickedness of their master, and presto, it is all changed. Slaves are yet in "their native barbarism!"

The sermon offers a lamentation over the supposed fact that there is "a disposition to lose sight of the first principles on which we sprang to arms, the defense of our Union, and our Constitution, and the supremacy of law," and to aim at "results" that is, the overthrow of slavery, "which the thoughtful and dispassionate portion of our people regard as wild, impractical and undesirable." It is certainly a great mistake to suppose that there is any disposition to lose sight of the Union, the Constitution and the Laws. It is to vindicate and maintain them that this war, on our part, is waged. The only thing the people are disposed to lose sight of, is, the sacredness of slavery and the claim its advocates put forth that it shall be protected by that Constitution which it is seeking to destroy. What is all this wretched twaddle about the right of traitors to hold their slaves, but an attempt, whether designed or not, to secure to them the means of doing the nation greater harm!

It is the imprudent demand of the assassin that his victim shall hold still, and let him take his life. The slaveholding rebels are to wield this engine of deadly power, and we, forsooth, are just to let them do it! You may take houses and lands, real and personal property of any kind but this; you may even destroy life, and be comparatively blameless. But if you touch this divine institution of slavery, you commit that sin which shall not be forgiven either in this world or in that which is to come.

Governor Pierpoint, of Virginia, border state man as he is, and being in the midst of slavery, has got his eyes fairly open to the nature of this contest. In his letter of July 16 to the Committee of Arrangements for the great [pro-Union] Mass meeting in New York, he utters these words which it would be well for every Northern man to consider:

"Say to them (i.e., the loyal soldiers) when they go, 'Use all the means God, and the nature, and circumstances have put in your power to suppress the rebellion and punish traitors.'" Rebel's property, in the rebel sense of the word, of whatever kind, sensible or insensible, should be made to contribute to the suppression of the rebellion in any manner that it can be made available.

"This war has been inaugurated and prosecuted by the rebels without reference to the rights of Union men. It is not for them to claim Constitutional guarantees. They have no rights, under the Constitution, save the infliction of the penalty of their crimes. They have grown insolent by their dominion over their own slaves, until they have adopted as their political axiom, 'that Slavery is the normal condition of the working classes.' Upon that principle, they are attempting to build their empire."

"This is the most gigantic rebellion the world ever saw. There is the most gigantic stake being played for. The question is: Shall Slavery or Freedom be Universal? There is no concealing it, this is the issue. The rebels have presented and forced it upon the nation. We have accepted, and it is to be tried at the point of the bayonet and the muzzle of the cannon; and were it not for the traitors in our midst, the verdict for Freedom would be rendered in three months. Every device that the devil can invent and put into the heads of traitors, seems to be brought forward to keep men out of the field, and to paralyze the arms of those already there. These traitors are tolerated in high and low places. It is the grasp of their hand now upon the body politic that partially paralyzes our strength. They are endeavoring to enlarge their grasp. This is our danger. But there were traitors in the camp of Moses, in the social family of Jesus Christ, in the army of the Revolution, and it would be wonderful if we had them not now in this country's struggle. They have ever received their reward, and they will, doubtless, in the present instance."

As the sermon, upon which these comments are offered, it addressed to the public through the press, and as it is adapted to place many of the best friends of the country in a false and invidious light, it is no more than fair that those who feel themselves attacked by it should have an opportunity to be heard in their defense.

---

[1] Lovell Harrison Rosseau served in the Kentucky state senate where he vigorously opposed secession. He resigned from his seat in 1861 to raise troops for the Union in Indiana. On September 9, 1861, he became colonel of the 3d Kentucky Infantry, and on October 1st he received a promotion to the rank of brigadier general of volunteers. Following the war, he served in the federal House of Representatives.

Chapter 7

Abraham Lincoln Loses In Morris County During Election of 1864

Although Abraham Lincoln failed to carry the state of New Jersey during the 1860 election, he did carry Morris County. But in 1864 he lost even in Morris County where popular support for the war had diminished amid mounting causalities and sharp Democratic criticism of the administration. The following article that appeared in the *True Democratic Banner* expresses jubilation at George B. McClellan's "victory" over Lincoln in Morris County — despite the efforts of local abolitionist clergymen who preached in favor of Lincoln.

Democrats Proclaim McClellan Victory

True Democratic Banner   *November 10, 1864*

THE DEMOCRACY OF MORRIS AGAIN TRIUMPHANT!
DEMOCRATIC MAJORITY FOR MCCLELLAN

The contest in this county was one that the Democracy may well be proud of. Never before did they make a better fight, although the "church and state" were arrayed against them. Lincoln's soldiers were sent home to vote, but Democratic soldiers denied that privilege; and greenbacks in abundance were scattered all over the county [to buy votes]. The Democracy felt this to be one of the most critical periods in the history of our country and determined, notwithstanding the fearful odds against them, to make a desperate struggle to change the administration, and so restore to the people, the government as it was when the constitution, the laws, the union, and economy were its distinguished, proud and glorious features, and nobly have they done their part, and triumphed in the effort. The true Democratic principles of the people of Morris may well be considered immovable and enduring after the vain but desperate effort just made by the abolition-republicanism to overwhelm them. The following table shows how handsomely they punished their enemies: [These figures indicate the margin of winning votes.]

Townships	Dem.	Rep.
Chatham	15	
Morris	37	
Mendham		4
Chester	131	
Roxbury	224	
Randolph	156	
Rockaway	10	
Jefferson	18	
Pequannoc		352
Hanover		72
Washington	173	
Total	824	428
	-428 [Rep.]	
Democratic Majority	396	

Chapter 8

Women and the War

Throughout Morris County and throughout the country, North and South, women played a critical role in the war effort by organizing soldiers' aid societies. They made clothing and other items for the soldiers and raised money for the sick in the hospitals. On a national level, the largest soldiers' aid society was the United States Sanitary Commission. Inspired by the British Sanitary Commission organized during the Crimean War, the organization attempted to remedy the poor sanitation within the camps, which bred disease and infection among the soldiers. It sent bandages, medicine, clothing, food, and nurses to the army. "Sanitary inspectors" from the Commission also trained soldiers in proper hygiene, sanitation, and cooking—despite the cold indifference of the Army Medical Bureau toward their presence.

Women also organized patriotic festivals and fairs to support the war effort and to raise money for the benefit of sick and wounded soldiers.

The following newspaper accounts of these activities include correspondence between soldiers' aid societies, an account of a patriotic festival organized by women, and an announcement of an organizational meeting where women made plans to hold a benefit fair.

Correspondence of the Soldiers' Aid Society

Jerseyman   *July 20, 1861*

The following letters of acknowledgment have been received by the Soldiers' Aid Society of this Town. Will the citizens of Morristown, as well as those in the vicinity, continue to send the contributions to any of the following named persons:

Mrs. Wm. N. Wood, President
Mrs. Sherman Broadwell, Vice President
Mrs. V. Dalrymple, Treasurer
Miss Robinson, Secretary
Managers—Mrs. Vail, Mrs. Mackenzie, Mrs. Miller, Mrs.
Cobb, Mrs. Headley, Mrs. Whelpley, Miss Jones, Miss
Rockwell, Mrs. Olmstead, Miss Emmell.

Headquarters N. J. Brigade
Washington, D. C.
May 24, 1861

Dear Sir:
   General Runyon wishes me to say that he has received your letter
and the box containing 245 havelocks, and is glad to know that the patriotic ladies of Morristown have so kindly remembered the soldiers of
New Jersey. The gifts they have transmitted are most opportune. In behalf of those for whom the presents were designed, he tenders the fair
donors their grateful acknowledgment.

Very Respectfully
C. W. Tolles,
Secy's, & c.

Trenton, June 18, 1861

To Mrs. W. N. Wood, President, Soldiers' Aid Society, Morristown.

My Dear Madam:
   I received your letter and box containing 230 havelocks on Monday,
for which I return our thanks for your very liberal donation. I visited
Camp Olden on Monday, to inquire whether there were any Morris
County troops that had not been supplied, but they were all out on drill;
however, one of the officers said he would let me know which were
without. . . . The lint and bandages were also very acceptable, as we
were just going to send a box with these troops. If I hear whether they
need any more, I will let you know.

Yours respectfully,
Caroline H. Fish

The Women's Central Association of Relief, Cooper Union, N.Y.

July 5, 1861

Madam:
   Please find enclosed a receipt of the articles received today from the
Soldiers' Aid Society of Morristown. I also annex a list of the articles
most needed at present. We have just entered into relations with the
Sanitary Commission at Washington, through whom the supplies will
henceforth be distributed. They have just made a requisition upon us
for hospital clothing for 300 patients. We hope your Society may feel

inclined to aid us again, that we may be able to respond to this appeal. With many thanks for your liberal donation,

> Very respectfully,
> E. H. Schuyler
> Member Ex. Com.

To Miss Robinson, Sec'y Soldiers' Aid Society:

List of Articles Received

23 Hospital Shirts, 8 Day Shirts, 8 Pocket Handkerchiefs, 42 Bandages, 1 Table Cloth, 10 Pillow Cases, 1 parcel Old Linen, 1 parcel Scaped Lint, 4 Towels, 32 Eye Shades, Pamphlet, Book Binders' Board for Splints.

List of Articles Wanted

Cotton Bed Shirts, one-and-a-half yards long; two breadths of unbleached muslin, one yard wide; open one-half yard at bottom; length of sleeve, three-fourths yard; length of arm hole, twelve inches; length of collar, twenty inches; length of slit in front, one yard; fastened with four tapes. Loose Drawers, 1 1/4 yards long, with a breadth of one yard wide muslin in each leg, with a hem and drawing string round the waist and bottom of each leg; length from waist to crotch on the back, 22 inches; and in the front 18 inches, with three buttons and three button holes. Soft slippers of different sizes. Light Flannel Dressing Gowns of different Sizes. Towels and Handkerchiefs. Abdominal or Body Bandages— Material, thick flannel; length 1 1/2 to 1 3/4 yards; to overlap in front; width, 10 to 13 inches, with narrow gores at the hips; 3 1/2 inches high, and 2 inches wide at bottom, with 3 broad tapes on each side, attached upon or above the gores.

Rockaway Women Organize Fourth of July Benefit Celebration

True Democratic Banner   *June 11, 1863*

FOURTH OF JULY AT ROCKAWAY—This celebration of the Fourth of July is for a purpose so humane—for the relief, by festival, of the widows and children whose misfortunes have been caused by the casualties of the war—that we must bespeak for it the earnest and conscientious patronage of the people of the county.

The loss in Co. L 27 Reg't. of some nineteen of the thirty-three out of this small township, who were drowned in the Cumberland River— added to the losses by the ordinary casualties of the war—seems to call for aid for the afflicted, upon the patriotic citizens of the county generally, and as a matter of duty.

The ladies of the Township of Rockaway are ever patriotic and vigilant; and are determined, in their festival purposed for the day, to greet all with such a reception as only the woman of New Jersey, in their sympathies for their sisters in this heavy sorrow, and for the many orphans thus cast upon their charities, can and will tender.

Rockaway has thus been made to bear a large proportion of the county's burden of the war. Most of the dead have left helpless families — and the aid to be given at home must be by few. Come, therefore, men and women of Morris County and help to lighten the sorrows of many — wipe away tears, and cause at least one ray of sunshine, each of you, to shine in upon desolated homes, and you will feel happier in your remembrances of the nation's Holiday of 1863.

An oration by an eminent speaker, with the other customary observances of the day, with Beckers' Brass Band of Morristown, may be relied upon. Again we say, "To Rockaway on the Fourth of July!" The name of the orator will be announced in our next issue, with other particulars of the proposed celebration.

Morristown Women Meet to Prepare Benefit Fair

Jerseyman   *June 11, 1864*

OUR SICK AND WOUNDED SOLDIERS— A meeting of the Ladies of Morristown will be held at the Session-Room at the First Presbyterian Church on Saturday Afternoon, June 11, at 4 o'clock, to make arrangements for holding a fair on the Fourth of July for the benefit of our sick and wounded soldiers.

The above call emanates from a number of our most public spirited and patriotic ladies. The object is one that must enlist the sympathies and hearty cooperation of all, and it is to be hoped that the attendance will be such as to furnish a complete guarantee of the success of the measure proposed. Certainly, at the present time, no one thing more demands the means and efforts of our citizens than the care of those who are doing battle for the country under whose beneficent institutions we have so greatly prospered and have enjoyed so much. Their needs are pressing and constant. Almost every mail brings us intelligence of additions to the list of wounded, and makes stronger appeals to our gratitude and our alms. Morristown, through our Soldiers' Aid Society and other benevolent associations, had done nobly thus far. She should not now be behind in encouraging our brave soldiers before Richmond with the assurance that those whom succor or alleviation can reach, through her efforts, shall lack nothing that can by any possibility be furnished to them.

Chapter 9

Letters Home

During the long stretches of time between major conflicts, soldiers had time to reflect upon the war in all its aspects. They expressed themselves in letters to friends and relatives, telling stories of life in the military, from the experience of battle to the monotony of camp life. Though firsthand accounts of war are generally accurate, their authors usually do not dwell on the grimmer aspects of battle to spare their loved ones needless concern—and, possibly, to avoid "editing" at the hands of military censors.

More than any other recorded document, letters reveal the humanity of those who participated in battle. They also express—at times with great poignancy—the tragedy of war. Of the three letters featured here, two were written by young men who left their families and friends to fight for their country, never to return alive.

Letters of William Van Fleet

William Van Fleet of Parsippany originally intended to enter the ministry, but when ill health prevented him from realizing his vocation, he became a schoolmaster instead. At age twenty-eight he was mustered into Company H (later Company K) of the 1st New Jersey Volunteers. He saw action in the Union assault at Spottsylvania Courthouse, May 11, 1864 — his first and only battle. Here he received a fatal wound in the knee. The following selections include some of the letters Van Fleet wrote to his wife and family; also a letter his wife wrote to him shortly before he died; and a letter from the military hospital to William's father, explaining the circumstances surrounding his son's death.

Letter from William Van Fleet to his wife, Anna Doremus Van Fleet.

Brandy Station
February 23, 1864

Dear Wife:

As Mr. John Hill[1] is here, I thought that I would write, although I have not received an answer to the last that I wrote. I am well except a cold and a slight touch of diarrhea. I will send you two of my cards, one for you and one for Father and Mother.

Last Sunday 27 of our men went out on picket.

The weather is fine here now. . . . I expect that we will be on the move soon. I heard that this regiment was going to be sent to Pennsylvania, to relieve the 10th regiment at the coal mines, but it is doubtful. The greater part of the old soldiers think that the war is not going to last much longer. Lee's men are deserting every chance they get, and those that come say that nearly all would do so if they had the chance.

A great many of the old soldiers are reenlisting.

Mr. Hill I understand is going to send a box for the benefit of the company. I wish you would find out, and if he does, I would like to have you send me some tobacco — smoking and chewing, and some tea, and if you have anything else to send, it will be accepted with pleasure.

There is a corps review today about two miles from here, it is ours, the 6th corps. I got clear for going out by chance, so that I have time for writing. I received a letter from John. He had been sick but was at work again. I suppose that you know that he is sexton of the Presbyterian Church, which pays him $1.28 per year besides the extras.

I would like to know if there was any difficulty in getting the state money.[2] We have heard that there is a report going around Boonton that our officers were good for nothing, and that they had not been in one night since we have been here. If so, it is false, I think that [they are] as good officers as any other company in the regiment

I will send a part of my journal home in this letter. This is all this time. My love to all. Kiss Mary Jane and Tillie for me. Good by from your Affectionate Husband,

Wm. J. Van Fleet

P.S. Please send me some postage stamps.

[1] Mr. John Hill, an assemblyman and well known abolitionist from Pequannock Township, served as a courier to the soldiers at Brandy Station.

[2] State money refers to a cash bounty offered by the state to volunteers.

Letter from William Van Fleet to his wife, Anna.

Brandy Station
March 4, 1864

Dear Wife:

As John Hill is not gone home yet and we are back into camp again, I thought I would write a few lines to let you know that I arrived in camp safe and sound but with sore feet. The regiment came in on the night of the 2nd but I did not get in till the next morning. I with two others of our Company stayed in a barn about two miles out. We marched about 25 miles that day. You will see a description of the march in my diary that you will find in here.

I wish that you would send me some postage stamps. I got the receipt for the box that you sent me. The next time you send anything direct it to me, c/o 1st Regiment N.J.V. in care of Quarter Master General Perrine, Trenton, NJ, and then it will come from there free of charge.

William Van Fleet (Courtesy of Parsippany Historical and Preservation Society).

I know not what is in the box, but I hope that there is a loaf of rye bread and some ginger cake in it. If you have a chance, I wish you would send me some tea. I think Mrs. Vincent sister's husband's brother is home on a furlough and maybe he will bring a small bundle with him. Things are so much higher than I thought and I have lent out some money that I can't get till payday, so my money is gone. I had to pay $5.00 for my cards. I have asked John Hill for $5.00 and will give him an order on you. He said he would see how he came out. If he could, he would let me have it, so that if he has an order, it is all right. This is all this time. Write often, it gives me pleasure to receive letters from home. We have been mustered for pay but I don't know how soon we will get it. Give my love to all and keep a good portion for yourself. Kiss Mary Jane and Tillie for me.

From Your Aff. Husband,
Wm. J. Van Fleet

Letter from William Van Fleet to his wife, Anna.

March 11, 1864
Brandy Station

Dear Wife:

I received your letter last night; it found me well as you hoped. I just came off picket yesterday A.M. about 10 o'clock.

13th

I was called away to go on fatigue, and yesterday I had to help to build the officers' cook house and this A.M. to go on inspection, so now I will try it again. Mr. John Hill is here yet; when he does come home you may call on him for two letters from me; one has my cards and the first of my diary in; the other has the second part of the diary. I received the box of tobacco and was glad to receive it. I have sold some of the smoking.

Dear Anna, I am glad to hear that you have a source of comfort in the Savior. I do think of you often and do pray for you too and have need of your prayers, for we have many temptations. Last Sunday we had communion here in our little chapel; it was crude but pleasant, but I don't know when we will have it again as our chaplain has left us. My cold is better than when I commenced this. Kiss Mary Jane and Matilda for me. In your next [letter] please send me some postage stamps. We expect to get our pay soon. My love to all, my friend, and a good portion for yourself. Write soon.

From your Loving Husband,
Wm. J. Van Fleet

Letter from William Van Fleet to his wife, Anna.

Brandy Station
March 30, 1864

Dear Wife:

I received your letter in due time and was glad to hear from you that you were all well. I got a letter from Mother. . . . She sent me a cake with a man that has been home on a furlough, and he brought it as far as Washington where it was stolen from him. He said that when he went to bed he hung the haversack up by his head, and when he awoke it was gone. It was him that brought me the letter. I want you to get an album to put cards in, and I want you to go to Boonton and get Capt. Fosters and Lt. Myers and Milner's. They will cost five schillings I suppose.

If you have any more money than Father wants, you can put it in the office at Boonton and get six percent interest I understand. We had target practice today. . . . William A. Wright made the best shot; there were two shots put in the "bulls eye." He put the one nearest to the center. . . . This William A. Wright lived at William Smith's. He is in the tent with me; we have built a new one. We just finished the chimney today, but I don't expect that we will have the pleasure of staying in it long, for the army will move soon I expect. We had rice pudding for supper last night and also tonight—some of my own making. We get a condensed milk . . . which is all ready prepared for such things, and then I boiled some rice and put that in it, which made it taste very good. I will send some more of my diary with this. I sent $40 with Mr. Hill. Did you get it?

Whenever you hear of the sixth corps, you will hear of us for we are in that corps. I believe that I can't think of any more this time. I wish that you would write once a week at least. I believe that I have done so, for if I have not, I will.

My love to all and a kiss for my little girls.

> From your Loving
> Husband,
> Wm. J. Van Fleet

Letter from William Van Fleet to his wife, Anna.

> Brandy Station
> April 18, 1864

Dear Wife:

I thought that I would write to you, although I had not received an answer to my last. I am well and hope that this may find you enjoying the same blessing. Did you get the two parts of my diary from Mr. Hill and the one that I sent in a letter? I have another part of it ready to send but will wait to see if you get the last or not. Mr. Hill is here again, and I will send it with him. He came very suddenly on us; we were not expecting him; in fact we heard that he was not coming. Ask Livingston if he will transcribe my diary with ink when he has time. I am afraid that it will get rubbed out; as it is, I have nothing but a soft pencil. When you go to New Brunswick you can take it with you and let them see it. There is a revival in progress here now. There are three of our C. F.[1] that have been hopefully converted. One was baptized yesterday. We had communion down here yesterday. We have prayer meeting almost every night, from 7 to tatoo (8:30 o'clock) after which Chaplain [Robert R.] Proudfit has an inquiry meeting. They are inquiring the way to salvation. Two of those that have given their hearts to God are from Boonton. The first, Dennis Brown, came and wished me to go with him to see the Chaplain who had given all who wished to converse with him on the subject of religion, the invitation to meet him from 1:30 to 3 o'clock, and I went with him and John W. Ford, who expressed a wish to go, too. D. B. said that his wife was the instrument in God's hands of his conversion, that she had prayed for him, but he had laughed at her, but she continued to pray and God has at last heard her prayers. This Ford has been one of the worst men in the company; he would drink and keep on drinking till he had fits; he has told me that he has spent nearly all his bounty for rum. Stood guard over him one night to keep rum away from him. He came into my tent and [I] asked him to go to prayer meeting. The next night I asked the prayers of the meeting for him, and the next night he stood and asked for them.

From your Loving
Husband,
Wm. J. Van Fleet

[1] Van Fleet probably used the abbreviation "C. F." to refer to a specific ethnic or religious group.

Letter from William Van Fleet to his wife, Anna.

April 29, 1864

Dear Wife:

I received your welcome letter last night and was glad to hear that your were all well. . . . You say that you will have to use some of the money that you have. That is what you have it for. I want you to get things to make yourself and the children comfortable and decent if it takes all of it. Take all, that is what I came here for, to leave something for to make you comfortable. . . .

We had a brigade service yesterday. The Captain said that there was not a company that did better than we did. Last Tuesday there was a man drummed out of service; he was marched along the front of the Brigade at drum playing the march, with 5 bayonets point[ed] at his back. There is nothing new here of consequence; how soon we will be on the move no one knows. But I expect it will be soon. Yesterday A.M. we had skirmish drill. You may send me some postage stamps if you please as they are a scarce article here now. We will soon be mustered for pay again, A.M. is the time. Dear Anna, I think of you often. I would like to see you all, but it can't be so now. I can't think of anymore now. My love to all and a kiss for my little girls. Write as often as you can, for it makes me feel good, too, to get letters from home.

From your Loving Husband
Wm. J. Van Fleet

Letter from Anna Doremus Van Fleet to her husband.

Parsippany
May 8, 1864

Dear Husband,

I received your letter on Wednesday night and was glad to hear from you and to hear that you were well. I would have wrote right away, but I had some coats to finish.[1] I have wrote every week for a good while and shall endeavor to do so as long as I can. They are all well except myself. I have got a very bad cold and have been sick for two days and don't feel much better yet. Mr. Brison came here on Friday, heard that the army was on the move and was going to fight. It makes me feel so bad. I feel very sad and lonesome. I would like to see you very much. Father and Mother went to Flemington last Wednesday and expected to go to New Brunswick yesterday and we expect them home tomorrow . . . . Matilda walks all over and talks quite some. Mary Jane is as mischievous as ever. I sent you some postage stamps in my last [letter] and will send you one in every letter.

I feel very weak and tired, so I will have to stop and finish it tomorrow and go to bed, so good night.

May 10, 1964—

Dear William,

Now I shall try and finish my letter. Father and Mother have not come yet. I feel a little better today, but I have a very bad cough yet. We have eight coats in the house to make for Mr. Brison. Matilda is very cross today. Cries all the time. Mary Jane often speaks about you and wants to go home to see you. I don't think I shall go to New Brunswick till June for I can't get ready to go before; I have so much sewing to do. I will tell you when I go.

I think of you often and would like to see you, but it will be all for the best. God's will be done. Remember me in your prayers. Write as soon as you can. I want to know where you are.

From your loving Wife,
Anna Van Fleet

[1] Anna Van Fleet worked at home doing piece work for Mr. Brison, a local businessman.

Private Van Fleet's Final Letter

Camp near Brandy
Station
[no date]

Dear Wife, Parents, Brothers, and Sisters:

I received your letter last Friday night. I was on picket at the time. I was glad to hear from you that you were well. . . . I expect we will soon be on the move and when we do move I expect that it will not be long before we go right into battle. When we do get on the move I don't suppose that I will be able to write so often. I have written nearly every week since I have been here. I should like to see you all but that is impossible now. I hope that I may be spared to see you all again but God's will be done. I don't fear death. If I should not see you again on earth, I pray that we may meet in heaven above. I have sent four parts of my diary; three of them I sent with Mr. Hill and one by mail. Did you get them that I sent by mail? I wish you would let me know whether you have got them. The last I sent with Mr. Hill when he was here the last time. I wish you would send me another book like that only smaller, about the size of an envelope or a little smaller. You may send me some postage stamps please. I believe I have nothing more to write this time. Love to all and a kiss for my little girls. Dear Annie. Don't forget your duty to bring them up for Christ.

An unidentified writer added the following postscript:

Dead at Fredericksburg May 25th from a fatal wound received in the battle at Spotsylvania, William S. Van Fleet son of Barrgan H. Van Fleet, New Brunswick, N.J. Thus, another Christian hero has gone to his rest. . . . Lain in his country's armor, he has fought the good fight, he has vanquished the last enemy. Written in a message to his wife, he said he feared not, for in God was his trust and he is gone to ware [*sic*] the Victor's Cross.[1] Blessed are the dead that die in the Lord.

A letter from the military hospital to William Van Fleet's father.

Connen Hospital
Washington, Ward 63

Mr. B. H. Van Fleet:

Yes, your letter of the weekend was received this day. I was sorry that it went to my regiment for it is so long for you to wait for an answer, but it can't be helped. I will tell you of the death of your son, the best I can remember. I went to the hospital in Fredericksburg the 14th; he was there at that time in great distress; he was wounded in the cavity of the knee and on the 21st, I think, his leg was amputated above the knee; before this I wrote a letter to his wife at his request. He was brought back beside me after his leg was off. He was in good spirits and his stump did as well as could be expected. It became corrupt with maggots, but the Doctor got them all out again and he looked well in the face. I was talking to him at times all the day before he died; did what I could for him. . . . He ate a good dinner of potatoes and beef the day before he died. It seemed to me that he was conscious of his position for he talked to me a great deal on religion. I think he told me he was a member of a church. He seemed to be happy and calm. I think he gave his heart to God, [and] not knowing what the result of his limb [surgery] may be, said he wanted to see his wife and friends. I shall tell you something I did not tell you in my first letter, that is, the night he died the bandage broke loose and he bled to death. I heard him screaming as the last drop of blood was leaving him. I called the nurse but he could not be found until your son was a corpse. Had the doctor been in the ward he could have taken up the artery and sewn him. He was buried to the left of the city and a head board with his name and his regiment on, and you can find it easy enough, but you can't move him till October. You can see me at Connen Hospital, Washington, Ward 63.

---

[1]"Theologically speaking, it is the victor's crown that the deceased should be wearing, but the cross and crown are associated with each other in many hymns of the period and may have been interchanged here," according to Pat Winship of the Humanities Division, Newark Public Library, who helped the editor research the origin of the phrase that

inspired the title of this book. In fact the *crown of life* is a very common Christian symbol. Artists frequently depict the crown intertwined with the cross, signifying that the endurance of trial and suffering leads to victory. This symbol appears in other Civil War writings. In *History of the Eleventh New Jersey Regiment* (Trenton, 1898, p. 139), Thomas D. Marbaker quotes an army chaplain who writes to the mother of a dead soldier that her son will "wear the victor's crown in heaven."

Letters of Josiah Quincy Grimes

Josiah Quincy Grimes was born in Parsippany, New Jersey, on March 15, 1844, son of William H. Grimes and Ann Elizabeth Grimes. As a young man Grimes was known to be studious, precocious, virtuous, and highly esteemed by all who knew him.

At age 17 Josiah went to Boonton to work in the apothecary shop of his uncle, Dr. John Grimes. Dr. Grimes founded the abolitionist newspaper, the New Jersey Freeman. *He was also active in the Underground Railroad. (See Chapter One.) Josiah, inspired by his Uncle's idealism, participated in meetings of Boonton abolitionists. At age 18 he enlisted in the Union army and entered the 15th New Jersey Volunteers. He fought in many major campaigns including the Second Battle of Bull Run, Antietam, Fredericksburg, Chancellorsville, and Gettysburg. Though he survived these battles, he died of illness on September 8, 1863, at Warrenton, Virginia. He was buried at the Vail-Parsippany Cemetery.*

Sixteen of the 37 letters that Josiah Quincy wrote to his family during the war appear in this section. Military censors subjected many of these letters to "editing."

Letter Number Two

Saturday, August 16, 1862

Dear Father and Mother:

I have been sworn in the service of the U.S., enlisted in Company "C", Captain [Ira] Lindsley. Thursday evening we were enlisted and sworn in, and each one got a bed tick and blanket. Then, as we had not got our tents yet, we marched down and slept in the stalls on the Hunterdon County Fairgrounds. Next morning we marched back again to Flemington and got our uniforms, knapsacks, haversacks, canteens, etc., then marched to camp and got our breakfast. In the afternoon, marched to the Raritan River and went in swimming.

They have very bad water around here, and it is very rusty. The soil is a red color, made from the crumbling down of what they call red shell.

The dust from it sticks to your shoes like mud.

I got my canteen filled with lemonade for twenty-five cents yesterday; went a great deal better than water. We slept last night in an open building belonging to the fairgrounds, laying crossways on shelves. I gave it up toward morning and walked around the fairground, found a lot of haystacks, went back, got Bill, and we went and slept between them on the hay.

We expect to get a furlough some time next week. Our company is full, 101 men, rank and file. We expect to be mustered in Mon-

Josiah Quincy Grimes (Courtesy of Rutgers Special Collections and University Archives, Rutgers University Library).

day. It is to be the color company of the regiment. We new fellows that came Thursday performed yesterday, and if everyone's words are to be believed, some bully marching, better than some companies that have been here two weeks.

I like soldiering first rate, so far. We have got a bully set of fellows in our company, got a lot of good singers in the company. The fellows are clearing out the brush and burning it around these woods, as we expect to have a meeting tomorrow in the woods.

I will try to get a furlough next week, as soon as possible. I forgot several things, such as towels, etc., that I need here. I sent my valise to Morristown in care of Garrett De Mott, to be forwarded to Parsippany. They may leave them at Ayers and Breeses' Store. Enclosed is the key belonging to it. No more at present.

From your son,
Quincy Grimes

Letter Number Six

September 7, 1862

Dear Lizzy:

I left Flemington on Friday, August 29th. We stopped at Lambertville and the folks of the place gave us a first rate dinner in the [railroad] cars. Then on to Trenton, from there to Camden, and then took the boat for Philadelphia, where we stacked arms, washed, and had the best supper we could have wished for. After supper we marched through the street to the Baltimore Depot. The ladies and girls stood along the line of march shaking hands with us. There was the greatest marching this time that I have ever seen. The boys would stop and shake hands and then run to catch up, officers just the same. We rode in the cattle cars all night. At one river, our train of cars were taken over by the boat. On Saturday morning we got into Baltimore, got breakfast there; didn't start from there until one o'clock, when we took the cars for Washington. Then we didn't get there until dusk, were quartered in a large building within sight of the capitol.

After a while we marched to a woods and camped there. Monday afternoon our whole company went out as pickets on the road to Edward's Ferry and relieved the pickets of the 173d New York. . . . We scouted around the woods and captured one of our own pickets. Our sergeant thought he was doing a big thing. Thought, I suppose, that we had taken a Rebel, sure. But we let him go when we found out who he was. Tuesday morning we roasted some corn in our fire, had some chickens boiled, and all together had a good time. We were relieved in the afternoon.

They are building a fort on the hill, and men are detailed from our company every day to help build it. Our company is composed of first rate fellows. Of course, there are a few hard cases, but the general run of them is first rate.

You want me to write twice a week. That is impossible. We have to drill six hours every day besides dress parade, and meals three times a day, and roll call morning and night. Besides the only time I can get to write is Sunday when I will try to write, but you must answer them regularly or it won't pay. I wish you would write as soon as you get this and let me know how everything is going on. I will try to get a furlough in a few months. Twenty days are allowed the soldiers in six months. Please tell Father to send me a dollar's worth of postage stamps. I would send the money for them, but I sent all the money I had home yesterday, except a dollar and some change.

I've got quite a nice present to send home to you. I want to get something else to send with it, and if you don't think it's nice, why, I won't make you another present.

> From your brother,
> Quincy Grimes

Letter Number Seven

> September 7, 1862

Dear Brother Willy:

I got your letter a week ago. I hope they will draft a lot of those Secessionists and those that are afraid to go. When we were at Camp Fair Oaks at Flemington, we drummed three Secessionists out of camp. One fellow got whacked over the head quite lively with a lot of dusty brush brooms.

I wish we had Abe Doremus and a lot of those Secesh [i.e., Secessionists] down here blowing. After that they would know enough to shut up. But I must stop.

> From your little brother,
> Quincy Grimes

Letter Number Twelve

> Camp Morris
> near Fort Kearney
> September 28, 1862

Dear Mother:

I received your two letters last week on the 25th and 27th. I received also the *Independent* and *Tribune*.

We have seventeen in our tent. It is a Sibley[1] with an opening that is only covered when it storms. A pole in the middle of it holds it up and is itself supported by the iron rods. Around the pole is a gun rack in which we place our muskets and equipment. The names of those in the tent are: Edwin A. Doty, Samuel D. Doty from Basking Ridge; Erascus Rikerson, Franklin Camp, Virgil Howell, Condit James Mc Mills, known as Boery; Hugh H. Layton, James Hathaway, William Oliver, Albert M. Armstrong, Silas Guerin, Charles H. Guerin, William B. Bailey, and two strangers. I believe their names are, respectively, William Trealese and Quincy Grimes.

I believe I told you in my last letter about my clothes and washing. I wash my own clothes. Generally [I] wash them first in cold water and then boil them. By this means I manage to keep them quite clean. I got a pair of shoes and kept my other ones and have them now with me but do not wear them because they are too small.

It is the expectation that we are to march tonight. Our cook is cooking two days rations. It is all conjecture where we are going. Some say to Frederick City, some to the Virginia Valley, while others say Harper's Ferry. They say we will leave our knapsacks and tents here. If that is the case, we are not going very far. We have forty rounds of cartridges apiece.

Don't delay in answering this on that account, but direct letters the same as before, as all soldier's letters must first go to Washington. We are kept pretty busy here drilling, working on the fort and road. We get but little time to write letters, and when we write we like to have them answered promptly. If they are not, it soon lags behind [i.e., the mail is not received when it is expected].

No more at present. I will write again as soon as possible.

Your son,
Quincy Grimes

[1] A Sibley was a light, easily pitched, conical tent invented before the Civil War by Henry Hopkins Sibley.

Letter Number Thirteen

[No Date]

Dear Father:

I received your letter postmarked the twentieth a few days ago. I wrote a letter from our camp near Bakersville a week or so ago home. We moved from our camp yesterday, marching about 15 miles to within 3/4 of a mile of the battlefield of Crampton['s] Pass. We are laying here expecting to hear the order every moment, "Fall in! Forward March!"

I have not much faith in McClellan, either as a general or a patriot. Anyone having such an immense army as he has, that has such poor results to show after having been in command a year and a half can't be much.[1]

I have enjoyed very good health ever since I have been to Dixie. Randolph is getting along quite well but didn't like the march very well. Says when I get old like him, I won't like it either.

But I must close. Give my respect to all the folks. Tell Willy I expect a letter from him soon.

From you son,
Quincy Grimes

[1] After the humiliating Northern defeat at Bull Run, Gen. George B. McClellan was given command of the Union force near Washington. A superb organizer and drillmaster, McClellan was also an experienced soldier who had fought in the Mexican War. His men idolized him because he refused to sacrifice their lives unnecessarily. But McClellan, a Democrat, was severely criticized by Republicans as he continued to drill his troops along the Potomac while hesitating to confront the Confederates, whose numbers he had overestimated. After six months of inaction, Lincoln threatened to "borrow" his army. McClellan finally moved his forces in an attempt to take Richmond. He succeeded in taking Yorktown, but as he approached Richmond, a Confederate force led by Generals Lee and "Stonewall" Jackson engaged McClellan's army and drove it all the way back to its base in Chesapeake Bay. Though the Rebels failed to defeat McClellan, the Campaign was abandoned. McClellan was assigned to a less active command, while the Union Army near Washington was put under the command of Gen. John Pope. But after the Confederates crushed Pope's army at the Second Battle of Bull Run, McClellan's command was restored. At Antietam on September 17, 1862, McClellan succeeded in halting Lee's advance into Maryland. Though militarily, the battle resulted in a draw, it appeared as a Northern victory, since, for the first time, the Union Army demonstrated its power. But McClellan's critics castigated him for not having pursued Lee. McClellan was removed from his command for the second and final time. Following his military career, McClellan went into politics. He ran against Lincoln in the 1864 presidential election and later served as governor of New Jersey.

Letter Number Fifteen

Camp near Bakersville,
Maryland
October 17, 1862

Dear Mother:

I received your letter last week dated the 5th. Our expedition turned out to be a march to Washington; from there in the cars to Frederick City where we stayed overnight. I saw Eugene Brighton in the 26th New Jersey in the street. He appeared to be well.

Did you get the letter I wrote from Frederick City Thursday afternoon? We started from Frederick City with our piece of shelter tent, overcoat, blanket, and three days' rations in our haversacks, canteens, equipment, etc. I had a coffee pot dangling at my side fast to my haversack. Bill Trealese [Grimes' friend from Chatham] had a frying pan on his back, as we tented together. We would halt to rest every two or three miles. Toward dusk we turned off in a big lot, formed in line, stacked arms, and stayed all night here—started early next morning—met a great many ambulances coming with the sick and wounded. The road on which we came was the same through which the Rebels retreated from Frederick City [during the Battle of Antietam]. Dead horses lay along the road and we passed over many rebuilt bridges that had been burned by the Rebels, passed through South Mountain Pass—rested there awhile and found a lot of inflammable cartridges, some shells, pieces of shells, etc.

I am in good health and spirits; haven't been sick since I have been here. I can stand the marches as good as any of them, and a great deal better than some. No more at present, so good-bye.

From your son,
Quincy Grimes

Letter Number Seventeen

Camp in Virginia at
Berlin, Maryland—Seven
miles from the Bridge
[No Date]

Dear Sister Lizzy:

We have just arrived on the sacred soil of Virginia. We left our old camp at or near Bakersville, Maryland on Friday, October the 31st, marched from our camp with our brigade consisting of the First, Second, Third, Fourth, Fifteenth, and Twenty-third New Jersey Volunteers. We were marched through with scarcely any rest some 15 miles to Crampton Pass [the place where Union troops broke through Confederate lines at the Battle of South Mountain], where we rested that afternoon and night. Next afternoon we started again. Passing through the battlefield of Crampton Pass, we saw the dead body of the horse Howell Cobb had shot from under him that was still lying there, and the steep hill up whose sides our boys charged on the Rebel batteries. Toward night we stopped and rested for the night. We drew out two day's rations of hardtack, salt pork, and fresh beef that night. The drum beat to arouse us at four o'clock this Sunday morning, and in a little while came the order, "Fall in!" We put on our equipment, haversacks, canteens, and our knapsacks, took our guns and fell in, marched to Berlin, crossed the railroad and canal there, and crossed the Potomac on a pontoon bridge that rested on 63 boats, into old Virginia. From there we marched some 7 miles to where we are now in a beautiful grove in which the whole brigade is encamped. Every moment or so we hear the boom of cannon coming from somewhere up the river. We may stay here and encamp and lay here sometime, and again we may march tomorrow morning before six o'clock. I wish you could have seen us as we marched from Bakersville. The whole army corps marched at the same time, and as far as we could see, before and behind, and on every side, the roads were alive with troops going to join, I suppose, in some of McClellan's grand movements. I wish McClellan was not in command of the Army of the Potomac, nor, in fact, of any other army of the United States, for I believe that he has cost the country more treasure and lives than that of any other, or all the other armies belonging to Uncle Sam. If we had only had [John C.] Fremont, [Joseph] Hooker, or some of the fighting generals in command, something would have been done and we should not have been talking about defending our lives as though we were the Rebels and had as much as we could do to defend ourselves from the tremendous power of the Southern Confederacy.

. . . . I got a letter from Tessie Burt last night, in which she wishes me to administer consolation to you for she says you lost your heart but found it again in a half cracked condition and ever since have been looking for every gent whose coat had a military cut. It's too bad Lizzy, but I will have to refer you to Tessie; as being acquainted with the circumstances, she better knows what consolation to administer.

Monday morning—We had roll call this morning at five o'clock and are laying around here expecting to be ordered out at any moment. There has been some fighting up above here; some of the sick and wounded passed here yesterday. I have stood the marches very well, so far. . . . But I must close.

Good-bye from your
brother,
Quincy.

Letter Number Nineteen

In the fall of 1862, Lincoln, exasperated at McClellan's failure to move quickly, relieved the general of his command, replacing him with Gen. Ambrose E. Burnside. Burnside rapidly moved the Union forces toward Falmouth (situated across the Rappahannock River from Fredericksburg) with the intention of moving from there onto Richmond. But a shortage of pontoons essential for river crossing delayed the advance. This gave Lee's army a chance to dig in along the hills south of the Rappahannock. When the time came to advance, Burnside opted for a frontal attack directly across the river instead of crossing the river above or below the enemy. This move proved fatal. The Confederates, occupying the high ground with a sweeping view of Fredericksburg, crushed the advancing Union brigades, inflicting 13,000 casualties, while they suffered fewer than 5,000 casualties. The horrible Union disaster at Fredericksburg caused many in the North to withdraw their support for the war. The defeat caused a terrible morale problem within the army itself.

Though Grimes did not participate in the ill-fated frontal attack at Fredericksburg, he did serve in a support unit. The actions that he describes in the following letter took place before and after the main conflict.

> In a ravine somewhere
> near Fredericksburg —
> Friday, December 12, 1862

Dear Sister Lizzie:

I received a letter from you a week ago today. The day before that, December 4th, we moved from our old camp near Stafford Courthouse about 18 miles, encamping about eight or nine miles from Belle Plain Landing, yesterday. We moved from there with three days' rations in our haversacks. On the way, we were ordered to load without priming. After marching a few miles through woods and brush, we camped upon a steep bluff overlooking the Rappahannock. Our Brigade formed in column by division, our Regiment being in front, while the First New Jersey artillery shelled the Rebels on the opposite side of the river. We crossed the river this morning at nine o'clock on a pontoon bridge. We laid there a while and the order came to lay down as flat as possible. About noon we marched in line of battle for a considerable distance to a ravine about 50 or 60 feet deep. We had hardly got there before zing, zing, zing, zing, went the shells over our heads. We laid low in the ravine, some shells whipping close to our heads and landing in the opposite side of the ravine. At night we marched a little farther down the ravine and laid up for the night.

Monday, December 15th, 1862—I haven't had a chance to write until now. On Saturday we marched out of the ravine, our Regiment having to go as picket on the right, an engagement being expected on the left, and we were posted along to keep our forces from being out-flanked by the Rebs. Part of our own company laid in reserve. I was with the reserve a little while in the morning, and was then sent to relieve a sick man. The Rebels' batteries were plainly to be seen along the line of hills and also the Rebel line of pickets about 300 yards off. By and by, the shells flew over our heads at a great rate. One exploded right by the corner of a fence about 50 yards off. The pieces passing close to our heads, we dropped down and laid low to the ground for a while. When we got up, they pointed their guns down and fired di-rectly at us. We laid very close, I assure you, but they fired two or three feet too high, only one striking very near, and that landed in the mud behind me and did not explode. We could feel the wind from the shot[s] as they passed over us. All this time we heard heavy cannoning and musketry on the left, and, now and then, cheering when we knew

Union Hospital, Fredericksburg

they were charging the Rebels. Pretty soon our batteries opened on the Rebel earthworks, and then they stopped firing at us, turning their fire to our batteries. I got up and could see the flash and smoke of their batteries quite some time before hearing the report.

We were relieved yesterday, Sunday morning, by part of a New York Regiment. We went to fall back on our reserve after being relieved, but it was not to be found. We went on a ways and found another company of our regiment and went back to the ravine with them. We stayed there a little while and then I took a few canteens and went up the brook to fill them. While filling them, some of our company passed along. One of them said to me, "Well, Quincy, Randolph is shot." Our orderly said, "You ain't wounded, are you Randolph?" "Yes," said he. And that was all he said. He was taken to the hospital and died yesterday afternoon. I had just written to his folks telling them of the sad news. Bill had his bayonet sheath ripped loose by a ball; also a button taken off his coat, and a hole put through two pair of pants he had on at the time, near the knee joint. Bill and myself divided Randolph's cartridges between us and intend to use them for him and those rascally Rebels.

By the way, I forgot to tell you that we received our colors, that is, our State colors, Jersey blue, the day before we marched here. Write soon, from your brother,

Quincy Grimes

Letter Number Twenty-Two

Sunday, February 8, 1863

Dear Mother:

I received your letter about a week ago, but having been unwell since, was unable to answer 'till now.

I enclosed ten dollars to pay for some little things that I wish you would send to me in a box. In the first place, Uncle John promised me some medicines. Please call over there and get for me a bottle of chalk mixture, a bottle of cordial, and a bottle of Essence of Peppermint. But I happen to think that I had better enclose a note to Uncle John and let you hand it to him, as he wanted me to let him know what medicines I needed. Please send me a washbasin, a good stout one without any handle, but with something fixed to it so that it can be strapped fast for convenience in marching. Also a short-handled tin cup. Send a good stiff blacking brush [for polishing boots], and a good large box of blacking. Send also four papers [i.e., paper containers] of black pepper, and two boxes of ground cayenne pepper. . . .Also send me a good pair of suspenders; also three or four cakes of pumice soap and a small bar of sassafras soap, and don't forget to send a good pair of boots, size number ten. . . . Send me some fruit, apples, or dried apples, or anything from home; a loaf of good bread would be a luxury. Send nothing, though, that will spoil under two weeks. Write the directions plainly or paint them so that they cannot come off the box, and don't forget to send me a pen holder and two or three pens, half a dozen large needles, two or three handkerchiefs, and anything you would like to send. Don't forget a coarse towel;

send me no clothing as we cannot carry much and I would probably have to throw it away on a march. Send me a pocket looking glass, pocket comb, and fine comb. The directions are: Company "C," 15th Regiment, New Jersey Volunteers, First New Jersey Brigade, First Division, 6th Corps. Don't, by any means, forget to send the medicines, as they often ward off a serious fit of sickness. Send me word when you send the box, and send a few stamps in your letter.

Quincy Grimes

[P.S.] Please send the box as soon as possible. Be sure and get the medicines. I enclose a ten dollar bill. Send word when you send the box and by what express it was sent. I forgot to say that Randolph Earle, instead of dying, as we all believed, the same day that he was wounded, lived until eight or nine days afterwards and died in the Soldier's Home at Washington — so a letter from Washington to our Captain states. Our Captain went off on a furlough the other day without letting the Company know anything about it until he had gone. But I must close, so good-bye.

From your son,
Quincy

Letter Number Twenty-Five

Saturday, February 28, 1863

Dear Mother:

Stephen Smith [the mail courier] arrived here night before last bringing a package for me containing a letter from you, box of camphor, and havelock. I was on guard that day and it was raining pretty lively at times, so I made immediate use of the havelock and found it to be a bully thing, keeping my neck and shoulders dry. This rain cleared off the snow that fell a few days ago, one of the heaviest falls of snow we have had, almost covering our little shelter tents. But it is all gone now.

I was unwell for some time with sickness and my stomach ache and diarrhea, but I'm nearly well now. I was at work on Tuesday on the road out by White Oak Church. There were 400 men at work from the three brigades of our division. We were making a corduroy road. The way we done it was this: we laid three logs lengthways with the road, one in the middle, the others on each side. Across these we laid other logs. Close together on the top of those, brush and then dirt. It makes a pretty good road, but it is slow work, and it takes a great deal of timber.

We have lost two more of our company, making eight we have lost since coming out.

We get fresh bread nearly every day and expect to get it regularly after this without missing a day. There are now eight ovens with iron tops, each baking 72 at a batch, so we will probably live a little more like civilized people after this.

We had brigade dress parade this morning, inspection and muster immediately after. We

Havelock

are now mustered in for four month's pay, which I hope we will get before long. On the first of May, we will have two months' more pay due us. If we get paid our four month's pay in one bunch, I shall send fifty of it home. I would like to come home on a furlough, but as the married men have the first chance, and there are eighteen of them in our company, there is but small chance for me. They draw for them in this way; they put a number of beans in a cap and one black one amongst them. Who gets the black bean is the lucky fellow.

Camp oven

As soon as I receive the box [of mail and parcels from home] I will write and let you know all about it. I expect we will get them in a little while now, if the mud dries up.

> But I must close, so
> good-bye,
> Quincy Grimes

Letter Number Twenty-Eight

Thursday, April 9, 1863

Dear Sister Lizzy:

I have just come from Corps Headquarters. . . . While on the way [to the Headquarters], we met Abraham Lincoln in a carriage drawn by four horses. Two citizens sat on the front seat, one of whom we thought resembled Seward. Behind them rode General Hooker, another general and a lot of staff officers, a body of lancers with their little red flags on their spears. Behind them all, bringing up the rear, Old Abe. Looks bully; he had a pleasant smile on his face, but is as homely as a brush fence. He reviewed our Corps yesterday. It was a splendid sight to see a whole corps, an army in itself, drawn up in line, or rather I should say, in close column, closed in mass. Just think of three parallel columns of troops in column by division, that is, two companies, each at least a quarter of a mile long, one quite some longer. Also remember that we were closed in mass, just room to move and that's all, and you will have some idea what a large thing an Army Corps is. Our Corps flag has a blue ground with a white cross in the center on which is inscribed a red Six. It took us about half a day to go through the performance. We were reviewed on the farm of Fitzhugh Lee, a Rebel general, said to be one of the finest farms in Virginia. . . .

Our company has been out target shooting lately. I have hit the target every time I have been out with them, which has only been twice. . . . But no more at present.

> From your brother,
> Quincy Grimes

Letter Number Thirty-One

In the following letter, Grimes describes his participation in the Battle of Chancellorsville. During that conflict, Gen. Joseph Hooker moved half of the Union army positioned south of Fredericksburg and marched them north around and across the Rappahannock River with the intention of surprising Lee's army at Fredericksburg from behind. In the meantime, Gen. John Sedgwick stayed

with the remaining Union Army south of Fredericksburg to create a diver-
sion as Hooker launched his main attack. But Hooker's plan did not fool Lee,
who, anticipating Hooker's move, split his army at Fredericksburg, and sent
part of it north to meet the Union foe. As Hooker's forces slowly advanced
through a wilderness, they met Confederate gunfire. Hooker ordered a re-
treat to a farm named Chancellorsville. Lee split his army again, leaving
10,000 men to face Hooker's front, while a force of 26,000 under Stonewall
Jackson marched 14 miles to attack the Union right flank. Jackson forced the
Union forces back to the field around the Chancellorsville farmhouse. Hooker's
army suffered badly, but it was not crushed. It still had a numerical advan-
tage. Meanwhile, Sedgwick's army near Fredericksburg became the main
force. After much fighting, Sedgwick took Fredericksburg but then aban-
doned it upon receiving a message from Hooker requesting help. Sedgwick
headed north to Salem Church, halfway between Fredericksburg and
Chancellorsville. Lee kept Hooker at bay with a line of relatively few troops
while concentrating his main force on Sedgwick. The fierce Confederate on-
slaught that ensued did not deter Sedgwick. Under his leadership, the 15th
and 26th New Jersey Regiments together with the 2d and 3d Vermont Regi-
ments completely routed the enemy at Salem Church. Sedgwick eagerly
wanted to counterattack. If Hooker had used his vastly superior numbers to
break through the thin enemy line facing him, he could have joined forces
with Sedgwick and the Battle of Chancellorsville might have been won by
the North. Instead he retreated across the Rappahannock. Sedgwick reluc-
tantly did the same upon receiving orders from Hooker. Lee had defeated an
army over twice the size of his own. Historians have called the Battle of
Chancellorsville Lee's most brilliant victory. (For more on the Battle of
Chancellorsville see pages 119 and 148).

[No Date]

Dear Mother:

You have no doubt wondered at my long silence and I hasten to break it. We cross[ed] the Rappahannock Wednesday, April 29th, at the same place we crossed last winter under Burnside. We were rowed across in pontoon boats. After our division had crossed, the engineers went to work and laid the pontoon bridges, laying three of them in about an hour.

Saw Henry Hutchinson, the fellow who used to study with Jacob Doremus' sons. He is in Company "K," Fifth Maine. About dark we filed out and relieved a regiment on picket in front. We laid behind the picket line and sent out two companies at a time to relieve those on post — these companies after four hours being relieved by others. That night

Pontoon Bridge over the Rappahannock

they kept the whole regiment awake and a tiresome night it was. Our turn to go on post came Thursday, between 10:00 A.M. and 2:00 P.M. With the exception of one shot fired at us, everything passed off all right. Thursday night, our Regiment was relieved and marched back to the rear of the rifle pits. In the edge of the block, near the river, we pitched our tents and rested for the night. Friday, May the first, we laid in the same place. Saturday, May the 2d, we packed up, struck tents, and laid down behind the rifle pits supporting a battery of brass pieces. The Rebs fired a few shells at first that exploded quite close to us but harming no one. They soon stopped it. Sunday, May the 3d, we marched out as far as the Bowling Green Road and supported a battery laying in the road where it had been cut through the bank. The battery lay [to the] back of us on a bank. In a little while the shells began to whiz over our heads, and an officer on the right called out, "Why don't the battery open fire?" They did open fire, and the canister went over our heads at a great rate. After a while, we moved down the road and filed in the rear of the battery and lay down behind the crest of the hill on which the battery was planted. The battery got out of ammunition and they sent the limbers back after more. When they had fired the last round, they ran the pieces back and we sprang up and advanced to the road. We laid some time in the ditch, the bullets and shells from the Johnnies humming past our ears at a great rate. As soon as our battery received their supply of ammunition, we marched back to the rear of it, took off our knapsacks, fixed bayonets, and waited for the Johnnies. They tried to flank us but a few charges of canister kept them back. When the battery had finished its last round, it retreated. From where we lay we could see the fortifications back of Fredericksburg, saw our troops charge on one hill and take the forts on it. Then we picked up our knapsacks and marched down the road; met the 26th New Jersey Regiment on the way, saw Eugene Righter and shook hands with him. He was all right. We rested just this side of the city for about half an hour, then marched through it and up the hill, and on some three miles until we came to the front. We fought at the foot of a hill and advanced to the edge of the woods, then fixed bayonets and marched through the woods until we received a volley from the Rebs. We stayed in there firing at a great rate for about two or three hours, when we were relieved by another regiment, and we fell back to the edge of the woods and rested for the night after marching off some distance.

I had my cartridge box belt shot off, a hole put in my pocket, but nary a scratch. At night, I, with several others, volunteered to go with the colonel and take the wounded to the hospital.

Monday, the Fourth — We laid down in line of battle all day and at night, retreated to the river and crossed about midnight. We are in the same old camp in our log huts.

Our company lost three killed and seventeen wounded, as follows: Killed — Capt. [Ira] Lindsley, Corporal Brokaw, William Storms; Wounded: Robert Lyons, Halsey Brennan, Edwin A. Doty, John A. Brawn, William F. Parrish, Robert Whitman, Henry Westfall, James Hiler, Stephen Smack; Smith C. Gage, died afterwards; John Tyson, Emmanuel Barton, William Beers, William Shipman, and three others, whose names I do not at present recollect.

I can remember nothing more of interest at present, so good-bye.

From you son,
Quincy Grimes

Letter Number Thirty-Three

White Oak
Church, Virginia
May 28, 1863

Dear Sister Lizzy:

I received your welcome letter the nineteenth. Since that time we have moved camp again about a quarter of a mile to where the woods were cut off last Winter. You may imagine we had a great time burning brush, cutting down stumps, etc. We have quite a nice camp. The tents are placed each side of the company street, and the tents are all single. They are not logged up, but the bunks are raised a foot or so from the ground, and the tent is fastened to the edges of the bunk, which lets the wind under the tent and makes it nice and cool. They are also fixing a sort of a bough roof over the roll tents for shade. One or two companies have fixed theirs, but we have done nothing toward it except putting up a few long crotches [i.e., props]. It was very hot a few days ago and is not very cool now.

By the way, our Paymaster is around, and Albert, just coming in, says he is paying off Company "A." Our turn will come in a little while for two months' pay, which we will be very glad to receive. I guess our Government intends to pay its soldiers regularly after this instead of waiting as it has from four to six months and longer. . . .

How do things go on in old Parsip? Are the Copperheads as sneaking as ever? I expect it pleases them greatly to see Hooker this side of the Rappahannock. I wish they were with the Rebels they like so well. They have made New Jersey appear Secesh. While her soldiers are absent on the battlefields, most of the other States have Committees to look after the welfare of its soldiers, and after each battle they come and take the wounded, and those who can are sent to hospitals in their own State. But New Jersey has no such arrangement.

They give our Regiment great praise for its conduct in the woods. It was the First Regiment that went in and stood their ground in the woods. I don't think you would recognize me if I should appear before you in the same plight I was at the time. Face and hands black with powder and sweaty. I looked a fright, as did the other boys. . . . But I must close.

From your brother,
Quincy Grimes

Letter Number Thirty-Five

Following the Confederate victory at Chancellorsville, Lee's armies moved northward through Virginia in preparation for the invasion of Pennsylvania. In June of 1863, the New Jersey 15th Regiment engaged in a counter movement along the Rappahannock River in an attempt to divert the Confederates from their objective. In the next two letters, Grimes relates his impression of events during this critical phase of the war.

Thursday, June 4th, 1863

Dear Mother:

I have just finished a letter for Eliza, and while I have my writing apparatus out, thought I might as well keep on scribbling. I am much obliged to Grandmother for the lemon she sent me, especially as it grew in Jersey. I received your welcome letter on Monday from Sergeant [Samuel] Rubadeau. I am glad to hear that all the folks are well. I expect strawberries are getting ripe about this time, for I have had two or three wild ones already. I should like to attend some of the Strawberry Festivals in Parsippany, but expect, instead of that, to attend a different sort of meeting on the south bank of the Rappahannock.

Sunday, June the seventh — Here we are on the bank of the Rappahannock. The Second Division is across the river. There are two pontoon bridges down, and I expect we will go across tomorrow. We left camp yesterday after having lain under marching orders for two days. All is very still here. Now and then our battery sounds a shot. What all this movement is for, time alone can tell, though the general opinion here is that it is only a front to keep the Rebs from throwing all their troops upon other points. But then, we may have more heavy fighting here. The Rebs have an advantage in drawing us into ambush, as the leaves are out, and they will have a secure hiding place in the woods, and Virginia, at least as much as I have seen of it, is covered with woods, though we have cut down the trees at a great rate since we have been encamped this side of the Rappahannock, and it looks a great deal different now than when we first came here. Imagine how it would look if Parsippany woods were all cut down from Powerville as far as they reached the other side of Morristown, and you will have some idea how it looks along the north bank of the river.

A fatigue party just passed armed with spades and shovels to throw up entrenchments on the other side of the river, I suppose.

I must close. Answer soon. If we get in any scraps with the Rebs and I come out all right, I shall try and let you know as soon as possible.

From your son,
Quincy Grimes

Letter Number Thirty-Six

Three miles from Fairfax
Courthouse, June 18, 1863

Dear Father:

You have doubtless seen by the papers that the Army of the Potomac has again started on a forward, or rather, backward, movement. We crossed the Rappahannock on Sunday night, the seventh, and laid behind rifle pits most of the time doing nothing much, but had to keep awake most of the night. On Saturday, the 13th, our Regiment went out on picket on the extreme left. It rained pretty lively when we first went out, but about midnight it stopped, and soon after, a lieutenant came and told us to go to the river. When we got there, they had taken up one of the bridges and part of the other one. After we had been ferried across, we took up the march and reached Potomac Creek in the afternoon, and after dark we marched over a rough road to Stafford Courthouse. We had but one rest on the way; when we reached it, we rested an hour, by which time it was daylight, and again we started. The road was very dusty and it was a hot day, but still they marched on. We had scarcely any rest, and the men began to fall out one after the other until there were scarcely any men left in the Regiment. I fell out for the first time. Our whole company fell out, Lieutenants, sergeants and all. Sergeant Rubadeau fell out, a corporal of the color carried the colors for him. . . . After a while they had to halt to let the men catch up. They say that there were but twenty men left in the Regiment when they stopped. They had to wait a good while. Our lieutenant gave up for good and hasn't joined us yet.

Before they started again, they told us that we were only going two miles and a half further; promised to let us rest five minutes out of every twenty. We stopped that night at Dumfries, started again in the morning, about three o'clock. They marched us as nearly as hard as they did the day before, rested us for two hours by a stream called Wolf Run or Bull Run Shoals. Bull Run empties into it two miles below where we rested. From there a few miles further on we reached Fairfax Station where we halted and rested that night and the next day. Today we marched a few miles, passed Fairfax Courthouse on the way, and rested in the woods about three miles from the Courthouse.

Tell Mother that William and myself would like to accept the invitation to the Strawberry Festival, but previous engagements render it impossible. We may have to attend a different sort of festival with Johnnie Reb in which lead ball will be the fare. Don't be at all afraid about using the money I sent home. I expect you to use what you want. Tell Willie I expect a letter from him before long.

What are the latest war news? We hear all sorts of rumors, but nothing that can be relied upon. Give my best respects to all the folks. But I must close.

From your son,
Quincy Grimes

Letter Number Thirty-Seven

Grimes wrote his final letter eight days after the Battle of Gettysburg. Here the 15th New Jersey Regiment was deployed as a second line of defense on a hill behind the strategic point of Little Round Top. Despite his participation, he makes no mention of the actual events that took place. Possibly, he originally included such information, but military censors may have expurgated it.

Near Boonsboro, Mary-
land July 11th, [1863]

Dear Mother:

We have had hard forced marches lately. In fact, we have not stopped a day since we left Fairfax, except a few days on the battlefield of Gettysburg, Pennsylvania. We have marched days and nights as well. Instead of ten miles a day, which was about the average of our marches last Fall, it is now between 20 and 30. We marched 37 the night and day before we arrived at Gettysburg. Day before yesterday, we marched from near Middleton, about eight miles to just the other side of Boonesboro, on the same road we marched on to Bakersville last Fall; formed a line of battle and stayed there the rest of the day. Yesterday we were marched about the same distance from Boonesboro where we are at present in line of battle. There are no signs of our moving as yet, and this is the longest rest we . . .

Grimes never finished the letter. It arrived home inside his trunk. After having survived the experience of war, he died of diarrhea, a common affliction of soldiers. This probably resulted from the ingestion of tainted food or contaminated water. The medicines his family previously sent him to treat his condition had failed.

The Siege of Charleston
As Described by James C. Vail

Between spring of 1862 and fall of 1863, James C. Vail, son of Stephen Vail (Morristown judge and iron works owner), was stationed on the Navy frigate and flagship, U.S.S. Wabash, where he served as Clerk to Adm. Samuel F. Dupont, Commander of the South Atlantic Blockading Squadron. In the following two letters, Vail tells of events surrounding Union attempts to subdue Charleston, South Carolina.

In the first letter, Vail expresses his dislike of military bureaucracy, and frustration at the government's lack of progress in the execution of the war. He also makes some favorable comments regarding the captured town of Beaufort, while lamenting its ruination at the hands of Union occupiers.

In the second letter, Vail describes an unsuccessful Union assault on a Confederate fortification. He also gives an account of a confrontation that took place early in 1863 between Union blockade ships and Confederate ironclads. During this conflict, the Confederate ironclads successfully cleared the harbor of Union ships, inflicting considerable damage to two of them, the Mercedita *and the* Keystone State*. Vail then describes a concurrent naval engagement on the Stone River south of Charleston, in which Confederates captured another Union gunboat, the* Issac Smith*. Vail counters these negative reports with accounts of several Union victories including the capture of two Southern ships — the blockade runner* Princess Royal *and an unnamed schooner. But overall, Vail's report indicates the frustration of the Union Navy in failing to overcome the enemy, which had successfully deployed the new ironclad ships in the defense of Charleston. Still, the Union persisted. Though the Confederate successes described in Vail's letter prompted Gen. G. T. Beauregard to declare the Union blockade officially over, the Union ships returned to resume the blockade within a day. Though Charleston held out for another two years, the Union captured many other strategic coastal points, while its blockade of those still in Confederate hands prevented vital supplies from reaching Southern armies.*

Wabash, Port Royal S.C.
November 25, 1862

Dear Uncle George,

I received your kind letter of the 31st . . . and hasten to answer it by this first opportunity I have. . . . Ever since my return from the North, I have been occupied constantly by the press of public business and have not had time hardly to let them at home know how I was. But as there is always a calm after every storm, so I have at last a little rest. I know now what it is to work for the Government, and I must say that I never want a government office of any kind as long as I can live without it. I think a government official is in worse slavery than any bondsman in the South.

I am sure I think Mr. [George T.] Cobb[1] is right in not wanting to run again. I don't think I would want the office more than once. But as I do not know or care anything about politics, I will leave them alone for the present, and write what I do know. I will say in closing the subject, that I think the Government is pursuing the wrong course in the closing of the war, or even, for gaining "confidence," either of the people as civilians, or soldiers. Indeed I know from actual experience that the course of the Government has estranged many a brave soldier and sailor from his true faith and allegiance to his country. They look upon this war as something that should have been ended long ago, and thinking and believing, as many of them do, that it is prolonged for the few that are making money; they loose all interest in it, and all they care for is their pay.

The Union flagship, **U.S.S. Wabash,** *where James C. Vail served as Clerk to Admiral Samuel F. Dupont.*

We have had some very bad weather here, but it is getting to be a little more settled and warmer as the stormy month passes away, and I hope we shall have some sunny pleasant days such as greeted my arrival here last winter when I first came from the frozen North to this land of Contrabands, mosquitoes, sand and secesh.

I paid a visit to Beaufort the other day, and what was my surprise at finding out that there were several young ladies there, officers wives and sisters who had come down to see their brothers. I tell you that I soon got acquainted with several and had a very pleasant time there.

Beaufort is a very pretty place and it is very nice to go up there once in a while, but it is fast going to ruin under the watchful care of strangers. It is an enormous waste of private property, and I have often wondered what could have induced the owners of it to leave it so suddenly.

Give my love to Aunt Mary, Grandma, Gramma and all the rest, and write soon to you affectionate nephew,

James C. Vail

---

[1] George T. Cobb, a Douglas Democrat Congressman who staunchly supported the war, was popular among Democrats and respected by Republicans. Everyone assumed he would win reelection in 1862. But Cobb alienated the conservative anti-war faction of the Democratic Party by supporting compensated emancipation in the border states and failing to vote against the abolition of slavery in the District of Columbia. At the party's district convention, Andrew J. Rogers of the anti-war faction presented an anti-abolitionist platform, which the delegates accepted. When Cobb refused to endorse it, the party, after much debate, failed to renominate him.

Wabash
February 1, 1863

Dear Mother,

I received your letter of [January] the 20 the other day and hasten to answer it.

I made application for an Accountant Assistant Paymastership, but not being 21 years old, the Department would not confer it upon me, so that there will not be much chance of my coming home yet awhile.

I have bad news and good news to tell you in this letter, and so much that I hardly know where to begin, but I will make an effort to get it all down.

First, you know that the *Montauk, Passaic* and *Ironsides* have arrived here. The *Montauk* went out a few days ago to the southward to attack a fort[1] and capture the *Nashville*. She attacked the Fort and almost knocked it to pieces, when her supply of ammunition gave out and she had to retire. She was struck 14 times . . . but did not receive the slightest damage. She will try it again in a day or so as soon as certain important preparations are made. The *Passaic* went out yesterday to stop the *Savannah* ram [a Confederate ironclad] from doing any mischief.

We have had numerous arrivals of transports and troops from Beaufort, N.C., and are to have all of General [John Gray] Foster's troops here in a few days (40,000) to operate against Charleston.

Then last but not least is the news which started and electrified ev-

The Ironclad Montauk *Beached for Repairs*

eryone yesterday afternoon.

The *August* was reported as coming in during the afternoon, and everybody was wondering what could bring her back from the blockade off Charleston, where she had gone a day or two ago, so soon. But our surmises were soon turned into sad thoughts, when it was reported that yesterday morning before daylight, two rebel ironclad steamers had come out of Charleston, captured the *Mercedita,* paroled her officers and crew, and disabled the *Keystone State* and two or three of her vessels, and then returned themselves uninjured. But this was only the rumor of the fact, which reached us a little later, and as I know all about it, I will give you the particulars.

About 4 A.M., the watch officer of the *Mercedita* saw what he supposed to be a steamer attempting to run the blockade approaching the vessel. He immediately woke the Captain, who came on deck and hailed the vessel, asking what steamer it was. No answer was returned; he then hailed a second time, they not giving any answer. He then said, "Answer, or I fire." When the answer was returned "Confederate Ram" – the name now being heard – Capt. [Henry S.] Stellwagen (of the *Mercedita*) then commenced to fire on him, he returning the fire and slowly approaching the *Mercedita.* A shot from the ram then entered the boiler of the *M*, several others passing quite through her. The ram finally got close under her quarter (stern) and the Captain of her cried out to Captain Stellwagen, "Surrender or I sink you. . . ." Captain S., seeing the uselessness of holding out any longer when he could only hit her with musket balls, surrendered, [and] sent one of his officers to the ram to ask assistance, as he was sinking. The rebel officer then paroled the officers and crew of the *Mercedita* and told her to take care of herself.

In the meantime the *Keystone State*, which was lying near, got underweigh and stood towards the ram with the intention of running her down, but when nearing her, the ram fired, hitting the *K. State* in one of her boilers, which disabled her at once; then the ram fired into her several times, doing her considerable injury. The steam rushing out of the boilers, and the shots, together wounded 20 and killed 20 including the surgeon. The Flag lost her Gunner and four men killed and several wounded.

The blockading vessels hearing the firing (they could not see far on account of the fog) came up to the spot and commenced firing on the rams, when they [i.e., the rams] immediately put about and stood into Charleston, disappearing in the fog. While all this was going on off Charleston, another bloody combat was going on in Stone River a few miles to the Southward. The *Issac Smith,* one of the North River cattle barges converted into a gunboat, went up the river on a reconnaissance, going up about the distance that she had done for some time, and was not troubled or molested in any way, but on returning she was fired on from three batteries on as many sides, and immediately returned the fire, moving down the river, but she got around, but kept up the firing for about fifteen minutes when a shot struck her boilers and thus crippled her; then she ran up the white flag and surrendered.

The loss amongst her crew officers must have been very great, as the rebel fire was very rapid, and the batteries close to the vessel. There was another vessel in the river, but she was also fired on when attempting to assist the *Issac Smith*, and was compelled to run back. We do not know that casualties occurred on the *Smith* as she is in the hands of the rebels, but they must have been very great.

The existence of the batteries on the river was not known, as they were masked, and undoubtedly, put up at night.

Now comes some good news as a set off to the above — Our blockading force off Charleston captured, the other night, one of the most valuable vessels ever taken during the war, the iron propeller *Princess Royal*, of which the New York papers have been speaking lately as having left Halifax to run the blockade.

She was loaded with steam engines, machinery, etc., and if she had succeeded in effecting an entrance, we would have just as many ships off Charleston at this moment as there was before the attack; and even more, the blockade is as effective; the fleet was not driven away as the rebels had hoped to have done, but on the contrary, it has the effect of making them more watchful of all vessels, and shows the rebels that they can hope for nothing of any good to them from such raids. We have the [ironclad] *Ironsides* laying there now; she would have been there before but was not able to get ready. The Government knew all about these rams long ago but did not give us the wherewith to combat them. We are slowly but surely effecting our preparations for a certain event as yet as nameable,[2] and you may expect to hear some more startling news some fine day.

The *Hope*, a little sailing vessel, used as a dispatch vessel, also caught a prize off Charleston the other day — a schooner. The Captain of the *Hope* was telling me about the capture; he says he ran after her until he got close enough to speak [to] her when he hailed her and ordered her to stop, which not doing, he fired his gun at her, a very small one about 1 1/2 inch bore, when the prize hove to and he took possession of her. But the best of it was that he had only one charge of powder on board and that was the one he fired away. He said he waited until he got very close so that one charge would tell.

We are having cold and warm weather here, by turns, but all the time very foggy. Just the opposite of the weather last winter when it was very mild and pleasant all the winter. I get up (or turn out, as the sailors term it) some mornings and go on the deck when I cannot see another ship in the harbor, the fog is so thick, so you see how much we are at the mercy of the rebel rams, which can get our bearings and be almost upon us before we see them. But we do not feel at all afraid, as we have a good crew and a few grim "dogs of war" to bark at them when they come, and which, we have deluded ourselves into the belief, the rams cannot withstand.

The *Princess Royal* is valued at over a $1,000,000, and the schooner I suppose is worth $10,000, so you see that we are almost paying the government for the expense of keeping us here, and when we get [to] Charleston I suppose they will release us from this arduous blockade and let us rest from our labors in this vicinity for a short time. I do not consider the two weeks I had at the North last October as being much of a leave from the uncertainty of their duration, which compelled me to forego several visits I had contemplated making. But I hope soon to see the shores of the North, although how soon or when, is more than I can at present say.

The Admiral has promised me one of his photographs, and I will send you one I have now.

I think I deserve great praise for the long letter I have written and hope that your answer will be longer than the last, which surprised me by its shortness.

Tell Aunt Eva that I have not been ashore since the 1st Dec., except on duty, as I have been very busy on board ship, but I will endeavor to get her the cotton seeds.

Give my love to all at home and remember me to all my engineering friends in Morristown. Sandy Mackenzie is quite well and working pretty hard at his duties of ordnance officer, but he gives satisfaction to the Admiral.

Give love to Georgie and write soon to your affectionate son,

James C. Vail

---

[1] Here Vail refers to Fort McAllister, a small seven-gun Confederate earthworks with an 11-inch mortar near the mouth of the Ogeehee River on the Georgia coast. Vail exaggerates when he contends that the Union monitor *Montauk* almost knocked the fort to pieces. According to most accounts, the *Montauk* inflicted little or no damage upon the Confederate fort. It did however, succeed in destroying the *Nashville*, a Confederate commerce raider grounded near the fort.

[2] This probably refers to the failed attempt to retake Fort Sumter in April of 1862.

Chapter 10

The Court-Martial of Brig. Gen. Joseph Warren Revere

Joseph Warren Revere, grandson of patriot Paul Revere, began his military career when he entered the Navy in 1826. In 1826 General Andrew Jackson appointed him Midshipman in the U.S. Navy. Revere participated in every major military conflict of the period including the Mexican War. In 1850 he resigned from the Navy and established a private shipping business. That same year, while commanding a merchant vessel, he rescued the passengers and crew of a wrecked Spanish vessel besieged by hostile Indians off the Mexican coast. The Spanish government honored him for his heroism by conferring upon him the title of "Knight of the Royal Order of Ysabel." Soon thereafter, he befriended Mexican president Don Mariano Arista who offered Revere a commission as lieutenant colonel of Artillery in the Mexican Army, which Revere accepted. During his service in Mexico, he received the Cross of Mexican Valor and other medals for having saved the Mexican army from defeat in a battle with revolutionaries.

Revere left the Mexican Army when Arista stepped down from office. In 1852 he moved to Morristown, New Jersey, to live in his estate known as "The Willows." In 1857 Revere travelled to Europe and India where he served as a military advisor to the British. During the Civil War, Revere reentered the American military. Governor Charles S. Olden of New Jersey appointed him colonel of the 7th Regiment of the New Jersey Volunteers.

After his promotion to brigadier general in October of 1862, Revere commanded the New York Excelsior Brigade at the Battle of Chancellorsville. Here, Rebel forces delivered the Union Army a crushing blow.

Originally, Maj. Gen. Joseph Hooker, the Union commander of the Army of the Potomac, planned to defeat the Confederate army at Fredericksburg through a strategy based on deception. He ordered part of the Union army under the command of Maj. Gen. John Sedgwick to remain south of Fredericksburg, facing the enemy across the Rappahannock River. He then marched his main army north, crossing the Rappahannock well above Fredericksburg. After crossing the river, he swung back south in the hope of attacking the Rebel army from behind. Hooker's plan did not fool the Confederates. Lee ordered part of his defensive forces at Fredericksburg north to confront the Union army. As Hooker's men advanced through a thick forest, they met Confederate fire. Hooker abandoned the high ground and ordered his soldiers back to Chancellorsville, which was not a village but a solitary house in a clearing surrounded by woods. Meanwhile, Lee split his army again, leaving a thin line along Hooker's front, while a larger force under Stonewall Jackson used an unfinished road to mount a surprise attack. Jackson hit Hooker's right flank with such force that Hooker's army assumed a defensive position throughout the remainder of the battle — even though they outnumbered the Confederates two-to-one and could easily have broken through Lee's thin line along the woods.

Jackson's army came close to taking Chancellorsville on the first day of battle, but Union artillery and the coming of night stopped them. Jackson prepared for a night attack, but as he and several of his officers rode out between the lines, Union pickets opened fire. Returning to Confederate lines, his own men mistook him for the enemy. They shot and mortally wounded him.

Revere's brigade, which had been kept in reserve, was brought forward to a defensive position to check Jackson's assault and to build fortifications in preparation for the Confederate onslaught that came the following day, May 3. Revere's brigade fought for several hours that Sunday morning, but the constant fire of Confederate cannon and musketry forced his shattered troops to fall back to a field in the vicinity of the white farm house that Hooker used for headquarters. Revere described the scene as one of chaos and "complete disorganization," with a constant flow of stragglers moving to the rear as fresh soldiers moved to the front. The field was so crowded that at one point in the conflict, an assistant to Maj. Gen. Daniel E. Sickles, commander of the Third Army Corps, requested Revere to remove his troops to make room. Revere, who had difficulty maintaining communications with his division commander, Maj. Gen. Hiram C. Berry, reported instead to Maj. Gen. William H. French, commander of the 3d Division, Second Army Corps. French advised him to help defend a line of abatis (a barrier made of felled trees with sharpened points), but Revere found this unnecessary since Union troops already occupied the line. Soon thereafter, Revere received word that General Berry had been killed. Revere assumed Berry's command.

Revere determined that additional troops would be needed to defend the road between Chancellorsville and the shallow crossing point in the Rappahannock River known as United States Ford. But first he needed to regroup the stragglers, provide them with food and rest, and return them to battle. Other commanding officers and members of the 3d Army general staff were engaged in the same activity under orders from General Sickles. But when Revere reported to the front with two thousand men, Sickles relieved him of his command for having acted without orders. Revere was unaware that Sickles had already given General Berry's command to 1st Brigade, 2d Division commander Maj. Gen. Joseph B. Carr, even though Revere clearly outranked Carr.

General Sickles filed charges against Revere for having left the scene of action and for abandoning military equipment to the enemy. The army subsequently court-martialed Revere. They found him guilty of conduct to the prejudice of good order and military discipline but not guilty of the two original charges. He was dismissed from the army.

Revere published a pamphlet countering the charges brought against him with a defense of his actions based on military necessity. He also criticized those who conducted the court-martial, maintaining that they violated procedure by altering and amending the original charges while adding additional ones. Revere staunchly defended his character by citing years of military experience in service to his country. He concluded by imploring the public for support in the hope of receiving another hearing.

The text of Revere's pamphlet appeared in the November 5, 1863, *True Democratic Banner*. The *Banner* stood by Revere, a fellow Democrat, against what they viewed as a politically motivated action by a Republican administration trying to find a scapegoat. There is some truth to this. During the war, the army court-martialed many other Democratic officers that had participated in loosing battles.[1] But in Revere's case, it was his commanding officer, General Sickles, more than any individual or political party, who probably felt the need for a scapegoat to exonerate himself of responsibility for the colossal Union failure in which he played a major role. In fact, Sickles often had difficulty admitting personal failure. For example, earlier in the conflict, when Sickles commanded an unsuccessful night attack against Stonewall Jackson, he reported it as a success. In all likelihood Sickles harbored jealous feelings toward Revere. This stemmed from the fact that when Joseph Hooker was appointed commander of the Army of the Potomac, he put Revere in command of the Excelsior Brigade to restore discipline to its ranks, replacing Sickles who had originally formed the brigade.

In the final analysis, neither Revere nor Sickles can be blamed for the Union defeat at Chancellorsville. The commander of the Army of the Potomac, Gen. Joseph Hooker, provided the real reason for the tragedy of Chancellorsville when he later wrote, "To tell the truth, I just lost confidence in Joe Hooker."

In 1864 President Lincoln exonerated Revere and restored his rank as brigadier general. In 1866 the Congress conferred upon Revere the rank of Brevet Major General—a special honorary rank usually granted to men in the field for acts of heroism.

The following is the text of Revere's defense.

Statement of the Case of Brigadier General Joseph W. Revere

At a General Court-martial ordered by General Hooker, commanding the army of the Potomac, held near Falmouth, Va., on the 12th day of May, 1863, for the trial of Brigadier General Joseph W. Revere, United States Volunteers, the following charges were preferred by General Sickles, commanding the Third Corps:

First Charge—Misbehavior before the enemy.

Specification—In this, that Brigadier General J. W. Revere, United States Volunteers, commanding Third Excelsior (Second) Brigade, Second Division, Third Corps, while the said division was engaged with the enemy at Chancellorsville, Virginia, did march his command an unnecessary distance to the rear to reform it, and did then march with his brigade, and such fragments of other regiments of the said division as he could assemble, to United States Ford, about five miles from the scene of action. All this without orders from his superior officers, about eight o'clock on the morning of May 3d, 1863. Charge Second—Neglect of duty, to the prejudice of good order and military discipline.

Specification—In this, that Brigadier General J. W. Revere, United States Volunteers, commanding Excelsior (Second) Brigade, Second Division, Third Corps, did allow public property to the amount of 189 muskets, 178 sets of accouterments, 259 bayonets, 28,440 rounds of small-arm ammunition, 1,779 knapsacks, 836 haversacks, 494 canteens, 2,000 shelter-tents, and fifty-five pioneer tools, in the service of his command, to be abandoned, and to fall into the hands of the enemy. All this without orders from his superior officers at Chancellorsville, Va., on or about May 3d, 1863.

And the finding of the Court was in these terms:

Of the Specification to first Charge, guilty, except the words, "while said division was engaged with the enemy at Chancellorsville, Virginia, did march his command an unnecessary distance to the rear to reform it," and "then" and "to United States Ford, about five miles from the scene of action," substituting for the latter clause, "to about three miles from the scene of action, towards United States Ford."

Of the First Charge, not guilty, but guilty of conduct to the prejudice of good order and military discipline.

Of the Specification to Second Change, not guilty.

Of Second Change, not guilty.

The finding of the First Specification, then is as follows:

Guilty, in this "that Brigadier General J. W. Revere, United State Volunteers, commanding Excelsior (Second) Brigade, Second Division, Third Corps, did march with his brigade, and such fragments of other regiments of the said division as he could assemble, to about three miles from scene of action, towards United States Ford."

The sentence of the Court was, that General Revere be dismissed from the military service of the United States.

This sentence was approved by the President on the 10th day of August, 1863, and made known to the accused on the 15th day of August, 1863.

General Revere responds to his accusers.

The court martial held the grave charges of neglect of duty and misbehavior before the enemy to be unfounded, and rested its sentence upon the far less disgraceful charge of "conduct to the prejudice of good order and military discipline." I make no comment upon the spirit which dictated an accusation fatal, if proved, to the honor of a brother soldier, yet unsustained by the facts: nor is it necessary to dwell on that large portion of the evidence in the case which relates to the second charge. The reader is capable of deciding for himself in what degree the facts warrant the finding, and to what extent the finding justifies the severity of the sentence.

No defense was offered by the accused on the trial. At the close of the case for the prosecution, my counsel, Gen. D. B. Birney, was so entirely satisfied with the evidence, as exonerating me from all censure, that, after offering the testimony of two officers for the defense, in explanation of some details, he advised the course of submitting the case to the Court, without making any argument, or any fuller explanation of the circumstances and motives governing my action. It was his opinion, as well as that of my friends present at the trial, that the case for the prosecution had completely broken down; and I received their congratulations upon the result without a doubt of my acquittal. Nor were any of us prepared for the extraordinary course which the Court adopted, in pronouncing me not guilty upon both the charges, yet framing another charge, fitting a part of one of the original specifications to it, and condemning me thus, in fact, unheard upon that particular accusation. "Neglect of duty," under the second charge, we were prepared to disprove, and did in fact disprove, by the very evidence for the prosecution. The more general charge of "conduct prejudicial to good order and military discipline" required a different defense, resting upon motives — upon special information and reasons for action known only to the accused; and if it had been fairly presented, it would have been met by such a defense. How far the Court was justified by military law in this peculiar finding, will be inquired in another part of this paper.

Some confusion may have been produced in the minds of the members of the Court by the ingenuity with which the chief witness for the prosecution insinuated the proof of an offense not really charged. Their testimony labors to establish two facts; one supporting the charges, and the other wholly irrelevant to them. The first is the offense of misconduct while commanding the division; the other, that of misconduct in unwarrantly assuming command of it. Now, while the latter, if proved, could have no effect upon the case as charged, it might very easily have fixed upon the minds of the Court an impression of insubordination, which must have affected their finding. No evidence was offered by me to disturb this erroneous impression. An attentive reader of the testimony can hardly escape the conclusion that the false issue thus craftily presented may have had this effect.

The occurrences which led to the situation at the time referred to in the charges:

The operations in which my brigade took part, during the few days preceding the battle of May 3d, at Chancellorsville, were peculiarly harassing and fatiguing. After several day[s] [of] continuous marching and countermarching, near Falmouth, on the north bank of the Rappahannock, the brigade crossed that river on Friday, the 1st day of May, and moved to the front at Chancellorsville, where they were stationed as a reserve, to support the troops then hotly engaged, and where, that night, they bivouacked under arms. It will be recollected that during that night and the following day, the enemy were busy in cutting a road through the forest, around our left flank and along our front, and in marching by it immense masses from our left to our right in preparation for the furious attack made from the westward towards Saturday evening, the 2d of May. The Second Division, after being under arms the whole of Saturday, were hurried forward about 5 P.M. to check this assault, and to restore the battle, which was fast turning into a rout, from the repulse of the Eleventh Corps which had given way on the extreme right. During the night between Saturday and Sunday, the brigade, while kept constantly on the alert from frequent alarms and the driving in of pickets, managed to throw up a line of log breastworks, expecting a renewal of the attack, for which we knew the enemy were massing their forces. The last communication I had with General Sickles was through General Berry, about two o'clock on Saturday afternoon, and the only

The Chancellor House

food my men received was at noon of that day—rest they had none. Going towards the rear during the night, I discovered that we had no second line there, and that our right was uncovered—a distance of half a mile, unoccupied by troops, intervening between it and the next force at White House.

The night we took prisoners—a captain and some twenty privates of the enemy, from whom we learned that General A. P. Hill commanded a large force directly in our front, intending to attack and gain possession of the crossroads at Chancellorsville; and that Stonewall Jackson had already thrown heavy masses of infantry and artillery towards our right, and intended to force his way at early morning between our army and the river. This most important information was at once sent to General Berry, my immediate chief; but whether it was forwarded by him to the generals of corps, or the general-in-chief, I do not know.

At daylight on Sunday, May 3d, the enemy drove in our pickets, and opened the battle with a heavy fire of artillery and musketry. The brigade fought steadily for several hours, until the enemy turned our left flank, and enfiladed[2] the breastwork, when they were forced by numbers to retire.

The country in which the battle of Chancellorsville was fought is a plain, overgrown with dense woods, through which a road runs southwardly from the United States Ford of the Rappahannock, intersected, at the hamlet of Chancellorsville, by a plank-road running westwardly from Fredericksburg to Orange Court House. This crossing-place was

Meeting Jackson's Flank Attack

essential to the safety of Lee's army to hold, and accordingly they had, as stated, during Friday and Saturday, put a road through the woods completely around our left flank and along our front, and had attacked us from the west with an immense force under their best leaders. Pushing this bold movement still further north towards the river, they confronted our army with a powerful line which stretched in a general direction parallel to its front; and to the road heading to United States Ford, threatening that vital point in our communications. It is clear then that, in a general sense, the scene of action became the whole extent of this road, from Chancellorsville to the river, and that the peril and the chance of conflict was no greater on our left than on our right, where the onset of Jackson might at any moment be expected. The distance from Chancellorsville to the White House is about three-quarters of a mile; from Chancellorsville to the ford is not less than four miles; and from the point to which my shattered brigade withdrew on Sunday morning, to the ford, is about three miles and a half. In the neighborhood of the White House, the forest thins out to a small clearing on about ten acres; and around the brick house near the ford is a much larger open space, while between these two points the woods are dense. The open space around the White House was crowded on the morning of Sunday, after the action, with troops moving in both directions, stragglers going to the rear, and artillery and infantry arriving constantly and debauching into it. It was also occupied by the fresh troops of (I think) the Second Corps. Such was the crowd and want of space, that I was requested by several staff officers, one, an A. D. C. [assistant division commander] of the general staff, to remove my troops in order to make room.

Into this crowded spot, then, the only open one within some miles, we had been driven in disorder and complete disorganization after the engagement of Sunday morning, there being no second line of battle in our immediate rear, behind which we might rally. I collected here five or six hundred men of the different regiments of the division who had straggled in after the action. The senior officer in command at that point being General French, I reported myself to him, and received from him the advice to occupy with my men a line of abatis. These, however, I found filled with troops, leaving no room for the addition of mine. Here, at this time, I heard from his A. D. C. of the death of General Berry my division commander who was killed at about half-past seven o'clock; and immediately afterwards I met Brigadier General [Gershom] Mott, the next in seniority in the division, going to the rear severely wounded. I at once concluded that I was the commanding officer of the Second Division, Third Corps; and in that capacity I directed all the officers of my division who could be found, personally, and through my staff, to rally and report to me. And as this new position devolved upon me, both the responsibility of directing the division, and the enlarged discretion which every general officer in such circumstances is supposed to possess, I determined upon my course of action in view of all the facts which have been stated.

The need of some action was urgent. I believed myself to be the division commander. I had no communication with any corps commander since noon of the preceding day, nor was any now possible. Nothing could be heard of him or of his staff from the numerous stragglers of the Third Corps who were constantly passing us to the rear through the woods flanking the road. I knew only that he had been engaged in the same action with ourselves, and supposed that he had shared the same disorganizing repulse. To reunite my small force to him through the inextricable crowds passing confusedly in both directions between us and the front would have been impossible, even had his headquarters been fixed or known. My men were worn with the marches and battles of four days, with want of rest and food for the last twenty-four hours, and with sharp fighting for the last four, and were nearly out of ammunition. Stragglers from all the regiments of the corps were passing in increasing numbers, adding constantly to the force which could only be collected by retiring, and could not have been reformed, if present, where we were. Add to this, that with my mind full of the intelligence received from the prisoners of the last night, I was convinced that there might be use for troops anywhere along the road to the ford; that the front of the battle had indeed been shifted far to the right; and that a large portion of the division, reorganized, refreshed, and resupplied, would be of more service there than a few hundred men could be, standing faint and idle where we were, or vainly striving to cross the torrent flowing past them. Or, if not needed at the right, surely the time would not be wasted which should be devoted to placing them in such force and condition that they could be marched back again to join in the battle which had ceased in our front, and which would meantime be sustained by fresh troops, if renewed during our absence. It was not so renewed, nor were we ever so far from the point we had left that it could not have been reached in a reasonable time.

My duty was to collect my division and bring it, ready for action, into union with its corps. Had I at that moment received any orders, they would have been the same which the corps commander states in his evidence that he gave to other general officers to report with my command. This could only be done by overtaking and rallying its debris, as they streamed towards the point where alone rest, and food, and ammunition, and space to form could be gained, and where as I at least knew, a chance of early action was to be looked for also; and then returning with it toward headquarters, which would by that time be established and accessible. At this moment they were not fixed, for Sickles states that only after Berry's death was the movement made for this purpose. I therefore, in the absence of orders, after reflection, sensible of the responsibility involved, but confident that it was the only course for bringing my troops speedily into efficient service, determined upon the movement for which I am censured by the Court.

Striking a direct course by compass through the woods, I moved a mile and a quarter towards a point on the main road about midway to the United States Ford, and then marched a short distance down the main roads to a position where the stragglers on both sides of it might be intercepted and rallied, and where orders from either flank might reach us with equal case. Arrived at this point, I halted the column, sent out patrols in all directions to collect stragglers, and obtained from the river, and distributed, food and ammunition. During this time I saw several general officers, and at least one major general engaged in the same duty of rallying troops who filled the whole space between my position and the river, in a vast and confused throng. At this time and place too, I saw and spoke with Lieutenant Colonel O. H. Hart, Adjutant General to General Sickles, who with two aides was busy in the same work. At noon, reports were called for from the different regiments, and 1,715 officers and men, in the aggregate, were reported present for duty. Anxious to avoid delay, I gave the men but little time to prepare their food, and then led the division towards the front again, increasing our force at every rod. Hearing while on the march that the Third Brigade was collected close to the ford, I sent one of my aides, Lieutenant Belger, to bring them up. Being thus joined by over three hundred men, more gathered from the different divisions of the Third Corps, I continued the movement to the front. When, within half a mile of General Stickles' bivouac, on this, his return march, I received orders (the first that were received by me from any one whatsoever during that day) by an aide from him, directing me to return, and shortly after, an order to the same effect from General Carr was handed to me. Major Burns testifies that he also met on this march an aide from General Sickles with orders to do exactly what we were doing—bring the stragglers to the front.

I reached the front at the head of about 2,000 men of the division, at half-past two in the afternoon by my watch. I reported there to General Sickles, who relieved me of my command. I at once offered to serve as a volunteer in any capacity in the battle that seemed impending. My request was refused, and General Sickles demanded an explanation, which I gave in writing.

It is here that I positively deny having ever sent an aide, or orderly, or any other messenger to General Carr, with orders to him to report to me at or near the United States Ford, as that officer has stated in his testimony on the trial.

To sum up all in a few words—after the fight was ended, I left without orders, and crowded off to the field, I led away a handful of worn and disorganized men towards a point where, in my belief, an action might even then be going on, and brought them back within six hours, after retiring less than three miles, two thousand strong, refreshed and resupplied. What this a breach of duty?

If the reader will now compare the original charges with the evidence on the record, and will also compare the finding of the Court with the facts as above stated, he may see reason to conclude, that, as the charges were not supported by the case made for the prosecution, so the finding would not have been justified if the matters just narrated had been offered by way of defense, fortified, as they could have been, by ample proof. For what is the substance of the finding! Let it be borne in mind that, by the law of courts-martial, "a prisoner must be acquitted or convicted of every part of each of the several specifications and charges of which he stands accused." The Court then "acquits me of those parts of the original specification to the first charge which in the finding are "excepted" from the conclusion of "guilty"—acquits me of "marching my command while engaged with the enemy"—acquits me of "marching an unnecessary distance to the rear." What is left in the finding thus emasculated? The simple fact that I "marched with the Second Brigade, and such fragments of other regiments of the division as could be assembled to about three miles from the scene of action, towards the United States Ford" — a fact in itself indifferent, implying no criminality nor neglect, and deriving its character only from the attendant circumstances and motives. I have shown from these circumstances and motives that the intention was right, and the act advisable — Something was required, beyond the facts so found, to give my conduct the character of a military offence. I believe that the incriminating element is to be found in the false impression on the minds of the Court, not derived from the charges, but artfully suggested by the principal witnesses, uncontradicted by me, and leaving its traces in the finding — the impression that I wrongfully assumed the command of the division. That would indeed warrant the find of "conduct to the prejudice of discipline and, good order." The reader can decide what the Court had no opportunity of doing, how innocent I am of this offence.

But the peculiar finding of the Court suggests a far graver question, as to the regularity and lawfulness of their mode of proceeding. The object I here make is not one of technicality, but one which, if well founded, vitiates and renders illegal the whole finding and sentence. It rests upon principles of military law, arising in former cases, and steeled by decisions recorded in the War Department.

By the rules and practice of courts-martial, military charges must be brought under some one or other of the Articles of War. When the specified facts and circumstances clearly point to a particular Article, the prosecution must be had under that Article, and the charge expressed in the terms used therein. Besides the various particular Articles of War, which assign a penalty for definite and specified offences, there is an Article known as the General Article (No. 99) which provides for the trial of all crimes not capital, and all disorders and neglects to the prejudice of good order and military discipline: and any offence not specifically provided for must be charged under this General Article. Accordingly, in my case, the first charge, that of misbehavior before the enemy, was specifically brought under Article 52, which provides for that offence, and the second charge, that of neglect of duty, an offence not provided for in any specific article, was brought under the General Article (99). The Court acquitted me on both charges, but then proceeded to frame a new charge, to connect with it a part of the specification to the first charge, under Article 52, and to pronounce a find of "guilty," under Article 99. This it was beyond their lawful power to do. A court-martial, after the prisoner is arraigned, cannot alter or amend the original charges, nor entertain additional ones. It must be remembered that charge and specification number two were both dismissed; they were disposed of, and were no longer in the case, and the only question was as to what the finding should be on the first specification. The law, as settled by the highest authority, the War Department, in the cases to which I have referred, holds that where a charge is laid under a specific Article, the accused must be found guilty of a violation of that article, or be acquitted. The court cannot find him guilty of the specification as an offense under the 99th Article. It is necessary that the offense against the 99th Article should be duly and regularly charged, in order that the accused may have notice of that which he is to answer. A charge of one of the specific offenses defined in other articles is not notice of a general charge of some disorder or neglect within the 99th Article. In another case, where the charge was made under Article 83, the decision says: "The court have acquitted the accused of the legal charge against him. At the same time they give judgement against him under the 99th Article of War. He was not charged with any offense under that Article. If charges are so drawn as to bring them expressly and exclusively under particular Articles of War, a court-martial cannot convict under other Articles. The sentence of the court-martial in this case is therefore void."

Again, in a case still nearer to the present, it is said: "The court find the prisoner guilty of the specification to the first charge, and not guilty of the second charge and its specification, and do sentence him, etc. The proceedings of the court in this case are disapproved; the court, although finding a part of the facts alleged against the prisoner, having acquitted him of both the charges preferred, proceeded irregularly in passing sentence upon him."

Nor can it be said that the Court here proceeded, in the exercise of that discretion which military law allows it, to substitute in the finding a lesser degree of the offense charged. That discretion is limited to the choice between offenses of a kindred nature. But cowardice, which is the essence of the charge of misbe-

Brig. Gen. Joseph Warren Revere (Courtesy of Morristown-Morris Township Library).

havior before the enemy, is a crime that stands single, and admits no shade of shame. There is no other offense of which it is an aggravated form. Between it and conduct to the prejudice of good order and discipline, the difference is one of kind, and not of degree; and it is not lawful for a court to adopt a difference of that nature as a basis on which to construct its finding.

On this high authority, I impeach the finding and protest against the sentence of the court-martial in my case, as illegal, and exceeding the power of the tribunal.

I have turned with reluctance from the merits of the case to a discussion of its form, and now proceed, with still greater unwillingness, to speak of some personal considerations. It is a painful necessity which compels an officer, thus dragged into public view for branding, to risk the blame of egotism by doing violence to his natural feelings of reserve. But the justice to myself and others which prompts this statement, demands that it should be complete.

Having received, from my own and other countries, testimonials, to me priceless, of my behavior as a soldier, I can smile at the flagrant vindictiveness of a charge which imputes to me cowardice on the field. But to the public, usually only half-informed through the newspapers, the opinion of those lately my companions in arms may be of value. The Court threw this charge aside, as it deserved, adopting, instead, the different and milder one of breach of discipline.

If it is difficult to make the finding of the Court consistent with law and evidence, it is still more difficult to reconcile either with the extreme harshness of the sentence. I am too old a soldier not to be aware that stern examples are needed in all armies, and that a general officer must sometimes suffer for errors of judgement in discharging the responsibilities which duty casts upon him. But some proportion should be observed between the offense and the penalty; and, in all armies, length of service, wounds, and imprisonment, may be pleaded in mitigation of punishment; and personal character may be made the ground of an appeal to the lenity of a court.

The greater part of my life has been devoted, in the profession of arms, to the service of my country, following naturally the traditions of a family which gave one not undistinguished name to the Revolutionary War, and which has offered two other of its members to death for the state, in this one. I have been for thirty years a sailor and soldier. Had I been a politician in epaulets, plying in the camps the arts of the caucus, and eking out by chicane defects in soldiership; or had I been lifted from some low employment to a rank won only by servility, and held only by pliancy, there might be retribution, though indirect, justice in this his sentence. But I have been more versed in war than intrigue. On all that Court, eminent as most of its members were, there was not one who was not my junior in length of employment in the United States' service. I am censured for conduct to the prejudice of discipline, after having served for twenty years, under the iron discipline of the old navy, without a reproach on that score—after having held in Mexico, in 1851, the rank of lieutenant-colonel, and instructor of artillery, confirmed in view of my fitness as a disciplinarian—after being appointed a brigadier-general of volunteers, on the recommendation of General Hooker himself, founded expressly on my known experience in discipline, and justified, before and since, by the severe and exact enforcement of that military virtue, for which I am well known in our present army, and which has borne its fruits in the brilliant reputation of the 7th New Jersey Volunteers, trained and originally commanded by me—after having served in the battles of the Peninsula campaign of [Gen. John] Pope, and at Fredericksburg, with wounds, but without a blemish upon my military character, in that or any other respect. Surely, the testimony of such a record to the improbability of the offence should have outweighed all but the most direct and absolute proof that it was committed. At least, with such a record, I had a right to expect from the Court, even with my defense unheard, greater lenity than is shown in this cruel sentence—and from the President, even though his attention scarcely rested upon my case, some indulgence for one who has given the prime of his life, without military reproach hitherto, to the service of the State. Upon that record, and his Statement, asking only an impartial hearing, I invoke the judgement of that public opinion to which all are amenable, and which seldom fails, in the end, to do justice.

---

[1] Other Democrat officers court-martialled by the army included Fitz-John Porter. As a brigadier general in the Army of the Potomac, Porter commanded a detachment during the Peninsular Campaign that sucessfully stopped most of Lee's advances during the "Seven Days Battles" including Malvern Hill where he repulsed the Confederates with heavy losses inflicted on the Southern army. Though recognized as an outstanding general by Northerners and Southerners alike, Porter was a Democrat and close friend of General McClellan. When Lincoln relieved McClellan of his command for having failed to decisively defeat the Confederates at Antietam, he also replaced Porter. Joseph Hooker took Porter's place as commander of the 5th Corps. Soon thereafter, General Pope, recently humiliated by his defeat at the Second Battle of Bull Run, scapegoated Porter by blaming him for the defeat. Though Porter and his Union contingent fought very aggressively during this battle, the Army court-martialed him on false charges. Porter has remained one of the most controversial figures in American military history. Historians have compared his case to France's Dreyfus case. Not until 1879 did an Army Board of Review exonerate him. At Porter's retrial, Pope refused to testify, successfully dodging a subpoena issued by the Board. But many others testified on his behalf, including James

Longstreet and a number of other ex-Confederate officers who had fought at the Second Battle of Bull Run. Porter and Revere became good friends after the war when Porter moved to Morristown. When Revere died in 1880, Porter served as a pallbearer in Revere's funeral procession.

[2] enfilade: To rake with maximum fire power in a lengthwise direction across the enemy's flank.

Chapter 11

The Civil War Diary of Edmund D. Halsey

Edmund Drake Halsey was born September 11, 1840, the youngest of nine children born to a prominent Rockaway family. Like his father, Samuel Beach Halsey, Edmund was known for his scholarly interests. From an early age he enjoyed reading and had a remarkable craving for knowledge. He entered the Sophomore class of Princeton College at age 17 where he demonstrated himself to be an outstanding student. Halsey loved literature and history and wrote extensively on local history. He authored the introductory and general section of *The History of Morris County, New Jersey* (Munsell, 1882), a book well known to all Morris County historians.

Halsey intended to enter the legal profession. But while studying for the Bar, he enlisted in the Union army, believing very strongly in the Northern cause. His brother Joseph, who resided in the South for health reasons, fought for the Confederacy.

Though Edmund had the opportunity to enter the service as a lieutenant in the local 27th Regiment, his father preferred that he enter the 15th Regiment as a private. He acceded to his father's wishes.

Early in his military career, Halsey demonstrated his great courage in a simple but significant act that would determine his fate for the remainder of the war. After having experienced the horror of battle and the defeat of the Union army at the hands of the Confederates, Halsey was given the chance to leave the field of battle permanently. The army offered him a detail in Baltimore as chief clerk to a medical doctor. He declined the offer, preferring to remain with his comrades in arms.

Halsey advanced himself to the rank of first lieutenant. As adjutant clerk he assisted his commanding officers, recording and transmitting correspondence between regiments and armies. He also served as judge advocate on courts-martial for one year.

Throughout his military career, Halsey's 15th N.J. Regiment fought in many major conflicts including Fredericksburg, Chancellorsville, Gettysburg, the Wilderness Campaign, Cold Harbor, Fisher's Hill, and Cedar Creek.

Following his return home, Edmund D. Halsey completed his legal studies and, in 1865, began practicing law in Morristown. Halsey prospered as a successful attorney and bank director. Active in local politics, he served one term in the state legislature.

Halsey married his sweetheart, Mary Darcy, in the spring of 1869. They had seven children, but tragically, only two survived to adulthood, and one of these died after graduating Princeton. On October 17, 1896, Halsey succumbed to pleurisy at age fifty-five. His body lies buried at the Rockaway Presbyterian Church Cemetery.

This chapter features excerpts of Halsey's diary in which he records and comments upon events of the war that he witnessed first hand. He relates how he decided to join the 15th N. J. Regiment, his initial impressions of camp life, and his first military encounters. This is followed by vivid accounts of battles and the hardships that the 15th N.J. Regiment had to endure in their fight to save the Union.

Entering the Fray

After the battles of July and August, 1862, I fully made up my mind to enter the service somewhere. I was very busy assisting father and the superintendent of his men then getting the hay on the Pleasant Valley Farm.

In the meantime, the people of Rockaway Township were training a company for the 27th Regiment, New Jersey Volunteers (9-month men), then organizing in Newark at a camp near Roseville. Henry Willis was proposed as captain and I was to be first lieutenant. As soon as the hay was picked, I went to recruiting vigorously. August 22—went to Newark to see the camp and my friends there. That night had a meeting in the church to raise volunteers. . . . Seven or eight joined the company that night. . . . I think of taking a squad of say 20 or 30—all that are ready to go—to Morristown to be examined in the morning and on down to Newark in the afternoon. I did not go to Newark but was about the neighborhood recruiting. . . .

During August and before, Companies C and F of the 15th Regiment, New Jersey Volunteers (3-year men) were being raised in the county, and I was urged to join one of them. Col. Sam Fowler was to be in command and Alanson Haines to be chaplain. I was offered the position of Adjutant Clerk [with] [r]ank and pay of a private but without exposure to the ordinary duties of a soldier. Father, who disapproved altogether of my entering the service at all, had discouraged the idea of accepting this position until he saw that the company of the 27th would soon be raised and I in it. At the dinner table, Monday, August 25, he said if I must and would go, he preferred I would take the place in the 15th. I at once declared it a matter of indifference to me, and if he preferred me to be a private in the 15th to a first lieutenant in the 27th, I would do as he wished.

DIARY,

of

EDMUND D. HALSEY.

Private-Co. K. — Sergeant Major,
2nd Lieut Co. F. — 1st Lieut Co. D.
1st Lieut and Adjutant,

FIFTEENTH   REGIMENT.

N. J. VOLS.

Aug 25th 1862. —— Jan. 12th 1865.

Title Page of Edmund D. Halsey's Civil War Diary

I had no time to see Captain Willis [of the 27th N.J. Regiment] or my friends, but telegraph[ed them] . . . to meet me at Morristown. Went down on the 2:40 train from Rockaway to Flemington. Father went with me to the depot and the worst of going away was leaving him. [My brother] Sam met me at Morristown and went with me. Stopped in Newark to be measured for a suit of clothes at Perry's . . . and thence by New Jersey Railroad and Central Railroad to White House [Station], which we reached by dusk.

From there took a stage eight miles to Flemington. This being crowded, several passengers, myself among the number, walked nearly all the way.

At the hotel in Flemington, met Col. Fowler, Dr. [Redford] Sharp, Lt. [John H.] Vanderver, the Mustering Officers, etc. At the desk at the end of the bar, I drew up and signed my own enlistment papers, dated them back to the 21st and was mustered in.

Aug. 27 — In Camp Fair Oaks [Flemington] all day. . . . [I]n the afternoon received orders to march Friday morning. Orders for Washington . . . . Busy carrying orders and attending to post office.

Aug. 28, At Camp Fair Oaks — The regiment is to start tomorrow at five o'clock — tents struck at 4 A.M. . . . We have been getting ready to move and the last candle is just glimmering out.

Aug. 29 — Our ride was triumphal, cheered all along the way, and the supper in Philadelphia was a splendid affair, perfectly free and neat and clean.

Camp Fair Oaks (from History of the Fifteenth Regiment, New Jersey Volunteers*)*

It seemed as if the people could not do too much for us, and the men long remember the march up to Flemington from camp — the drum corps playing their only tune, "The Girl I Left Behind Me," the warm reception and heaps of good things at Lambertville, and the kindness of the ladies who furnished the supper in Philadelphia.

Aug. 30 — The regiment marched through Baltimore from depot to depot. . . . The cavalry we passed was the 6th N.Y. The trains of sick coming from Washington were not pleasant to see, and the low booming of artillery, more and more audible as we came nearer Washington, were the first sounds of war. The supper at the Soldiers' Rest was simply coffee, bread, and a piece of meat. Most of the men declined it altogether.

Aug. 31 — Wrote father an encouraging letter promising that when I did return I would stay with him.

City [of Washington] full of rumors. All the carriages impressed and sent to Alexandria returned empty, showing that the enemy held the battlefield.

The day was as rainy and dismal with reports from the battlefield. The Regiment marched up to Tenallytown and pitched their tents . . . as well as they could in the rain. With the adjutant I went around to the different hotels and learned what we could of the battle just fought. Colonel Fowler was at the St. Charles. A new regiment from Pennsylvania passed up Pennsylvania Avenue with bucks tails in their caps or hats. Long trains of wagons and ambulances were running about the streets. At this time the river side of Pennsylvania Avenue was built up with shanties or tents only, and the sight was dismal enough in the rain and the mud.

Went out early to camp at Tenallytown near Georgetown (with the adjutant in a carriage). . . . Passed a cold, uncomfortable night—no covering but an overcoat and [slept] on bare boards under which the water ran as a stream.

Sept. 2, Tuesday—Camp at Tenallytown—Camp Kearney—Busy writing all the morning. In the afternoon, regiment got an order to march at a moment's notice. . . . News that [Gen.John] Pope had been driven back and we would be attacked perhaps. . . . All in camp lay on their arms.

Sept. 3, Wednesday—At Camp Kearney—Immediate danger passed. In the afternoon [Maj. Gen. Edwin V.] Sumner's whole army corps came up and encamped near us, a distressed lot—had not changed their clothes since leaving Harrison's Landing, four weeks before—dirty and ragged—officers and men lost all but what they had on.

The contrast between these troops and our men [was] most striking. Our men looked at them with amazement, little thinking that they would shortly look exactly like them—browned by the sun almost to blackness—no baggage but a blanket each and not appearing to need any. A black cup or tin plate their only cooking utensil. Regiment the size of one of our companies but with muskets bright as silver and maneuvering their whole corps with less fuss and in less time than our regiment would require. Exhausting the pump in a few minutes and then drinking the water in the ruts in the road, they established their camp all about us, relieving us all of sense of danger.

It is my impression that all offensive movements on the part of our army for the winter are not to be thought of, and all we can expect to do is to keep the rebels out of Maryland.

Sept. 8, Monday—Bad news. Rebels all around us—four miles from Rockville and eight miles from here. Crossed the Potomac in three places.

Sept. 10 — At Camp Morris — Drilled under Lieutenant Benton (once) of Ninth New Jersey with some five officers in manual of arms from 5:30 to 6:30 P.M. First time I ever drilled.

In letter [home] acknowledged receipt of clothes, etc. "I have been getting two or three meals a day at a farmhouse nearby, but 75 cents a day is too expensive for a man on $13.00 a month. . . . There isn't much style to meals in camp but I have come to a very philosophical contempt for form. . . . I have a great deal of writing to do. . . . All the orders pass through my hands and Jackson, they say, has gone up through Maryland to the west of us. Burnside and McClellan are close behind him and he won't come back, you may depend. Sunday night we could hear troops nearing all night. The rebellion is on its last legs and nothing but starvation drove the Rebs into Pennsylvania. . . . Banjos and fiddles abound and all goes merry as a marriage bell. . . . Some men who

Sketch of soldiers quarters drawn by Edmund D. Halsey.

ran the guards for whiskey and got caught have been standing on barrels with knapsacks in the company street today.

Sept. 21 — [Wrote home] "My health is perfect. The Colonel and Major have told me I am growing fat and I feel so myself. . . . We have so far had good bread and coffee, fresh meat once a day, rice or beans once a day, with money to get potatoes, catsup, ginger cake, etc. I get along first rate."

Oct. 1 — Regiment embarked on train about 3 A.M. . . . Reached Frederick, [Maryland], at 6 P.M. . . . Slept at night in the baggage car. . . . Some of the people of Frederick showed themselves very generous to us. Some of our men went to private houses and were hospitably entertained by those who refused to take anything in return and who fed as many as they could possibly. The people were very pleasant spoken and good looking.

Oct. 3 — Marched 16 miles over South Mountain through Boonsboro, across to Antietam and through Kedersville to Bakersville. Passed tree marked by balls — ambulances, hospitals, dead horses, fresh graves; and some of the men saw dead rebels yet unburied.

Oct. 16—Near Bakersville, Maryland—In a letter to Father, after acknowledging the kindness of family in writing, etc., [I wrote] "You have no idea what effect it has to think—to know, that one has friends who are thinking of him and willing to do what they can for him if he needs assistance. Perhaps this is the reason I have never felt discouraged or downhearted since I entered the service. The nearest I ever came to it was when I received your first letter in which you seemed to feel as though I had deserted you. This now is the only reflection, which causes me to think I may have mistaken my duty. I surely did not intend to do so. This is a time when every one is expected to make sacrifices and I cheerfully do what is required of me. The danger is not so very great as many suppose from the statistics at hand. True—of the thousands who went into the old regiments only hundreds remain. The First New Jersey Brigade now numbers only 1/4 the number it had at the beginning. However, many enlistees were discharged within a month or two as unfit from the first. Many go home sick. . . . Many die in hospitals from diseases caused by their own imprudence or from diseases, which would have caused their death anywhere. Not a few desert and but few are killed in action."

"You will be mistaken if you think our life is one of unmixed hardship. . . . You would smile to see us seated around a coffee pot steaming hot, a frying pan full of meat, a loaf of bread (so far we have generally managed to get that) with the cup and plates scrupulously clean—thanks to Cato [a black man who cooked for the soldiers]."

Oct. 31—Reveille beat at 3:30 A.M., and by sunrise we were two miles on the march. . . . The march was a hard one and the road was strewn with blankets, which the men threw away.

Nov. 3—Marched about six miles with Capt. [Ira] Lindsley as usual—went about six miles and camped on the Leesburg and Winchester Road in a grove.

In the afternoon the brigade was drawn up to witness the drumming out of five men for cowardice at Crampton Pass. They were pushed along rapidly, holding their hats in their hands to show their shaven heads, the provost guard holding their bayonets at their back.

Nov. 6—Met a gentleman named DeLancy (who had friends in Burlington, N.J.) and knew Joseph [Edmund Halsey's Confederate brother] and said he was a captain in the Virginia cavalry. . . in [Gen. James] Longstreet's division; that he heard from him lately; that Joseph and his family were well, the latter in Richmond. . . . He evidently sympathized with the rebels and knew all about them. He said his whole stock of sheep [and] poultry were taken [by Union soldiers] from under his eyes the night before; that coffee and sugar were unknown and that

Edmund D. Halsey as a private (Photo courtesy of Rockaway Borough Free Public Library).

the last whiskey he saw sold was not 10 weeks old and brought $10 per gallon.

Nov. 18—Marched southwest to Stafford Courthouse. Fell out during the march with Alanson at a farmhouse to get something to eat. The lady of the house was willing to give us some biscuits and boiled cabbage, but stragglers stole her apples, pigs, chickens, etc., while she was getting ready. . . . It was very late when the wagons came up as the roads were horrible, made so by the rain. Ten mules were at one train and could not budge it. The soil is clay—blue, yellow, and red, greasy and sticky.

Nov. 27—Thanksgiving Day. A clear, beautiful day. Was busy nearly the whole day. Dined on a mince pie and ginger cake eaten on the run.

The road to the landing was alternate mud and corduroy, but the sight of the Potomac, a railroad and steamers, etc., in the river amply repaid me. Bread sells at 25 cents a loaf and other things in proportion. I do not wonder at delays and halts since I have been here. Railroads are torn up and a regiment 10 miles from its supplies with only its two or three teams to haul them would starve to death.

Dec. 4—Reveille at 4 A.M. In line at 6 A.M. . . . The march was a hard one on the regiment, being made rapidly and with scarce a halt. We supposed we were to cross the Rappahannock below Fredericksburg.

Dec. 5—A long steady rain commenced about 9 A.M., which turned to snow in the afternoon. . . . The men work hard to get the tents up.

Dec. 6—Pvt. [Robert] Sylvester, Company E, died of typhoid fever and not to be wondered at. He was barely alive when we left last camp, was jolted 16 miles in an ambulance and then put in a cold and wet tent.

Fredericksburg

Though Gen. George B. McClellan succeeded in halting Lee's forces at the Battle of Antietam, he did not immediately follow up his "victory" with further action against Confederate positions. Instead he continued to move the Army of the Potomac cautiously and slowly, which gave the Confederates time to place themselves in a position of logistical superiority. Lincoln, frustrated over McClellan's lack of progress, relieved him of his command (for a second and last time) replacing him with General Ambrose Burnside. Burnside, under pressure from the administration and the public for a quick victory, moved quickly toward Falmouth across the Rappahannock from Fredericksburg toward his major objective — Richmond. But a long delay in obtaining pontoons needed to cross the Rappahannock gave Lee the opportunity to secure the surrounding hills with 75,000 men. Assuming that Lee expected an attack above or below Fredericksburg, Burnside launched a "surprise" frontal attack, which the Confederates easily repelled with disastrous consequences for the North. In the words of one of General Longstreet's artillery officers preceding the battle, "a chicken could not live on that field once we open on it." The Confederates inflicted thirteen thousand casualties upon the Northern Army.

Edmund Halsey's regiment saw action for the first time at Fredericksburg, not as part of the frontal assault force, but as a part of the left wing under the command of Gen. William B. Franklin, who fought "Stonewall" Jackson's forces below Fredericksburg. This flanking action met with some initial suc-

cess but was ultimately ineffective since Franklin, confused by Burnside's garbled orders, moved too slowly and with too few men. Halsey's regiment sustained a loss of four men killed, 20 wounded, and five missing. Though the causalities may seem light, it was the first time that the regiment met with death among its ranks. When they later received news of the slaughter of their comrades in the main assault force to their north, a sense of doom pervaded the ranks, which Halsey relates in his description of these events.

Dec. 11, Thursday — Reveille at 4 A.M. Regiment started about 6 A.M. . . . in sight of Fredericksburg about 4 o'clock. We were kept back out of sight of the enemy but a battery . . . was firing from the edge of the hills. At sundown we were moved forward and descended the hill as if to cross the river, but our brigade was sent back about nine o'clock and went into camp for the night in the hills. . . . The night was cold. There was hardly any wood for fire and I caught a terrible cold. . . .

By general orders, we left in camp our sick, including the fewest possible attendants. The result was the dying from freezing and want of attention of two, at least.

Dec. 12, Friday — We crossed the Rappahannock at "Franklin's Crossing" on pontoon bridge, about a mile below Fredericksburg, at about nine o'clock (Gen. [William T.] Brooks . . . stopping our band playing "Dixie,") and were formed in line of battle on the South bank while other troops cross[ed] behind us.

Late in the afternoon the brigade formed . . . and moved forward. . . . The brigade had not moved far before the enemy opened on us, the first shells exploding high over our heads. They soon got their range and would have hurt us considerably had it not been for Deep Run Ravine, which we reached, and down which the lines moved. The first line ascended the south bank and commenced to form anew when we were ordered back into the ravine.

Dec. 13, Saturday — The cannonading and fighting about Fredericksburg and the heights above was continuous all day. Chaplain was in the town where shells were bursting in the streets. . . . After nightfall the scene was terrific — the cheers of the men, flashes of musketry and roaring of guns, etc.

About five o'clock in the afternoon, the rebels had crossed our pickets and a charge was made by the 4th and 23rd in which Colonel Halet was mortally wounded and the Fourth lost about 100 men. They captured as many of the rebels.

Dec. 16, Tuesday — Roused up at 12 [midnight]. . . . As quietly as possible, we moved out of the ravine and stood in line on the north side. Troops were moving over the river behind us.

It was cold and dark. In my hurried and sleepy condition, I had put my right boot on my left foot and could not tell what made my feet hurt so. After an hour or two waiting, we moved to the bridge and over it, our brigade being the last to cross. Marched to the hills, then east along their foot for half a mile and then by a road up the hill. It was then getting daylight and rained in torrents. As it grew light we moved into a wood west of the road and went into camp.

We could see the rebs advancing cautiously over the ground we had left, and advancing a battery there, fired shells at us. The last of our whole army had crossed in the night; The last of a movement, which had been going on since the attempt to turn their flanks on Saturday, proved unsuccessful.

Dec. 20, Camp near White Oak Church — Cold and raw — Felt cold and sick all day with headache, no appetite, etc. . . . The 28 sick we had left behind at King George Court House were sent for and had a terrible story to tell of the privation they had endured. One died in camp from exposure and one in the ambulance on the way here. These things and the memory of our defeat threw a gloom over the camp. We look for a retreat to the Potomac line, and General McClellan, "who always took good care of his men," grows in favor.

Dec. 23 — Never saw so many discouraged and discontented men in the regiment before.

Dec. 25 — Made a Christmas dinner of wheat cakes with butter and sugar and piece of steak.

Dec. 31 — Received note from Emery at Baltimore offering me a detail there as chief clerk to the medical doctor. Answered it in evening, declining it.

Jan. 2 — Since December first, twelve men have died at camp or in general hospital, four killed and five missing — total, less 21. Virgil Howell froze to death, and we have others whose feet were frozen in hospital. Things looked blue here for a time.

January 4 — [Lt. John H.] Vanderveer from Chester who is quite sick of typhoid fever is to be moved to the General Hospital tomorrow and will probably from there have leave. His father and brother-in-law are here.

Jan. 6 — We are . . . ordered to have three days rations on hand and be ready to march at 12 hours notice. The weather keeps good, though I am in hopes [that] if it is going to rain, it will do so before ordered to march, for I am afraid of being stuck somewhere.

We still live at the top of the market; had splendid doughnuts last night and this morning.

I've hoped the paymaster would be around, but the chance is getting slim. I have about 75 cents on hand.

Stuck in the Mud

Following the Union defeat at Fredericksburg, Gen. Ambrose Burnside decided to march his men up the Rappahannock and flank the Confederates from the left. As they proceeded, it started to rain. The soil turned to a sticky mud, so thick that mules drowned in it. As men, wagons, and horses became stuck, the Confederates on the opposite side of the river taunted their adversaries with a sign reading "Burnside stuck in the mud." After three days, Burnside abandoned the futile "mud march." The 15th N.J. Regiment spent a dismal winter encampment at White Oak Church where many died of typhoid fever.

Jan. 21, on Burnside's Mud March — Marched in a drizzly rain (it had rained all night), halting every hundred yards or so in the mud, toward the river about two miles, and camped again.

Jan. 22 — Burnside's Mud March — It has rained all night and we understand the movement has failed and we are to go back to our old camps. Beaten by mud. It cleared in the afternoon and a whisky ration was given out. . . . It was a dreary day, wet and with nothing to eat but fried pork without side dishes.

Jan. 23 — Burnside's Mud March — Clear. Companies D & I were detailed for fatigue and were at work hauling pontoons back from the river through seas of mud.

Jan. 24 — Burnside's Mud March — We were in line at daylight expecting to move back to White Oak Church where it is reported the paymaster is waiting for us. But we were marched to and from the river through the mud (probably to deceive the enemy) and were hauling pontoons all the morning.

Alanson, Dr. [George R.] Sullivan and I went to the house of Mrs. Sweetman of Locust Grove (who has a son in the rebel army and another in Orange Co., N.J., and remembers Joseph's wedding — knows him, etc.) where we had a good dinner of bacon and hoe cake. I went to a neighbor's to get soda for her, and with this she was going to make us biscuits for supper.

While sitting on the piazza waiting for them to cook, the regiment with Col. [Edward L.] Campbell at the head of it waded by, and I was called in — without my supper. The regiment marched back to the camp of Tuesday night and pitched camp for the night. Alanson and Sullivan remained at the house. . . . It rained again in the night. The rebs are said to have a board up across the river marked, "Burnside stuck in the mud."

Jan. 25, Sunday — Burnside's Mud March — Dr. Sullivan joined us at

11 bringing in cookies and a hoe cake from Mrs. Sweetman for me. She seemed to have taken a fancy to me, probably on Joseph's account. The hoe cake was all Colonel Campbell and I had to live on that day, and it was good.

Regiment got marching orders about now and reached the old camp at White Oak Church by 8, through the mud and without rations for most of the men. Here, we found all in confusion. The cavalry, who had occupied our camps in our absence, had burned up the chimneys and stockades.

A whiskey ration was served as the camp was in a pandemonium. Army generally demoralized.

Feb. 2, Monday, near White Oak Church—[Wrote to sister Sue] "The army seems thoroughly demoralized. Officers and men cursing the administration and the war. The disasters of Vicksburg, Fredericksburg, Galveston, Stones River, and the *Monitor* [recently lost at sea while being towed] etc., all cast a gloom over the army, which puts me in mind of the descriptions of the dark days of '76. The men in their shelter tents and but barely supplied with shoes have become disheartened and begin to think they can never succeed." "The *New York Times* of January 26 has a good account of our last move. It was, I believe, a great plan well laid and would have been successful but for the elements."

Awaiting the Renewal of Battle

The 15th N.J. Regiment spent the remainder of the winter and early spring preparing for the summer campaign.

April 3, Friday, Near White Oak Church—Grand review of the division by General Hooker . . . [who] looked older and less dashing than I supposed from what I had heard of him.

April 8, Wednesday—Grand review by the President of four corps — ours, Sedgwick's—Meade's—[Maj. Gen. John] Reynolds'—and Sickles'. We left camp at 8 and marched about three miles to near the Fitzhugh house where we were drawn up in three lines of Regiments. . . . Over a hill could be seen the black masses of another corps, their bayonets giving them the appearance of being frosted with silver. Lincoln, whom I had a good opportunity to see, appeared very pale and careworn. He rode up and down the line with General Hooker and a crowd of staff officers . . . and we passed in review in division columns.

April 13—All the tailors at work cutting out red crosses for the men's caps, this to be the mark of our division hereafter. . . . All is haste and a general clearing for action.

April 30, Thursday—On picket until relieved about 5 P.M. or later. . . . We could see the enemy on the hills evidently watching us, and there was some artillery practice toward night.

The order of General Hooker announcing that "the enemy must either come out and fight on our own ground or else ingloriously flee" was read to us.

When relieved from picket duty, we fell back to the little rifle pit, which had been occupied by the rebs on the south bend of the river.

Gen. Joseph Hooker (from Pictorial History of the Civil War)

Chancellorsville

At the Battle of Chancellorsville, the Union Army again met with defeat, despite its superior numbers. Outmaneuvered by Lee, General Hooker retreated from the offensive and settled into a defensive position early in the conflict, even though he could easily have broken through the thin Confederate lines at his front. But while Hooker hesitated, a Union force south of Fredericksburg under Gen. John Sedgwick had considerable success. Under Sedgwick's leadership, the 15th and 26th N.J. Regiments broke through at Fredericksburg. Later they made a heroic charge near Salem Church, halfway between Fredericksburg and Chancellorsville. Here they held their ground until nightfall when four regiments of Alabama infantry under Brig. Gen. Cadmus Wilcox drove them back. The following day, Lee commanded three Confederate divisions numbering 21,000 in a counterattack against the Union forces, but Sedgwick successfully repulsed them. If Hooker had used his numerically superior forces to break through the Confederate lines at his front, he could have joined Sedgwick's forces, and Chancellorsville may have resulted in a Northern victory. Instead he retreated. Sedgwick reluctantly did the same.

Chancellorsville was Lee's greatest victory and Hooker's biggest defeat.

Halsey begins his account of the battle with a moving description of the two opposing armies on opposite sides of the river cheering each other, perhaps in recognition of the special bond that all soldiers, even enemies, share by virtue of their experience of war—an experience that sets them apart from other men.

May 1, 1863—At "Franklin's Crossing"—We lay in the rifle pit near the landing all day, the only excitement being occasional picket firing, and once in a while a rebel shell going over our heads and bursting behind us.

At sunset, pickets of our division were relieved by [Gen. Abraham S.] Piatt's Brigade. All the other troops of our corps . . . were paraded on the Stafford side of the river in full view of ourselves and the rebs. Bands were playing, and there was a general cessation of firing. Directly, we heard the rebel bands playing "Yankee Doodle." Our brigade band . . . responded with "Dixie." The rebels could be seen on the flats and on the hillsides. Both armies cheered. It was a strange sight, and the sun going down at the moment made a deep impression on everyone.

May 2, 1863—At Franklin's Crossing—We remained at same place; . . . occasional shells and picket firing . . . kept us on the alert.

In the afternoon, heavy firing, cannonading, and musketry could be heard in the direction of Chancellorsville. On the hills we thought we could see the rebel regiments on the march, but their uniforms made them hard to be distinguished from the gray side hills.

Toward evening the pickets were advanced to the edge of the wood or to the Bowling Green Road, a very spirited affair, which seemed not at all like fighting. The rest of the corps moved quickly to the river, crossed and passed us marching toward the ravine where we lost sight of them in the darkness. We thought the enemy had left, and we had only to move in and occupy their places.

May 3—At daylight we moved out by the flank, inclining to the left to the Bowling Green Road. . . . Marching along this road we were suddenly greeted by half a dozen shells from the edge of the wood. Instinctively, men ducked their heads, but General Brooks riding alongside the regiment noticed it, and his "Tut, tut, men" stopped the involuntary movement.

Company B, with which I was, was in the extreme left flank, and here the ditch was full of water so that we had little room. Suddenly the rebs advanced their line and the regiment was rushed over to the south side toward them.

Something struck me in my boot and I tumbled into the water. I was getting out of it to find the regiment rush past me and back of the battery so that it could play on the advancing line. Supposing myself to be wounded and hearing the voices and steps of the rebs, I lay perfectly still in the road. For what seemed an age, the batteries played over my head. Pieces of shell struck the ground within an inch or two, and a bullet passed between my face and the ground. I heard the groans of one of our men growing less and less audible in the ditch south of the road till they stopped altogether.

The firing gradually slackened, and from our position back of the battery we had a fine view of the Fredericksburg Hills and saw our second division carry them in fine style. It was a great sight to see the long blue lines advance steadily up the sides of the hill, not checked by the fire of the rebel pits in front of them. After their success, our line was withdrawn and we moved by the flank along the road towards the city. We had lost several men, one by the accidental discharge of one of our muskets, which the colonel ordered to be broken.

We passed through Fredericksburg, meeting here and there one of our dead in the street—over the hill—down a hill and up another and then along a pike toward Salem Heights. Troops were laying on either side of the road, making way for us to pass. . . . Captain [Henry P.] Cook met us coming from the wood with his hand on his shoulder where he had been struck by a minié.[1] He said, "They nipped me. . . ." The regiment then advanced over the fence. As I was crossing, a minié ball struck the fence between my legs. I don't think we had advanced 20 yards before we caught a terrific volley. The command was given, "Fire by file— Commence firing!" But the regiment really fired by volley. . . . One man of Company G was shot in the body close to me and turning to leave the field, his blood went over my boots. The wood was full of smoke and firing continuous. Seeing and hearing, both difficult.

At dusk the regiment came out of the woods, picked up their knapsacks, and moved from the woods to the east of the pike. . . . I went to gather what news we could of our wounded in battle. It was bad enough. Captain Lindsley and Lt. [John] Fowler were left dead in the woods with Color Sgt. [David E.] Hicks, and many others, and our advance had been checked. Our loss was 25 dead, 125 wounded, and four missing.

Many incidents in other regiments which occurred under my eyes will not soon be forgotten.

May 4, Monday at Salem Heights—In the morning we were first to one side and then to another as an attack seemed imminent. Most of the morning we were on the south side of the pike, in line parallel to it, supporting a battery near a small house. From where we were, we could see very little but heard a great deal. Heavy musketry was heard behind to the right of us. Next, in front, and, as it moved nearer and nearer, to our left. In great anxiety, we watched the latter as it moved nearer and nearer to our left until it was between us and Fredericksburg. We knew we were cut off.

The last position was in one of the lines of battle massed behind the church, and here we lay till dark. Then commenced the retreat to Banks Ford.

Skirmish lines were formed one behind another, the first line holding their own till the last minute and then [the] other taking the line in the rear. Our artillery mowed down the advancing rebs with great slaughter apparently, but darkness seemed our best defense.

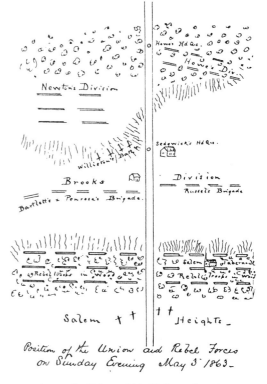

Map drawn by Edmund D. Halsey showing Union and Confederate positions on the evening of May 3, 1863.

As we marched along, we could hear the rebels yelling in our rear. Arrived near the ford, we lay for a time in an old rifle pit probably dug out by the rebels—afterwards to the woody bank of the river where most of us fell asleep, a bullet whistling over our heads occasionally and shells thrown at random.

We were to be the rear guard, it seemed, but just before daylight we were roused and moving upstream to the pontoon bridge; we crossed simultaneously with a New York regiment. . . . Shells struck the water either side of us, but we were too sleepy and tired to notice them. As we went up the road on the north side, it became daylight and the rebels saw and shelled us as we gained the top of the hill.

May 5, Tuesday, Banks Ford—Cloudy and rainy. Moved back a mile or so from the river and found ourselves in or near our camp of Jan. 22 . . . tired, hungry, sore, and dirty. The camp was filled with the unburied carcasses of horses and mules that had died in January, and the enemy occasionally reached us with a shell. . . . Wrote girls of my safety.

May 6—Near Banks Ford—Made out reports of our losses. We hear that Hooker has fallen back with the rest of the army and that all are marching to their old camps again.

May 7 — Near Banks Ford — In the afternoon — [the] regiment moved to a clearing (away from the dead horses) and camped for the night. Commissary whiskey was abundant in the camp that night.

May 8 — Marched back to our old camp at White Oak Church where we arrived in the middle of the afternoon — tired, footsore, dirty, and demoralized.

May 9 — The probability of another retreat to Washington and a third Bull Run discussed in camp.

May 10 — Benajob Wear died at two o'clock in the morning of chronic diarrhea. He had been with us on the march though unfit to do so. Sent the $11.50 found on him home. . . .

---

[1] A minié ball, named after French army officer Claude Étienne Minié, was a rifle bullet with a conical head that revolutionized warfare. Due to its small size, the minie ball could be loaded faster than conventional rifle shot. This made the rifle, with its greater accuracy and longer range, a practical alternative to the far less accurate musket.

Gettysburg

Gettysburg marked the turning point of the war. The bold Southern attempt to defeat the North on Northern territory began with some success early in the conflict, but the Union held the strategic high ground during the heavy sustained Southern onslaught. Northern commanding officers under Gen. George G. Meade demonstrated a remarkable degree of skill and coolness under fire as they executed a well coordinated defense. Lee, on the other hand, underestimated his enemy and overestimated the invincibility of his own army. He made a bold move that turned into a fatal error when he ordered Gen. George E. Pickett to charge the middle of the Northern line. The North crushed the Rebels under a heavy barrage of artillery and rifle fire. The remainder of the battered Confederate army retreated to Virginia. Halsey describes Northern troop movements preceding the battle and describes the battle from the vantage point of the 15th N.J. Regiment — as part of a second line of defense behind a stone wall at the crest of a hill, north of the important strategic point, Little Round Top.

June 12, at Franklin's Crossing — The last five days . . . men have been under arms all the time and when not on picket, large details were kept awake to rouse the rest.

The ground we are compelled to lay in has been camped on so much that it is infested with vermin, which plagues every officer and man.

The rebels appear in force on the hills and we hear their bands at night.

June 14 — On the March — Moved rapidly to Stafford Court House about 3:30 in the morning. The men lay down in the road and slept till daylight. I lay in dirt two inches thick, my head on a stack of muskets.

June 15 — The March to Dumfries — After half an hour's sleep, we fell in and resumed our march at daylight. This was the severest day's march we ever had. The heat was intense. The fine dust hung like a cloud in the air and was inhaled at every breath.... [N]ot a company left in line. Men were laying along the road sunstruck and panting for breath, in scores. A half of an hour or so revived the men, and by slow marching with frequent rests, the troops marched into Dumfries at dusk in good order.

June 16 — On the March — Hot and dusty. [M]arched on to Wolfe Run Shoals when we came within the "Defense of Washington".... I took a bath in the stream, which refreshed me. Here, [Pvt. William] Kelsey was shot in the neck by accidental discharge of a gun — but his life was saved by presence of a surgeon.

After a bath we marched on to near Fairfax Station where we camped for the night and had the first good night sleep since the 6th. Very foot-sore.

Here we first heard of Lee's invasion [of Gettysburg] and the cause of our mysterious movements became plain to us. We saw evidences of quantities of stores destroyed and abandoned.

June 26, Friday — Marched till noon through mud and rain. . . . The march was a hard rough one, and I was footsore and annoyed by unwelcome visitors in underclothing.

June 30, Tuesday — In the last five days we have made 84 miles. The boys stand it well and I never saw them march better. There is hardly a straggler. . . . We are now eight miles from Pennsylvania and the rebel cavalry have been and are all around us.

July 2, Thursday — Daylight found us marching as rapidly as possible toward Gettysburg. No time allowed for coffee. Halts barely 10 minutes. We passed the wagon trains — first where we heard that the battle had been going on for a day or two — then the wounded, who reported we have been getting the worst of it. The citizens, especially at Littleton, were very kind. Large pails of fresh, cool water were kept on the horse blocks in which the men could dip their cups as they passed along. Citizens were seen carrying off the wounded in buggies. . . . At a place between Littleton and Gettysburg, we filed to the right into a field and lay for an hour from one to two. No one thought of cooking, but every man slept the hour in the blazing sun. . . . We had made 32 miles in about 15 hours.

[A]bout 5, we heard roar of musketry and on our left to the south the cheers of the men, etc., apparently getting nearer. An officer rode in and inquired for headquarters, 6th Corps. We pointed across the brook where Sedgwick's Corps flag was flying, but every man rolled his blanket and slung it. The officer scarcely reached headquarters, it seemed, before we were ordered to fall in. The order was half obeyed before it was given. We double quicked toward the firing, passing a few wounded, and shells bursting over our heads. We reached the edge of a wood back of Roundtop [a strategic knoll defended by Union forces] as it was getting dark. The "reserves" had turned upon the enemy and driven them from the hill. It is said that both they and the enemy saw our lines advancing.

July 3, 1863 — The morning was very quiet. The wood in front of us prevented our seeing much of the field, and we were laying in it very much at our ease when a little after noon, several shells came crashing in among us. In a moment we were back in line, which was formed at once, and then all lay down. For an hour or two, the cannonading was terrific. [Gen. James] Longstreet's charge was made to our right. We could not see the rebs, but we could see our own men and our batteries. Horses and men were rapidly killed in the latter, and one of the two caissons blew up. From Roundtop we could hear our men cheer, and a heavy gun posted up there seemed to be doing heavy work.

The rebs were everywhere repulsed. Our reinforcements were coming up, and thousands of deserters and prisoners came in.

The 1st Regiment in our front had taken their cartridges out and put them on the rocks beside them and had picked up extra muskets. They had no design to leave.

Pieces of shell fell thick among us, and we lost in the Brigade one killed and ten or twelve wounded. That night slept with [1st Lt. Nehemiah] Tunis on top of a very large rock, which lay behind our line, without blankets or anything. July 4, Saturday — Rain. I visited 4th and 11th N.J. who lay behind Roundtop. The 11th lost 60 to 100 men in charge of the adjutant. Both are terribly cut up. Payson Berry is missing. E. Sturtevant is wounded [in] arm and leg. Logan is killed.

All was quiet along the lines except a recognizance, which amounted to nothing. We had 80 men on picket under Maj. [Lambert] Boeman and in the night, which was so wet, we could neither sleep nor make a fire burn.

A Deserter's Grim Fate

Following Gettysburg, Lee's army escaped southward across the Potomac, much to the dismay of Lincoln, who believed that General Meade should have pursued and defeated him once and for all. During the following months, a series of indecisive actions continued in the area south of Washington. Throughout this period, the army was plagued by the problem of desertion. Halsey, now a first lieutenant, describes the consequences of desertion in the following account.

Aug. 10, [1863], at Warrenton—Priestly of Company E, who deserted and was returned at White Oak Church, had been under guard ever since; [he] was drummed out and sentenced to two years at hard labor.

The man is young and seems a simple, ignorant fellow, hardly responsible for his acts. He has had hundreds of opportunities to escape on the march if so minded.

August 14—Regiment marched about two miles toward New Baltimore where . . . [Pvt. David] Jewett, 5th Maine, was shot for desertion in presence of the division.

The division formed three sides of a square in two lines. . . . The prisoner was finally brought out sitting in his coffin in an open army wagon drawn by four horses and rode slowly around the inside of the square. He was then taken out and shot in the open side of the square. The division then filed by him by the right flank and away. The body was laying on its face. The balls had come through the back of his head and between his shoulders. Came back with a headache from the heat to find Headquarters had been moved to the top of the hill.

Line Officers of Fifteenth N.J. Regiment including 1st Lt. Edmund D. Halsey who is standing in the middle row, second from the right. (Courtesy of the Hunterdon County Historical Society).

Surprise Attack

During the fall of 1863, the 15th N.J. Regiment participated in many advances and retreats as opposing armies maneuvered for position. In early November, the regiment joined in a surprise attack on a Confederate occupied, Union built fortification along the Rappahannock River. Halsey describes the attack.

Nov. 7 — Marched to near Rappahannock Station where we fell in with enemy's pickets. Dispositions made for the attack, which commenced about the middle of the afternoon. The 2nd and 3rd Brigade supported by us and the remainder of our corps . . . gallantly assaulted and took the pits and works north of the river with 1650 prisoners, four cannon and nine or ten flags.

This attack appears to have been entirely unexpected by the enemy. Our men sprang over their men in the rifle pits. . . . Our brigade advanced handsomely. . . . The 15th had a good line. Major [James M.] Brown riding in the rear on the left, Col. [William] Penrose in the center, and myself on the right. A shell struck under the Major's horse but did no damage. He was smoking his pipe as he rode.

Just after dark, a battery on the edge of the wood east of the railroad about opposite us was opened, the flashes of its guns making a very brilliant appearance.

The Wilderness Campaign and the Battle of Spotsylvania Courthouse

Throughout the winter of 1864, the Armies of the Potomac and Northern Virginia camped on opposite banks of the Rapidan River. Early in May, General Grant began moving his forces across the Rapidan hoping for a showdown with the Rebels south of the Wilderness, the place where Hooker met defeat a year earlier during the Battle of Chancellorsville. Though the Union army of 70,000 far outnumbered the Confederate force of 40,000, the Southerners knew the woods far better than the Northerners, who blundered about in confusion, firing upon their own men, while exploding shells ignited the underbrush, burning alive many of the wounded.

After four days of heavy fighting in the Wilderness, the Union sustained 17,000 casualties, the South, 10,000. Despite his heavy losses, Grant pushed forward, attempting to march around Lee's right and seize the crossroads village of Spotsylvania 12 miles to the south, which would have placed the Union Army closer to Richmond, forcing Lee to either fight or retreat.

The 15th N.J. was among the first regiments to fight at Spotsylvania. On May 8, together with the 3d N.J., they courageously charged the fortified

Spotsylvania Courthouse, but the Confederates repulsed their attack, inflict-ing 101 casualties. On May 12, the 6th Corps made a deadly assault on the "Bloody Angle" at Spotsylvania with the 15th N.J. Regiment on the ex-treme right of the front line. Along several hundred yards of Rebel trenches, soldiers engaged in hand-to-hand combat as it steadily rained. So intense was the fighting that an oak tree behind Southern lines was cut down by minié balls. The 15th N.J. eventually had to fall back, having lost more than half its men and seven of its best officers. Of the regiment's 429 infantrymen and 14 line officers who crossed the Rapidan on the 4th, only 122 men and four officers remained. From May 5 to May 12, the Army of the Potomac lost 32,000 men killed, wounded, and missing. Halsey recounts the story of these grim days.

May 4, Wednesday — Passed Brandy Station and crossed the Rapidan at Germania Ford before dark. Marched about a mile and went into camp for the night, sending six companies out on picket.

May 5 — Broke camp a little after daylight and moved out, but soon had evidence of the enemy in close proximity. . . . We were moved about in the wood and brush in a confusing manner until afternoon when we were formed, 10th New Jersey on right, and the 15th on left of the front line.

. . . . Our orders were to "guide left." Advancing, we found ourselves crowded, and the orders on our left were to "guide right." Col. P. sent me to Col. [Henry W.] Brown to tell him this during a temporary halt, but Brown, who was sitting on a log with his staff about him, said he would be up presently. [Sgt. William J.] Cooke and [Lt. Charles R.] Paul were annoyed but said nothing. Again we advanced and found our-selves alone with the 10th. I rode back and forth between Colonels Penrose and [Henry O.] Ryerson to keep the two in line. At another halt, each of these Colonels urged the other to assume command of both. The firing grew heavier and minies whistled about as but another line seemed ahead of us. Directly we came into an open field on a hill. Here, General Sedgwick and Capt. Cook each gave us orders, the latter trying evi-dently to get the Brigade together again, but Sedgwick ordered our regiment forward into a gap and we went in, seeing no more of the 10th or the rest of the brigade. Where we went was to the right of [Col. Emory] Upton's Brigade where two companies of the 95th Pennsylva-nia had been holding the ground. The leaves were on fire, and scat-tered over the ground were dead and wounded of rebs and 5th Corps men. . . . In front was a clear field, with the rebels on the other side. Our right was in bush, which prevented anything being seen. The 7th Wisconsin was on our right.

At nightfall when things had apparently quieted down, an awfully exciting scene was enacted. Beginning off on the left came a roar of musketry growing nearer and nearer, both armies evidently firing, caused, we supposed, by an advance of the enemy. Every officer of our command shouted, "Don't fire," and struck up the muskets such of the men as offered to do it. This stopped the firing along the line. Shortly after, the same thing came from the right, coming up to within a regiment or so of us. There was no advance, but each army in close quarters believed the antagonist moving to attack.

This over, we settled for the night—Capt. [Ellis] Hamilton took a few men a half dozen yards to the front and formed a picket line. The enemy were so near that their muskets, Col. Penrose thought, were ours, and twice sent me to tell Capt. Hamilton to make his men stop firing, and I brought back word (I had only 10 paces to go) that it was the enemy. In this way we passed the hours of darkness. I slept a few minutes, waking between two half-roasted bodies—one reb and the other a 5th Corps. [Wrote to sister] "The dead lay thick about us, and some wounded out in a field to our left between the lines kept crying out for water and to be carried off. This night was perfectly hideous."

May 6—As new pickets came in, Hamilton was hit in both thighs from which wounds he afterwards died. The musketry and shelling were almost incessant on either side of us all day. The open field at our front prevented the rebs from attacking us. Their officers could not get them into the open. In the afternoon things grew more quiet and tools were brought up with which we threw up a rifle pit. Colonel Penrose also had our horses brought up.

At nightfall we again heard the roar of musketry on our right. This time an advance in earnest by the rebels. We could hear their yells and firing passing around to our right, and directly, balls were coming from front and behind. Col. Upton took his second line and moved off towards the right and Colonel Penrose was left in command of the front line. General [Horatio] Wright came along, and I sang out to him, "We are all right here, General!" to which he responded.

Darkness by this time had come on. Colonel Penrose and myself rode off tonight a little way, but found the wood filled with our men—some with prisoners, and all in confusion.

Late at night the regiment was aroused, and moved quietly to the left, on to the road and down it for a mile or so. Men stooped and trailed arms, and held their canteens with the hand to prevent their rattling. The enemy were in easy call.

Moving down the road a mile or so, turned to left, crossed a clear field and then to right, going into a position parallel to the turnpike, and facing north. It was about daylight when the position was taken. . . . We made the charge under Colonel Upton, and did not hear of losses or doings of the other New Jersey regiments until the next day.

May 7th, Saturday—Hot and clear. At daylight we began to dig a rifle-pit along the road and sent pickets to the front. I went out to the line, and found they connected with nothing on the left; passed along that way, and came to a line of pickets facing ours. Found officer of the day and reported. Made my way back to the regiment from left. An attack was made and handsomely repulsed to left of us, early [in the morning]; but the rebs felt our picket line all day. We lost 5 men on the skirmish line during the day. Capt. [Cornelius] Shimer was out on the line. In [the] afternoon both armies cheered. Firing was all about us. . . . [W]e were in the rifle-pit expecting an immediate attack, but [the enemy] were only engaged by our skirmishers.

After dark we moved along the road to the right to near the. . . . turnpike, where we halted for an hour or two. Moved from here with the rest of the New Jersey brigade, with which we had again fallen in. We had been under Colonel Upton two days.

About midnight we moved on the pike toward Chancellorsville. Nearly two thousand prisoners at one time marched alongside of us. On roads to the south could be heard the rumble of wheels.

May 8, Sunday—About seven o'clock we passed through Chancellorsville, with about 2,000 prisoners marching alongside of us.

The rifle pits, etc., of the old battlefield are all in shape. Noticed a skull lying in the road.

We were countermarched and moved up to a piece of wood, sloping eastward behind where General Sedgwick was afterwards killed. Here we lay down in the wood for a little while, the enemy shelling us rigorously.

[T]he 15th was ordered to advance across the field to develop the enemy in the opposite wood. . . . As the line ap-

Gen. John Sedgwick (from **Pictorial History of the Civil War**).

159

proached the wood, it was evident the Fifteenth was too short. [Wrote to sisters,] "We started in good shape, the 3d [N.J. Regiment] deployed as skirmishers. About one-half the way across the field, Colonel Penrose sent me for another regiment to cover the left of ours. I rode in, got the first and was showing Col. [William] Henry the way when we were met—when half way across the field—by our regiment coming back— or what was left of them. They found a fort and three lines of battle in front, and nothing was left but to get back, which they did, leaving their dead and most of their wounded behind them. We reckoned up our losses. Captain [Lewis] Van Blarcom missing and over a hundred men killed, wounded and missing. . . . That night we had little sleep— watching the enemy and caring for our wounded."

May 9—[Samuel] Rubadeau, our color sergeant, was shot dead. . . . General Sedgwick passed by us and, inquiring why we were massed as we were, ordered our brigade out. Colonel Penrose started me at the head of the column to lead it; he, remaining to start each regiment successively as the one before, filed out. I had reached the outer edge of the wood, perhaps a hundred yards, when [the] Colonel rejoined me, and in a low voice said the general was hit, and put his finger to his face, shaking his head to indicate there was no hope for him. He had ridden to the edge of the wood and was standing in the wood on his horse a little back of where Colonel P and I slept (perhaps 20 feet) when he was almost immediately shot. Colonel Penrose was directed to take command of the brigade, irrespective of rank.

May 10—In [the] morning our line was advanced over the road swinging to the right, keeping up our connection with the other pickets. . . . The 15th being deployed [as skirmishers] continued to press the enemy, moving towards "the Angle" and almost at right angles with charge of the 8th. . . . Gen. [Gershom] Mott of the 2d Corps brought up two regiments of the Excelsior Brigade, and they with the 1st New Jersey made a charge, but the "White Diamonds" broke at the first fire and did not stop. Our skirmishers came back with them but stopped at a brook . . . and proceeded to make coffee. After dinner . . . again charged . . . and as . . . the White Diamonds again broke and fled for miles, the 15th came back in good order and lay down in the wood till dark.

Between 3 P.M. of the 9th and night of 10th, we lost 22 men killed or wounded.

May 12, Thursday—[Wrote to sisters,] "A sad day for our regiment."

Early in the morning, we moved to the right where we were massed for a short time, the 2d Corps making their charge on the "Angle" at McCoull's [house]. We were hurried back to the former place and there an order was read that the 2d Corps had captured 10,000 prisoners and 28 guns ([Maj. Gen. Edward] Johnson's division). The cheers were interrupted by rebel shells, which showed they were still in position.

It was raining furiously. The road was lined with wounded. The musketry in front was continuous. Suddenly we moved to the right of the Angle by the flank, and then, facing and in a single line, charged.

Confederate Entrenchment at Spotsylvania

The next 20 minutes were horribly fatal to the 15th, which was on the extreme right. . . . [F]rom all along to our right . . . as well as in front came a blaze of musketry. It seemed to me as if the right wing was swept away in an instant. The left wing got to a rifle pit, captured a flag, about a hundred prisoners, and got back—some of them—but not in line.

[Capt. James] Walker, Shriver, [George C.] Justice, and Vauvry were killed. Justice had just waved his hat on top of the rifle pit when he was killed. Vaurvy was wounded in the wrist and died shortly after. I saw him, but did not think him badly hurt. . . .

[We lost] over 150 men. Only one man was left in the color guard, the other color being brought off by [the] sergeant of Company H.

The brigade was soon rallied, say 300 men, and moved to a position just back of the Angle where we lay till dark. Here I remember a man of Company G was shot in the arm. The white oak tree was being cut off by bullets a few yards in front of us.

First Lieutenant Cummings, instead of coming back with the regiment, had crept along the pit and joined the men still holding the line, and stayed with them the balance of the day. At night we were moved back through the woods and back and forth and moved about, finally laying down in the wood near Shelton's.

Here we lay in the rain in silence, balls striking the trees with a dead thud all about us.

It was a grievous day for the 15th.

May 13, Friday, at Spotsylvania—We lay in the same position till afternoon about 2. Counting up our losses. Since May 5, of the 429 men we then had, but 150 remain, and but four line officers [of the original 14].

I tried to get noncommissioned officers to go in the color guard, but could not. I got two or three privates and they were to be made corporals.

[Wrote to father,] "We have suffered terribly in the past eight days we have been fighting. . . . When I think of what we have gone through, I have to be very thankful to Providence that I am spared."

"The fighting has been unusually desperate and continuous. Beats the seven days peninsula fighting. The odds have been first on one side and then the other. It is believed that we have the decided advantage now on the whole. The army is, however, almost exhausted, and I am afraid a slight reverse would be terrible in its consequences."

About 2 P.M. we moved down to battle ground of yesterday, relieving the 10th New Jersey in the rifle pit. The tree cut off by bullets was in our line. The other side of the pit, the trench, was filled with the dead and wounded, mostly rebel. A leg or an arm could be seen moving in the mass. These were being taken out as they were

Burial Squad, Spotsylvania Courthouse

found, though the rebs kept firing at us all night. . . . The chaplain and a detail were burying the dead in our rear.

May 14—Passing the Anderson house [marching on the Fredericksburg road] a rebel sharpshooter cut the ground directly under my feet on horseback, evidently shooting from a tree quite far off.

The regiment passed a wounded man sitting on a stone—the most horrible sight I ever saw. His arm had been taken off and his whole face seemed hanging in a mass in front of him.

May 15, Sunday—The men are listless and feel doomed. An order was sent tonight caused by this feeling, exhorting the men by the memory of their losses not to be discouraged but to crown their efforts by victory.

May 19—[Wrote to sisters,] "Yesterday sleepy and tired. Last night we were quiet, and this morning, moving out to our picket line of Tuesday night, have been digging rifle pits. Tonight we are expecting orders to move. . . ."

"Of 2,800 men of our Brigade but 1,100 are left. . . . Our whole division is cut up the same way—but our Brigade is very much demoralized, having lost so many officers especially."

"I welcome photographs of our old chapel . . . and of Capt. [William] Cornish as a civilian. I value the former as being the place wherein I made profession of my faith. This has been a great comfort to me I assure you, and often during this terrible campaign I have thought that were it not for my friends, the condition of those we have left behind us was to be envied. Recollect that passage from Thessolonians, 'He the more fortunate, yea he hast finished, etc.' But I trust that He who hath watched over me thus far will continue His watchful care, and whatever fate is in store for me, I know it will be for the best."

May 22—At nine o'clock last, after the firing had ceased, we moved out of our pits. . . . We were all short of rations. . . . Colonel Campbell, Chaplain, and I had nothing but popped corn and coffee for dinner, and nothing for supper.

. . . . This was the first day since May 4 that we were not under fire.

Cold Harbor

Following his failure to take Spotsylvania, Grant marched his army south, attempting to lure Lee's army into open combat. Lee evaded Grant through a series of countermoves, placing his army in well entrenched positions from which he waged defensive battles. Lee intended to wear down Grant and prolong the war to frustrate Northern hopes of a decisive victory. Grant resigned himself to fighting on Lee's terms. He mounted an offense against Lee's heavily fortified army at Cold Harbor. Here the Rebels fought from a complicated, confusing zigzag of trenches. From their positions, they easily cut down direct assaults in the most crushing Union repulse since Burnside's assault of Fredericksburg. Grant deeply regretted the attack in which 7,000 Union soldiers were killed or wounded compared to fewer than 1,500 Confederates. Edmund Halsey vividly describes the horrible bloodbath.

June 1, 1864, Cold Harbor—Started at daylight and reached here where the cavalry were fighting about noon. The air was filled with dust, which made everything—men, horses, brush—all one color.

About noon our lines were formed — the 3d Brigade and 2d Brigade to right of the wood; 1st and 4th Brigades left of wood, and to our left, the 2d Division. Our regiment was in the third line, and as the rest of the division advanced, we lay still.

As the line passed the skirt of wood, the musketry began. . . . Directly an officer appeared at the edge of the wood and beckoned us forward. We rose and advanced through the wood where we got a view of the whole field.

The line which had charged ahead of us had disappeared, obliquing to the right. The 1st New Jersey was coming back by the road. A rebel battery to left of our front at once opened fire. . . . We moved rapidly forward to a small knoll about 150 feet from the battery where we halted and opened fire . . . silencing it more or less effectually.

A little to our left and behind the top of another knoll was the 3rd New Jersey (Capt. [Charles A.] Wahl being conspicuous, waving his saber, and with the top of his hat torn with a bullet) who were firing into the enemy. . . . To our left was nothing, and we apprehended that the enemy would soon flank us, as a wood a short distance off in that direction would enable them to do so easily. To increase our danger, a battery of ours to the right of where we started opened fire, its shells dropping in among us. Word was sent back without success. [Pvt.] Ogden Whitesell ran back by the colonel's order but the stupid or frightened captain insisted upon his fratricidal work until threatened with being fired into by us. At least I suppose Whitesell delivered that message he was told to.

We kept at this fire till night, the muskets getting, in some cases, too hot to hold. Under this fire the 10th came up with little loss, and fired behind us.

Between the firing, which kept up till late, the men dug a sort of pit with their tin plates, and later, spades were brought up, and we dug a good rifle pit. . . .

In this charge we lost thirty or forty men, among them Sgt. Maj. Voorhees Wyckoff, one of the very best men of the regiment, of a frank, open countenance, always in good humor, undergoing every hardship without murmuring and never shirking from either danger or work. His death was an irreparable loss to the regiment. I believe he was a perfectly consistent Christian man and I had been most intimate with him since we were at White Oak Church. He was a beautiful writer and caught as well the proper way of doing the work of the Adjutant's office, relieving me to a great extent of the drudgery of the office.

June 2, Thursday, at Cold Harbor — Lying behind works under or-

Entrenching at Cold Harbor

ders to charge at dark, but postponed by rain. . . . My recollection of this day is that we lay in our pit, anxiously looking at the wood on our left from which the enemy could at any time rake our position. The enemy in front keeping up an almost constant fusillade.

We had lost one of our men this way. He had been digging a grave in the hollow behind the pit for one of our men and came up to the line and asked Colonel C. to send a man to help. . . . Instantly a musket ball struck him in the face and he fell dying at our feet. He was laid in the grave he had dug, widened for two.

We could see the shells in the morning when the sun rose behind the battery from the time they left the gun, and it gave us a feeling of relief to see them pass over our heads. The dust and smoke were such that the sun could be looked at any hour of the day nearly all the time we were here.

June 3, Friday — Early in the morning we had orders to charge, General Russel standing in among us and ordering the advance. Colonel Campbell said, "We will when the line gets up to us," referring to the line of battle seen approaching from our left rear. It was [Gen. John] Gibbons' division of the 2d Corps. As we first saw them, the rebels saw and opened fire. . . . They had to cross the same wide field we had passed on the 1st [of June], every inch of it swept by the enemy. In this line was a new heavy artillery regiment, which advanced in a handsome line but was cut down like grass. A few reached the rebel rifle pit and were there probably taken prisoner. It was the most sickening sight of the war, and the sight of those bodies strewed over the ground for a quarter of a mile, and in our sight for days, will never fade from our recollection.

After dark we moved over into the front line, relieving the 10th New Jersey. A charge was made to our left at night as we could tell by the musketry and the fusillade continuing along the line.

After the charge of the morning, our men held the wood to our left, and a rifle pit was dug across the intervening space during the day. First a man crawling on his face threw up a little dirt to cover him. Behind him, others followed until a respectable pit was made joining our left. We could see the rebel bullets fall in the loose dirt thrown up, but they did not stop the work.

Another incident. The ground behind us was as dangerous as that in front. To get water, our men would run the gauntlet of the enemy's fire. A man could take a dozen canteens and run as fast as he could to a little building halfway back and have a rest. His comrades watched the race, the bullets striking the dirt sometimes close to the feet of the runner and one after another asked permission to go, until Colonel Campbell said he "believed they had enough to swim in."

[S]o far as sleep was concerned, Colonel Campbell and I took turns. . . . It required the greatest effort of the officers to keep the men awake.

June 4, Saturday, Cold Harbor—Just at daylight or a little after, orders came up that reenlisted veterans of the 3d New Jersey would be assigned to the 15th, the rest of the regiment being ordered to New Jersey. Colonel Campbell ordered me to go to the rear and take charge of them.

I ran the gauntlet of rebel bullets, which whistled around me as I ran, having a feeling that if I was maimed and fell, I could not get away in safety. . . .

At dark I took the command up to the line, getting them between the fusillades of the enemy. The men mingled with those of the 15th (were ordered into the same companies of the 15th they belonged to in the 3rd) and I lay down and slept, entirely unconscious of fusillades and of a heavy shower, which left me in a puddle of water in the morning.

June 5—We lay behind the pits all day, exchanging shots with the enemy's sharpshooters. Their rifle pits were not 20 yards off. (By the scale of the war map we were not 132 feet distant.)

One man, David Husted of the 3d, running after water, halted behind an apple tree. The enemy fairly barked this tree and would eventually have hit him had not our men risen up and opened a general fire on the enemy, which gave them something else to think of. Husted watched his chance and ran in. He understood what his comrades were doing for him.

We number now (with the 2d and 3d), 216 muskets, having lost 52 men since the morning of June 1.

At night we were taken from the front line and put in the third where we had comparative quiet, though the enemy kept up their fusillades, and the balls dropped in among us or whistled by us.

June 7 — In the afternoon a flag of truce was exhibited and a general cessation of hostilities took place. The flag was flying from three to eight, during which time our dead were removed and buried.

It was a singular sight to see the men of both armies standing up, looking at each other curiously, while between the lines, both parties mingled, exchanging [news]papers, etc.

At 9 o'clock we were moved back into the first rifle pit, relieving the 4th. All was quiet during the night.

June 8, Wednesday — All was quiet during the day, by tacit agreement both parties desisting from firing. Papers were exchanged and the rebs appeared very friendly.

The Shenandoah Valley Campaign

Following Cold Harbor, the Army of the Potomac continued its assaults on Confederate positions, but it fought with less and less enthusiasm. On June 15, during the initial Union assault of Petersburg, a force of 40,000 Union soldiers failed to break through a Confederate line of only 2,500 men commanded by Gen. Pierre G. T. Beauregard. After Lee arrived with reinforcements, the Union Army carried on their assault so halfheartedly that General Meade called off the attack. Meade asserted, "[O]ur men are tired and the attacks have not been made with the vigor and force which characterized our fighting in the Wilderness."

The war-weariness of the Union soldiers is easy to comprehend. Since May 4, 63,000 Northern men had been killed, wounded, or missing. This amounted to three-fifths of the total number of casualties suffered by the Army of the Potomac during the previous three years. The assault of Petersburg continued in a long drawn-out siege that lasted through the summer.

The inability of Grant's forces to end the stalemate at Petersburg dismayed many Northerners at home. But in early September, news came of Union victory on another front. Atlanta had fallen to Gen. William T. Sherman. This was followed by another Northern success, this time against the Confederate army of Jubal Early, who during the summer, made a daring raid into Washington, bringing his men within five miles of the White House. Gen. Phil Sheridan led a successful attack against Early's 15,000 Confederates at Winchester. Early retreated south to Fisher's Hill where Sheridan pursued and successfully engaged him. Early's army fled 60 miles south to the Blue Ridge Mountains. Sheridan's forces proceeded to the Shenandoah Valley where they waged total war against the civilian population by destroying barns, foodstocks, and livestock. "The people must be left nothing but their eyes to weep with over the war," ordered Sheridan.

On October 16 Sheridan left his forces at Cedar Creek as he went on to Washington for a strategy conference. During Sheridan's absence, Jubal Early launched a devastating surprise attack, forcing the Union forces four miles down the valley. Despite this terrible blow, part of Sheridan's army remained intact. When Sheridan returned to the battlefield, he reorganized the hundreds of stragglers to reinforce the army. With his calvary and infantry acting in unison, he chased Early's forces across Cedar Creek, transforming a rout into victory, thus ending Confederate control of the Shenandoah Valley.

Throughout this period, the remnants of the 15th N.J. Regiment were placed under Sheridan's command. Halsey describes the 15th's participation in the battles of Fisher's Hill and Cedar Creek.

September 22 — Fisher's Hill — At 3 P.M. the lines were ordered forward, our regiment in the second line. Moved forward in line of battle to about the edge of the wood. From a road on our right flank, we could see cleared fields to the front. Every shot fired by the enemy passed over and among us — we were so near — but no heavy loss was experienced.

Later from the far side of the cleared fields ahead of us, rebels were seen running, and behind them Crook's men cheering and pursuing. At once, the whole line went forward. As we approached, the rebels ran, leaving guns, etc., in position. Crossing the works we wheeled to the left and advanced rapidly diagonally toward the pike across the fields. The plains were covered with men fleeing and pursuing. Our men seemed wild with excitement. But our brigade preserved their order and was about the only one that did.

It was dark when we reached the pike in back of the rebel position. Here the crowd was reorganized. 8th Corps this way — 6th Corps this way, each to different sides of the pike. Our brigade was at the front and in order, ready to repulse any attack of the enemy while our men were in disorder, but they did not think of such a thing.

One officer of the 4th who had been in an arrest for some little escapade, I remember rushing along with a handkerchief tied around his head where he had been slightly wounded, brandishing a hickory stick, cheering and shouting with all his might. His sword was given to him the next day, I believe.

Men seemed wild with joy and enthusiasm, and men of the 8th Corps were warmly cheered by the 6th for the important part they had taken.

After a time spent organizing, we moved in cautiously to Woodstock where we arrived at daylight.

On Sept. 24 — From the high ground . . . we could look across a level flat around which swept the Shenandoah, and see the rebels on the hill beyond. Our artillery practiced on them with some little effort, but their right was turned by our cavalry and we were soon in motion across the plain—halting once or twice in line of battle at right angles to the pike. . . . Once across this plain we fell in with the rebels in full retreat, and we pursued them till dark through New Market and Sparta—in all, 20 miles.

This advance was one of the magnificent sights of the war. From the top of the hills we could see their long lines of battle stretching across the valley and moving away from us. Passing over cleared or ploughed fields, their lines could hardly be distinguished from the ground save by the flashes of their musket barrels in the sun. Behind the lines of battle were their skirmish lines, which a line of our cavalry skirmishers continually attacked. Behind the cavalry skirmish line was an infantry line of skirmishers, and when the front line was checked, [they] immediately came up with it and the rebels moved on. Behind the infantry skirmishers was the long black first line of our infantry, behind which was the second line moving by the right of regiments to the front, ready to swing into line.

At dusk the enemy seemed to make a stand. We found our lines and were about to attack when they moved in again and went into camp.

Sept. 25 — [T]he enemy withdrew during the night. Marched . . . to Harrisonburg. . . . Two or three caissons with spokes of wheels cut with an axe were standing in the street, abandoned by the enemy . . . [T]heir wounded were in the hospital.

At night, the appearance of the camps lying about the town, from our hill, was beautiful, like that of a great city.

Sept. 26 — Harrisonburg — A few minutes ago, one of our men was brought in with his throat partially cut. He had been out for apples and some men attacked him from behind, attempted to murder him, and took some $300 he had with him. The wound is not considered mortal, but the affair is not a pleasant one. He thinks they were citizens who attacked him, but I guess it was some of our own men. Possible men of our own recruits who knew him to have the money, his recruit bounty. There were some hard men among our substitutes and recruits.

Sept. 30 — Our men were out foraging and some of them, I am afraid, pillaging. . . . Many refugees, both black and white, accompany our trains toward the north star, feeling that this country, beautiful and productive as it is, is no place to live in. As usual our forages covered the country for miles bringing in forage — sheep, chickens, grain, etc., lots of preserves, clothes, etc. . . . Everything they seem to think can be made use and they are able to carry, they bring in. The rest they demolish. . . . [S]ometimes vengeance follows speedily, and the man who breaks through discipline to satisfy his cupidity is gobbled up by [Confederate] guerillas, and his fate depends upon the humor of his captors.

Oct. 4 — Dayton, with every building within five miles, was burned by order of Sheridan for the murder by a guerilla of Chief Engineer [Lt. John R.] Meiss.

Oct. 6, Thursday — Started at half past five A.M. and marched till half past four in the afternoon with only a few ten minute halts — to the hill South of Mt. Jackson and between it and New Market (about halfway). As we marched along the pike or by the side of it, our cavalry swept either side of the mountains, burning barns and driving sheep and cattle. Smokes were seen far southward. As usual many refugees, black and white, accompany our trains.

Oct. 9 — It seems that yesterday evening, Gen. [A. T. A.] Torbert remarked to General Sheridan that the enemy were following him up pretty close. Sheridan replied, "A good deal closer than I like to be followed. With this, General Torbert acted today, and, laying a trap for the reb cavalry, captured eleven of their twelve guns. Gen. [Thomas L.] Rosser is said to have gone through Middletown in the morning, boasting to the citizens that there would be a charge and that his cavalry from the Army of Virginia would not run, etc. A few hours after, he went through the same place, chased by a squad of our cavalry on a dead run.

Oct. 11, near Front Royal — Rode to the top of the hill in front of our camp and took a view of the Luray Valley, Front Royal, the juncture of the North and South Forks, Manasas Gap, Wapping Heights, and in the rear, the camp of our corps. One of the prettiest pictures I have yet seen in this region.

In evening, foolishly invested in a horse raffle.

Oct. 19 — Battle of Cedar Creek — Under orders, the brigade was roused before daylight and stood, each regiment on its color line in the darkness, the men shivering with cold, until objects grew distinguishable. When it became broad daylight, ranks were broken and men sent to make coffee. Directly, the bugle blew and Colonel Penrose called out "Pack up." Tents, etc., were hurled into the regimental or brigade wagons, which Cooke at once rushed to the rear. The brigade started at once in the direction of loud firing past Sheridan's (subsequent) headquarters. The stragglers of the 8th and 19th Corps were streaming to the rear in columns.

The line was formed on the ridge beyond. Here Colonel Penrose and Colonel Campbell were wounded. Major Boeman commanding the 10th was killed. Falling back, a stand was made back of where our camp was. Going through a piece of wood, [Sgt. John] Mouder, carrying the state color, which was not unrolled, was killed. No one noticed the loss till too late to get the color. The enemy did not pursue after this last stand, and the division moved by the flank of regiments to the rear.

Suddenly this order was countermanded, and we were marching in the other direction. Capt. [Charles R.] Paul told me that General Sheridan had gotten back. We formed a line in the wood, the Brigade as one regiment, no effort being made to distinguish companies.

We halted long enough to get something to eat. A regiment of the 19th Corps came up and formed on our right. Moved by some impulse, they commenced firing by volley, and were, with some difficulty, stopped. Our pickets were in front of them.

Here Sheridan came along the line with a word to every part of . . . [the regiment]. "It's all right, We'll flank—out of there yet. . . . You'll be back in your old camps tonight." The men cheered and the rebels answered with a shell or two.

[T]he advance was made through the wood. At the edge of it we could see across to a ridge opposite of which were the enemy behind a stone wall. Their fire checked the first line, and the second came up and

Battle of Cedar Creek

171

merged with it.

Across the field and up the hill, the line went, the enemy firing at it, and we losing some men, but they abandoned the fence before our men reached it.

[Sgt. Peter] Gunderman carrying the colors was struck on the right shoulder with a solid shot, which broke the staff in splinters, tore off his sleeve, and rolled him backward down the hill. But he was up in a moment, and seizing the color, went ahead with it.

The rest of the advance was like the evening at Fisher's Hill on the 22d of Sept. The whole plain seemed covered with running men. At nightfall the only possible order was for every man to find his camp of the morning.

Around our camps, fires were built, large pots of coffee made, and wounded were searched out and brought in. I think seventeen badly wounded men were around our fires that night. . . . And yet with the exception of a man in Company F who was shot in the head and groaned unconsciously, dying before morning, I did not hear a groan or word of complaint from one of them.

Oct. 20, Thursday — Our wounded were being taken away in ambulances all day, the last going about 4 P.M.

Charley Hall and I went over in the afternoon to see the "trophies." In one line were forty-seven pieces of artillery. Close by were thirty wagons — some our own; some high-backed farm wagons and ambulances with 2nd and 3d Corps badges on them, etc., and about 1,000 prisoners.

Oct. 21, Friday — Camp near Middleton — Our state color, which was captured October 19 and recaptured by the 4th New York Cavalry, [George A.] Custer's division, was presented to the regiment. Speeches were made by Gen. [Frank] Wheaton, Gen. Torbert, Custer (I think he was present).

The regiment presented a sorry sight. Gunderman was in line with his blouse half torn off and holding the other color by its shattered staff. In all the speeches, only good of the regiment was spoken and no blame attached to them.

Our loss at present stands 13 killed, 58 wounded, 13 missing.

Returning Home

Following the Union victories in the fall of 1864, it was clear that the war was coming to an end. The prospect of Union victory encouraged Northerners. But for soldiers of the 15th N.J. and other regiments who had suffered the greatest casualties, the war had gone on too long. 240 men of the 15th had died in combat, more than in any other New Jersey regiment. Nation-

*wide the 15th New Jersey ranked 12th in fatalities among two thousand
Union regiments.*

*Understandably, the initial enthusiasm of soldiers who originally volunteered
for service in the 15th N.J. had long since waned. Not only had they seen the
slaughter of their comrades in battle; they had also participated in the devastation wrought upon Southern civilians by the Northern army under the command of General Sheridan.*

*Halsey himself had grown war weary. He had seen too many of his friends
die. Besides, his family wanted him home. Halsey's father was in poor health; he
needed Edmund to help manage his business and care for the family, including
an invalid sister whose poor health had brought her close to death.*

*In November of 1864, Halsey applied for resignation from the service. In a
camp near Winchester, he wrote in his diary, "There is but one officer who came
out with us May 4 who has not been wounded, killed, detailed, or mustered out.
I feel like a stranger. Alanson [Haines] intends to go home, and Dr. Hall is
getting a long sick leave." A month went by without a response. He resub-
mitted the resignation on December 19. On Christmas Day Halsey finally
received word that his application had been approved. His official discharge
papers came January 8, 1865. The following day, as he prepared his departure, the enemy attacked his camp near Petersburg, wounding one man.
Halsey records this and other happenings that occurred during his last days
in the army before his homeward journey.*

Jan. 9 — Camp near Petersburg — Cold — The rebels again attacked our
picket line. To protect the line from these sudden incursions, abatis were
taken up to the line. The rebels saw these being placed for a while quietly, but suddenly opened fire, wounding Earl in the leg.

Fixing up court business etc., and making arrangements to leave tomorrow.

Quite a jubilee at brigade headquarters. [Dr.] Sullivan and [Capt.
William] Cornish coming up from the 39th. Gave Dr. [Redford] Sharp
my silver watch.

Jan. 10 — Went to City Point by rail to get transportation for "Ned"
[Halsey's horse] but was disappointed in getting off. Coming back —
shut up with half a dozen other passengers in a boxcar full of freight.
The train broke in two, and our part went on a mile or two, while we
stopped in the first hollow. Got back very late.

Jan. 11 — Camp near Petersburg — My last day in camp and waiting
for opportunity to get away.

Jan. 12, Thursday — Started for home — Left City Point on boat with
. . . our men who were furloughed.

Jan. 13 — Arrived in Washington. . . .

Jan. 14—Washington—Went to Oxford, a low mean place, with the crowd, to pass the afternoon. Stayed all night at Willards.

Jan. 15, Sunday—At Washington—Went to Church morning, and evening with Captain Slater's family (and had rather a quiet day).

Jan. 16, Monday at Washington. Nothing to be done at the departments because of Edward Everett's[1] death, so wasted the day. . . .

Jan. 18—At Washington—Finished my business and drew my money. Went to Ford's [theater] with Paul, Ellis, etc., but broke away from them and left . . . for earliest New York train.

Jan. 19—Left Washington at six or seven and reached New York in Evening.

Jan. 20, Friday—Went over to Brooklyn (to see Uncle William and with message to Nettie and [Alanson] Haines). To Rockaway on afternoon train.

---

[1] Edward Everett, a famous American clergyman, orator and statesman, once ran as vice-president on the Constitutional Unionist (Whig) ticket.

Chapter 12

The Andersonville Memoirs of Charles F. Hopkins

Throughout most of the Civil War, the problem of housing large groups of prisoners had been obviated by a North-South prisoner-exchange agreement. But in early 1864, the North discontinued the prisoner-exchange agreement, primarily over Confederate refusal to exchange black prisoners of war. This action reduced the number of seasoned Confederates on the battlefield, much to the North's advantage. It also resulted in the deaths of countless soldiers from both Northern and Southern armies in prison camps noted for their brutal conditions.

Camp Sumter in Andersonville, Georgia, by far had the worst reputation. Originally built to hold 10,000 men, this 16.5 acre plot of open land enclosed by a 15 foot stockade was later expanded to a 26 acre yard that contained more than 32,000 Union prisoners. Designed by Gen. John H. Winder and commanded by Capt. Henry Wirz, the notorious camp provided little in the way of housing, clothing, medical care, or sanitation. Water came from a stream that entered the prison yard after it had first flowed through a Confederate military camp. The downstream end served as the camp latrine.

Soldiers died in massive numbers at Andersonville, primarily of disease and starvation. Of the 45,000 Union soldiers imprisoned at Andersonville, 13,000 never left its confines alive.

The following account of Andersonville is taken from the memoirs of Charles Hopkins. Many consider Hopkins Morris County's greatest war hero. He won the Congressional Medal of Honor in July 27, 1892, for "distinguished gallantry under fire" at Gaine's Mill, Virginia. Here he tried to save his badly wounded sergeant from capture by carrying him nearly a mile through enemy crossfire, though he himself received two wounds. The Confederates captured Hopkins and his sergeant, but they soon released them as part of the prisoner exchange agreement.

Almost two years later, during the Battle of the Wilderness, the Confederates again took Hopkins prisoner. This time, he was not so lucky. With the prisoner exchange agreement no longer in effect, the Rebels sent Hopkins to the dreaded Andersonville Prison. Hopkins relates his prisoner-of-war experience in memoirs written almost three decades later. These memoirs provide a vivid first-hand description of the suffering inflicted on Northern prisoners of war. The account excerpted here begins with the march toward Andersonville.

Life in Andersonville

We passed through Macon where some officers were confined. Our stop was short, closely guarded, and here again the guard was increased. This was the last straw needed—creating a reality, not suspicion, that all was not well with us. Only fifty-five miles between us and a Hell of Hells of the Confederacy. One night and part of a day we traveled and then on "The Sabbath," May 22, 1864, we found ourselves in our refuge! No, not refuge—but a place of suffering torture and death, beyond description, to die a death that no language can express. Andersonville! Oh, that name that sears the hearts of mothers, widows and orphans! That chills to the marrow of the living, who once knowing its horrors can never forget them! The name that has gone to the most remote corner of the civilized world as the most inhuman spot on God's footstool! The Apache savage was a cruel tormenter but he was not enlightened, and death at his hands came quickly; but at Andersonville torment equal to that of any barbarian of the past ages was prolonged.

Under a still stronger guard, we left the cars and looked about us in order that we might discover any ray of hope, one bright spot on Nature's face—there was none!!! . . . Stronghearted, brave men who had almost gleefully faced the cannon's mouth, spouting death and wounds in their ranks, here, sank almost in helpless despair—some actually did, and died—yet, the thought was "where others can live, we will not die!" The few only succeeded.

. . . .That human being[s], civilized, could systematically plan a death so horrid and cruel—starved, sick, and wounded men, barbarians would disfigure and torture, and thus cause death in their anger; but to coldly calculate and compass the destruction of human life by slowly starving, killing piecemeal as a result of such calculation, was beyond conception by any but those who knew its contact.

The huge gates became more and more distinct as we solemnly marched—as it seemed to our own funeral—and to many thousands it was literally true. We reached the "Stockade." How that name compels a shudder. . . .

After some delay those big gates yawned before us like the cavernous mouth of some great monster; and we were "lockstepped" in by fifty and sixty at a time, or all the "lock" would hold; the gates in our rear would close and a similar pair of gates would open in our front. Our gaze was riveted to the inside moving thousands; all who got near us as we passed in, crowded that single street—if you can term it—to a "pack" twenty or more deep, each watcher intent to discover some comrade, brother, father, or acquaintance among the incoming "fresh fish," as the

Charles Hopkins (Photograph courtesy of Gerald F. Hopkins)

prisoners before us termed us. Oh, what misery was there depicted upon so many of those gaunt, hopeless faces, filthy and black from pine smoke; ragged and almost nude with the vermin plainly seen upon the poor apology for clothing! Some begged to know the fate of friends, others to learn of the death or capture of someone close to them by some tie of relationship; some met a brother or friend as unfortunate as themselves, and bemoan their fate. Indeed, this picture in its great stockade frame was a rival to Dante's picture of Hell. The stories of those who had tasted the bitter realities of this place were enough to chill the swift warm stream that made the hearts of heroes beat so rapidly now. A beautiful May day, and Sabbath, yet, we could not rejoice while marching into "Hades" with those awful gates creaking a sad requiem behind us, and to so many, forever. Well may the "legend," "He that enters here leaves hope behind," have been placed over the entrance, for truly it was so. The prison was a parallelogram of about two to one as to its length and breadth of about eighteen acres at this time — was enlarged July 1 to about twenty-seven acres — and one third of this not habitable, being a swamp of liquid filth. This was enclosed by wooden walls of hewn pine logs, from eight to ten inches square, four feet buried in the ground, eighteen feet above, braced on the outside, crossbarred to make one log sustain the other, and a small platform making comfortable standing room for the guards, every one hundred feet, with about waist high space below the top of the stockade, reached by a ladder. A sloping roof to protect the men from the sun and rain had been placed over them. Later in 1864 the second line of stockade was built and a third was partly built for protection — it was said if attacked by Federal troops, but we knew it was to discourage us from "tunnelling" — the distance being too great. The Florida Artillery had cannon stationed at each corner of the Stockade, thus commanding a range from any direction, four guns were so placed near the south gate as to command the gate, and over the depressed section of Stockade, which at this point was about forty to fifty feet lower than elsewhere, and at this point the little stream entered the enclosure. The "dead line," so much talked of and feared, was a line of pine, four inch boards on posts about three feet high, and seventeen feet from the stockade walls, thus leaving the distance all around the enclosure an open space, and incidentally reducing the acreage inside, and giving the guards a clear view all about the Stockade — or the name given it by [Gen. John H. Winder,] its inventor and architect, "Bull Pen". . . . To intrude inside this deadline was instant death, or wounds that would cause death by the rifle of a watchful, ready, willing, murderous guard; provided he did not miss his mark intended and kill or wound someone not aimed at in camp. As to missing some victims, [this] was almost impossible in that crowded place.

Inside the camp death stalked on every hand. Death at the hands of the guard, though murder in cold blood, was merciful beside the systematic, studied, absolute murder inside, by slow death, inch by inch!

As before stated, one third of the original enclosure was swampy—a mud of liquid filth, voidings from the thousands, seething with maggots in full activity. This daily increased by the necessities of the inmates, the only place being accessible for this purpose. Through this mass pollution passed the only water that found its way through the Bull Pen. It came to us between the two sources of Pollution, the Confederate camp, [and] the cook house; first, the seepage of sinks; second, the dirt and filth emptied by the cook house; then, was our turn to use if for all purposes, until later. Near the deadline, all took water for all purposes, and drink being a necessity, hence, other purposes must be limited as to quantity, and the hours which taken. I have known over 3,000 men to wait in line to get water, and the line was added to as fast as reduced, from daylight to dark, yes, even into night; men taking turn of duty with men of their mess, in order to hold their place in line, as no one man could stand it alone, even if in the "pink" of physical condition; the heat of the sun, blistering him, or the drenching rains soaking him, not a breath of fresh air, and we had no covering but Heaven's canopy. Air-loaded with unbearable, fever-laden stench from that poison sink of putrid mud and water, continually in motion by the activity of the germs of death. We could not get away from it—we ate it, drank it and slept in it (when sleep was possible and exhaustion compelled sleep). What wonder that men died, or were so miserable as to prefer instant death to that which they had seen hourly

Issuing Rations at Andersonville

taking place, and so preferring, deliberately stepping within the dead-line and looking their willing murderer in the eye, while the shot was sent crashing through a brain that was yet clear. This I have seen and know; the victim intended to close the door that led to doubt as to how he would die. Others, not mentally balanced because of a starved brain and system, wandered inside the fatal line and were ruthlessly slaugh-tered. One poor demented comrade, not instantly killed, lay for hours in full view of his comrades — gasping and struggling with death, but no one could go to his rescue for fear of the same kind of death. Men, who at one time, were lionhearted, brave in battle, shuddered at the sight, and wept like children, and cursed the murderer. This victim was a demented, starved, one-legged veteran who had lost his leg at Chickamauga; hence, his name by all who spoke to or of him. Very frequently some poor fellow was shot upon one pretext or other, none of them valid among "men." Three, we personally know of, met this fate while getting water — ignorant of the danger of forgetting them-selves, touched the deadline and died of their wounds in a short time. The "Silent Reaper" was busy on every hand and in so many ways, and some so pitiable, that a heart of stone would relent toward the victims in their loathsome misery and suffering.

The cases of insanity were numerous. Men, strong in mentality, heart, and hope were, in a few short months, yes, often in a few weeks, re-duced to imbeciles and maniacs. Today they know you and look upon you as friends and comrades; tomorrow they are peevish, whining, child-ish creatures, or raving maniacs. Some would beg for something to eat; others asked for wife, mother, children or other relatives; some, in their delirium were home talking to their friends, enjoying the good eating that mother set before them — they seemed happy, many forever talking of hunger, and a goodly number were furiously wild, and had they been strong they would have been dangerous — not knowing their closest friend, trusting no one, raving and cursing in fearful language. Happily, may I say it, all such died soon, worn out and exhausted by this emo-tion. Yet, there was never a time that these terrible scenes were not en-acted. It was piteous to see, but compelled as we were, it filled every waking moment. . . . These scenes caused much depression and added to the inward mental note — if not audibly spoken — "when shall my turn come and must it be as this?" The mental anguish of those days and months was the slowest torture to him who still had a clear brain — a cruelty to which the barbarian was a stranger. Just think and imagine, if you can, what your thoughts would be to see a father, son, a brother, or even a comrade, not related, slowly but surely becoming a mere skel-eton, a maniac, appealing continuously for something to eat, talk of home, friends, in his delirious spells; knows you not—you, helpless to do more than endeavor to live yourself, cheer him up when your heart is breaking, and so not believe your promised hopes to him. Under such circumstances was it not wonderful that suicide was little or not known to any except demented ones? These were the hours that tried the mental strength of the "man," and were a hundred times worse than the thoughts of a hundred Gettysburg or Chickamauga battles! One was to die in glory under the folds of that flag which he was sworn to defend, and be among his comrades, dying at post of duty. The other was to rot in misery, a degradation among blood of our blood, kin both by blood and Country, yet they had forgotten all the ages had praised them for "Chivalry and Civilization."

The average deaths per day for seven and a half months were eighty-five. But during the months of July, August, September, and October, the average was one hundred per day. One day in August, following the great freshet [i.e., a rising of the water flowing through the camp as a result of rain], I counted 235 corpses lying at the south gate and about it. Many of those had been smothered in their "burrows" made in the side hill in which they crawled to shield themselves from sun and storm, the soil being sandy, became rain-soaked and settled down upon the occupant and became his grave instead of a protection. Others, who had no shelter, in whom life was barely existing, were rain-soaked, chilling bone and marrow; life flitted easily away, and left but little to return to clay. These holes or burrows in both the flats and up the north slope, were counted by thousands; no doubt there were some that never gave up their dead but lay there as buried in their self-made sepulcher. No effort was made to search unless the man was missed by a friend, and of such are these that are "unknown" upon the records for some 12,000 at the "Hell of Winder's."

Chapter 13

Remembering the Dead

The Civil War had cost over a million lives, more than any war in our nation's history. For the families of slain Northern soldiers, the sense of loss far outweighed the triumph of victory. In their shared grief, these families came to understand the necessity of honoring their dead as a community.

The custom of decorating graves of soldiers during the spring actually began in the South as early as 1865. By the following year, the custom appeared in the North, where it became widely observed. Memorial Day was eventually declared a Federal holiday largely through the efforts of the veterans organization, the Grand Army of the Republic. The G.A.R. also encouraged the construction of local monuments honoring the dead.

This final chapter features an 1868 editorial from the *True Democratic Banner* commenting on the G.A.R.'s involvement in the celebration of Memorial Day—followed by an 1871 account of the Morristown Civil War Memorial dedication ceremony, which appeared in the *Jerseyman*.

Democrats Criticize G.A.R. Efforts to Memorialize the Dead

Though founded as a nonpartisan veterans organization in 1866, the Grand Army of the Republic served the Republican cause. Its leader, John A. Logan, a U.S. senator and former Union general from Ohio, successfully garnered substantial veteran support for the Republican party. Logan and his compatriots avoided partisan symbols and speeches but kept the memory of the war alive by reminding Americans of the losses incurred during the war. The G.A.R. encouraged the commemoration of Memorial Day, originally known as Decoration Day, and formalized its observance, which helped make it into an official federal holiday. Throughout the nation, G.A.R. posts held ceremonies that combined religious and patriotic observances. Orators often gave speeches extolling the heroism of those who died for the sake of liberty, while reminding their audience of the South's responsibility for starting the war.

Emphasizing the need to protect the reunited Republic, Logan and other Republicans saw the G.A.R. as a bulwark against forces within the government that might pose a threat to the fragile Union. During the impeachment crises of 1868, Logan even developed plans to mobilize the G.A.R. if Andrew Johnson should use the regular army to dissolve Congress or evict

Secretary of War Edwin Stanton from his War Department Office.

The willingness of Republicans to even consider the use of such extralegal force alarmed Democrats. Many Democrats viewed the G.A.R. as a political army organized to overthrow the government. They feared the establishment of a Republican monarchy or empire that would grant voting and other rights to freed slaves without the consent of the people.

During the 1870s, the G.A.R. deemphasized its connections with the Republican Party, placing greater emphasis on securing better pensions for disabled Union veterans. Consequently, many Democrats joined the organization, though they remained a minority.

The following is a Democratic commentary on the role the G.A.R. played in the 1868 celebration of Decoration Day. The author's views typify the Democratic view of the veterans' organization during the late 1860s.

True Democratic Banner   *June 4, 1868*

The Grand Army of the Republic (so-called) has just been engaged decorating the graves of the Union soldiers, according to orders given by General Logan who nominated Grant at Chicago for the Presidency. Since the last Presidential election, the remains of the soldiers lost in war have been allowed to rest in quiet neglect where they fell, or have been collected in cemeteries where they have lain in undisturbed repose until the eve of a Presidential election.

While we yield to none in disposition to confer lasting honors upon the victorious dead, especially those who have sacrificed life upon the altar of their country, it is but proper to expose this sudden ebullition of love for the deceased soldier as a piece of political claptrap devised by a party organization for the purpose of stimulating a temporary excitement and ostentatious display. Look out for more claptrap, more humbugery, more mockery, hypocrisy and heartless pretence. Radicalism has been reduced to such mean and dishonorable shifts to keep up appearances.

The Dedication of Morris County's Civil War Monument

The Civil War Memorial on the Morristown Green remains one of the best known public monuments in Morris County. The 24 foot obelisk surmounted by a statue of a soldier commemorates those men of Morris County who lost their lives fighting for the Union.

Originally not everyone wanted a memorial. Some preferred to forget the war. But by the late 1860s, many expressed their desire to publicly honor *the dead. Though the majority of freeholders initially voted against allocating funds for the memorial's construction, members of the public who wanted the memorial outnumbered those opposing the monument. When election time came, they voted in new freeholders favoring the project. Construction on the $15,000 monument began soon thereafter.*

The dedication of the monument took place on July 4, 1871. At that time politicians delivered speeches extolling the dead and the cause for which they fought. They spoke of the fight for freedom and the need to preserve the Union. They did not specifically mention slavery, since many Democrats still believed the war should never have been linked to emancipation. They preferred to keep the celebration nonpolitical. Speechmakers instead talked of reconciliation and the need to heal the nation's wounds. Despite this, blacks were not completely ignored. The organizers of the dedication did make at least some effort to recognize African Americans by including a black band among its host of featured musicians.

The following article, excerpted from the Jerseyman, *reports this event and quotes many speeches. Two of these speeches are included here — one delivered by New Jersey's Democratic governor Theodore F. Randolph, the other, by Morris County freeholder E. E. Willis.*

Jerseyman   *July 8, 1871*

FOURTH OF JULY IN MORRISTOWN, DEDICATION OF SOLDIER'S MONUMENT — Notwithstanding the unpleasant weather, which doubtless kept thousands from participating in the exercises, the celebration of the Fourth in this Town was one of the most imposing ever witnessed in this section of the State. The town was early filled with people from all parts of the County, and many former residents who for years had been unknown upon its streets came from distant States to join in the jubilation. Governor Randolph presided over the exercises, and his staff was present in uniform. The Procession comprised a large number of civic societies from various parts of the county, the fire department of the town, organizations of G.A.R., ex-soldiers and sailors, companies D and E, 4th Regiment; from Jersey City, the Orange Veterans, and county and town officials. A noticeable feature was the turnout of the members of the Stanley Public School in carriages, under charge of George Shepard Page, and a white horse ridden by its present owner, Captain Bunting of Madison, which was once given by the ladies of New York to Gen. T. F. Meagher, and was in the battle of Fair Oaks and other contests. Music was furnished by four brass bands, headed by the famous Governor's Island band, brought by the Jersey City companies. The other bands were Becker's of Morristown, the South Orange band, Huff's (colored) band, and ex-Sheriff [William W.] Fairchild's martial corps. Major Thomas J. Halsey commanded as Marshal, and the procession, numbering, probably, 1,000 persons, with a squad of police at its head under Chief [John] McDavitt, marched through the principal streets of the place.

Upon the arrival of the procession at the stand, Governor Randolph assumed his seat as presiding officer. . . . Governor Randolph then delivered the following address:

Neighbors and Friends of Morris County. Fellow Citizens of New Jersey:

It is fitting that the descendants of a people of the State that severed its allegiance from British authority days before the Provincial Congress proclaimed the National Independence—of a people that had fought upon their own provincial soil at Princeton, the great and turning battle of the war—of a people that had succored and sheltered upon these very hills and within these beautiful valleys of ours, the distressed, half-clad and nearly starved army of the patriots of that era, whose steps from yonder camp ground to the Headquarters of the Great General [Washington]—still preserved to us—thanks to the patriotism of an honored family—were marked on the pure snow by the bloodstained tracks of unshod feet—it is fitting, I say, for these and scores of other reasons, the mind of every true Jerseyman will promptly suggest, that the National Anniversary of the Independence of these old thirteen States, as well as that of those who have been born of them, should be celebrated in our midst, surrounded as we were by historic recollections, with full and appropriate ceremonies.

'Tis not so much the achievements of the great and unequal Revolutionary struggle we celebrate, noble and memorable as they were, as it is the act which declared us free, and which, though long preceding Peace itself, was the first great step towards it. Then, as now, the true object of war, waged by a Christian people was, and ever should be, the establishment of speedy peace—Peace that comes with healing on its wings, peace that buries the sorrowful past and opens wide the doors of love and reconciliation.

We come to celebrate our Ninety-fifth National Anniversary—at peace as a Nation with all other nations; with that great nation from whose allegiances we severed ourselves after seven years of great suffering and heroism, we are not only at peace, but by a recent treaty, [we] have arranged our differences, and as far as human feeling can be suppressed by National compact, have joined hands in promoting the peace, good will, and prosperity of two great peoples.

The Morristown Civil War Memorial remains a focal point where people gather to express their patriotism during times of national crisis. This view of the monument was taken during the 1991 Persian Gulf War. (Photo by David Mitros)

No bitterness of strife was ever greater than that 'twixt Great Britain and these Colonies, and yet no peaceful compact has more promise than ours of today. The lesson is suggestive.

My friends, you know it has been the custom of all enlightened nations to establish and keep commemorative days, distinguished from all others by omissions and commissions singular and apart from all other days of the year.

As one weary of ascending and descending the rugged paths of travel finally reaches the broad summit—standing out clear in the sunlight and apart from the general landscape—yet to other and more distant eyes being the crowning feature of a beautiful whole—so we, upon this Anniversary day, should be lifted up in our patriotic purposes, and leaving for the time the plodding daily life, to take from this controlling point of Time, views perspective and retrospective, profitable to us as American citizens, and to our entire country and its welfare.

My province, however, today, is not that of your orator. Happily for you this duty falls upon one of our most distinguished as well as most eloquent fellow citizens, who, though placed at the head of one of the chief departments of the Federal Government, that of the Navy, will never forget that the grand old State of New Jersey bore him, whatever loving Federal care shelters and protects him in his present lone bachelor life.

I say, in all sincerity, that it gives me a great, though melancholy satisfaction, to be able to assist in dedicating a Monument to the memory of those brave and patriotic men who, as your sons, brothers, neighbors and dearly loved ones, gave in defense of their principles, all they could give—their lives.

There will be to them again no stubborn contest in the thickets of the Wilderness under Grant; no other gallant charge under the fiery [Philip] Kearny in the midst of a no less gallant foe; no life struggle, eye to eye, and hand to throat, as in that most bravely contested and terrific contest of the war, on the hill of Malvern, led by your own brave and gallant townsman, Fitz-John Porter. [See footnote on page 133.]

Passed from life, beyond human recall, it is for us, not so much by yonder beautiful, appropriate heavenward reaching shaft, to keep green their memories, as by the evincement of patriotic principles and fitting acts of public and private life to show our appreciation for and guardianship of the great Constitutional rights their lives were given to perpetuate.

[Following some introductory remarks by Freeholder Director E. E. Willis, crediting those who created the monument,] Mr. John Thatcher, by an ingenious arrangement with ropes, unveiled the statue, the flag that had covered it floating off with the breeze to the top of the adjoining Liberty Pole amid loud cheers, music from the band, and general rejoicing — the Jersey City companies saluting the monument with three rattling volleys of musketry and dipping their flag.

Mr. Willis continued,

Fellow Citizens:

In the year 1861, ten years ago, we, some of us at least, stood with aching hearts to witness the departure from among us of a band of brave and noble men, who, at the first announcement of peril to our country and our Union, sprang to arms, rushed to their aid, and not stopping to count the cost, unhesitatingly proffered in their defense, their services, their all, even to life itself, remembering only "their country, first, last, and always."

Again and again during the next four years, our hearts were saddened by the recurrence of the same scenes, until hundreds of our best and bravest had left us, many of whom we shall never meet again until the sound of the last trumpet.

They died of starvation in southern prisons. They slept in hospital cemeteries all over the land, from Maine to Texas.

Of many, no record whatever remains upon earth, except in the mourning hearts of those who watched and waited so long in vain for their coming.

A few returned, bearing within them the seeds of death, implanted by wounds and sickness and exposure, and after lingering a few weeks or months, long enough to make the parting more bitter, breathed away their lives in the arms of friends and kindred, only more fortunate than others that the tears of those weeping friends can be shed over their graves.

These are the men, the heroes, to whose memory, with grateful recollection of their sacrifices, their sufferings, their death, in behalf of us, who remained at home, sitting in ease and comfort; these are they, to whose memory we have erected and now dedicate this Monument.

We have assembled here, on this an anniversary of our nation's birth — a day most appropriately selected for the purpose — to do honor to those who contributed so much to preserve it from destruction. Surely they are worthy of this, and all the honor a grateful country can offer. We have come to prove that we are not unmindful of the sacrifice they made, that we appreciate it, and that we have endeavored to show that appreciation by erecting this enduring Monument, to keep their memory green before us, until granite and marble shall crumble into dust.

Their names, in the lapse of years, may become dim in our hearts, but this Monument will still remain to impress upon our children and our children's children, this one great truth, that our liberties, our Union, our nation, were cemented and consecrated by the blood of our best and bravest, and that treasure, purchased as such costly price, should never be lightly given up or thrown away.

Fellow Citizens of Morris County, the Board of Chosen Freeholders, through me, their representative, now formally tender to your affectionate care and keeping, this Monument to the memory of your departed heroes, feeling a lively gratification in so doing, and trusting that memory shall never fade in your hearts, or [in] the hearts of those who succeed you, so long as this Union stands, which, God grant, may be as long as its granite and marble shall endure.

Epilogue

By the end of the Civil War, over 380 soldiers from Morris County had given their lives to preserve the Union. In so doing they also helped eliminate slavery, the cause of the split between North and South that had led to the war.

Abolitionism had triumphed. Radical Republicans, who had gained control of Congress following Lincoln's death, established military governments throughout the South. They succeeded in enforcing black suffrage, while disenfranchising thousands of Southern white leaders.

In Morris County and elsewhere, Democrats reacted predictably. The *True Democratic Banner* ran numerous editorials condemning "Black Republicans" for giving African Americans political power. It also featured racist humor and satire ridiculing blacks as unfit to participate in government.

Morris County's Republicans responded by defending the policies of the Radicals. On September 21, 1867, the *Jerseyman* featured an editorial entitled, "Catechism for Copperheads" that asked the rhetorical question, "Who are the men who have saved the nation from the blighting curse of slavery; who have carried the country triumphantly through the rebellion; who boldly and defiantly faced the peace criers and traitors, North and South, during the war; and who are now willing to meet the same enemy, either with bullets or ballots, as occasion may require?" Answer. "The Radicals."

Despite Republican idealism, Reconstruction became associated with graft and corruption at the hands of Northern "carpetbaggers." Still, the new state legislatures of the South included many intelligent and responsible legislators, black and white, who successfully passed much progressive legislation that has survived to this day. But disenfranchised Southern whites grew increasingly resentful not only toward the Radical Republicans but also toward the moderate Northern Republicans who supported black suffrage and other reforms in the South, while rejecting the same reforms at home. In fact, the legislatures of most Northern states withheld the right to vote from their African American minorities until the passage of the 15th Amendment in 1870, which granted suffrage to males of all races.

In New Jersey, the Democratic legislature (which had regained control from the Republicans in 1868) *never* ratified the 15th Amendment, and it rescinded the state's ratification of the 14th Amendment, which granted citizenship rights to everyone born in the United States, including blacks.

As conservatism prevailed, Northern whites grew more sympathetic to their Southern counterparts, and moderate Northern Republicans gradually withdrew their support for reconstruction. Anti-black Southern whites regained positions of power in state governments.

In the following decades, white Southerners flaunted the 14th and 15th Amendments. Beginning about 1890, they openly disenfranchised African Americans through fraud, intimidation, and unfair literacy tests.

The economic condition of blacks deteriorated. If the federal government had seriously taken measures to rehabilitate the South by redistributing former plantation land to landless farmers of both races, as some abolitionists had advocated, reconstruction may have succeeded. Instead, an agricultural economy based on sharecropping developed, which tied blacks to land they did not own, keeping them in debt to the white landowner who forced them to purchase seed, supplies, and food at exorbitant prices. Though blacks fared better when they migrated to the industrial North, they still confronted racism, especially among working class whites who viewed them as a threat to their jobs.

The Civil War had reunited America. But reconstruction failed to reconcile Americans. In both North and South, the legacy of slavery retained its hold on the nation.

Appendix

Civil War Veteran Grave Sites

Name	Cemetery	Regiment	Company
Abell, William	Evergreen Cemetery (Morristown)	1st NJ Militia	E
Aber, Jacob	Old Walnut Grove Baptist Cemetery (Randolph)	33d NJ Vol.	B
Aber, Peter (Wagoner)	Center Grove Methodist Cemetery (Randolph)	27th NJ Vol.	F
Abram, L. Johnson	Evergreen Cemetery (Morristown)	22d US Colored Troops	
Ackaley, Charles	Pleasant Grove Cemetery (Chester Twp.)	11th PA Cavalry	C
Ackerman, Charles	Evergreen Cemetery (Morristown)	1st NJ Light Artillery	Bat. C
Ackerman, John	Evergreen Cemetery (Morristown)	26th NJ Vol.	H
Ackley, Joseph	Evergreen Cemetery (Morristown)	26th NJ Vol.	D
Adams, J. Sylvester	Hilltop Cemetery (Mendham)	30th NJ Vol.	I
Adams, Sylvester	Denville Cemetery	150th NY Vol.	K
Allen, Augustus	Evergreen Cemetery (Morristown)	PA Emergency Militia	E
Allen, D.S. (Capt.)	Orchard Street Cemetery (Dover)	39th NJ Vol.	K
Allen, Erastus	Evergreen Cemetery (Morristown)	1st NJ Militia	E
Allen, George W.	Mt. Freedom Methodist Cemetery	US Sharp Shooters	
Allen, James	Greenwood Cemetery (Boonton)	23d NJ Vol.	K
Allen, John C.	Locust Hill Cemetery (Dover)	1st NY Engineers	K
Allen, John L.	German Valley Rural Cemetery	27th NJ Vol.	G
Allen, John S.	Locust Hill Cemetery (Dover)	102d NY Vol.	K
Allen, Wilson	Orchard Street Cemetery (Dover)	40th NJ Vol.	G
Amerman, John B.	New Vernon Cemetery	1st NJ Light Artillery	Bat. D
Anderson, John	Evergreen Cemetery (Morristown)	11th NJ Vol.	H
Andrew, Crosby	Evergreen Cemetery (Morristown)	29th CT Vol. (Colored)	C
Andrew, William C.	Succasunna Presbyterian/Methodist Cemetery	1st NY Engineers	K
Anglum, John	St. Mary's Cemetery (Boonton)	US Regular	
Ansom, Joseph	Center Grove Methodist Cemetery (Randolph)	1st NJ Vol.	K
Armstrong, Alfred	Evergreen Cemetery (Morristown)	15th NJ Vol.	C
Arnett, James	Flanders Methodist Cemetery	27th NJ Vol.	C
Atkins, Nicholas	Locust Hill Cemetery (Dover)	30th NJ Vol.	K
Atno, John	Stanhope Cemetery	27th NJ Vol.	K
Axtell, Charles (Cpl.)	Evergreen Cemetery (Morristown)	NJ Militia	E
Babbit, Dayton L.	Evergreen Cemetery (Morristown)	NJ Militia	E
Babbit, Hampton	Evergreen Cemetery (Morristown)	2d NJ Vol.	H
Babbitt, Sydney	Rockaway Presbyterian Church Cemetery	40th NJ Vol.	G
Babcock, G. W.	Stanhope Cemetery	22d NJ Vol.	H
Babcock, James	Evergreen Cemetery (Morristown)	1st Rgt., Hancock's Corp.	G
Babcock, Manard	Cuff Cemetery (Newfoundland in Jefferson)	25th NJ Vol.	E
Babcock, Matthias	Hanover Road Cemetery (Hanover)	1st NJ Cavalry	E
Baldwin, Noah	United Methodist Church (Montville)	39th NJ Vol.	K
Baldwin, Stephen Y.	United Methodist Church (Montville)	27th NJ Vol.	G
Ball, Henry M.	Hanover Presbyterian Church Cemetery	7th NJ Vol.	B
Ballantine, Samuel B.	Hilltop Cemetery (Mendham)	24th NJ Vol.	B
Bam, George A.	Evergreen Cemetery (Morristown)	127th US Colored Troops	B
Barkman, John C. (Cpl.)	German Valley Rural Cemetery	8th NJ Vol.	F
Barnes, Edward	Union Cemetery (Marcella in Rockaway Twp.)	4th WI Cavalry	C
Bartington, John	Rockaway Valley Methodist Cemetery	27th NJ Vol	C
Barton, Emanuel	Denville Cemetery	15th NJ Vol.	C
Barton, Luke	Denville Cemetery	2d DC Vol.	D
Barton, Paul	Denville Cemetery	26th NJ Vol.	D
Barton, William (US Navy)	Denville Cemetery	Mississipian Squadron	
Bastedo, Gideon	Union Cemetery (Marcella in Rockaway Twp.)	27th NJ Vol.	L

Name	Cemetery	Regiment	Company
Bastedo, Joseph H.	Parsippany Cemetery	3d NY Light Artillery	Bat. C
Bates, Edward	Zeek Cemetery (Marcella in Rockaway Twp.)	8th NJ Vol.	A
Batson, George D.	Stanhope Cemetery	2d NJ Vol.	C
Bay, James B.	Evergreen Cemetery (Morristown)	32d US Colored Troops	C
Bayles, George	Evergreen Cemetery (Morristown)	7th NJ Vol.	K
Bayles, Theodore	Evergreen Cemetery (Morristown)	7th NJ Vol.	K
Beach, Amzi	Evergreen Cemetery (Morristown)	27th NJ Vol.	I
Beach, Henry O.	Center Grove Methodist Cemetery (Randolph)	11th NJ Vol.	H
Beach, John	Rockaway Presbyterian Church Cemetery	11th NJ Vol.	A
Beach, John H.	Rockaway Presbyterian Church Cemetery	135th IN Vol.	H
Beach, Jonas	Rockaway Presbyterian Church Cemetery	15th NJ Vol.	E
Beach, Joshua	Rockaway Presbyterian Church Cemetery	11th NJ Vol.	E
Beach, Moses	Rockaway Presbyterian Church Cemetery	27th NJ Vol.	L
Beach, Robert N.	Hanover Road Cemetery (Hanover)	7th NJ Vol.	G
Beam, David	Middle Valley Cemetery (Washington Twp.)	27th NJ Vol.	C
Beam, John	Rockaway Presbyterian Church Cemetery	15th NJ Vol.	B
Beam, William H.	Evergreen Cemetery (Morristown)	4th NJ Light Artillery	
Beavers, George S. (Cpl. in Color Guard)	Hilltop Cemetery (Mendham)	15th NJ Vol.	A
Becker, William	Evergreen Cemetery (Morristown)	1st NJ Brigade Band	
Bedeu, William E.	New Vernon First Presbyterian Cemetery	27th NJ Vol.	I
Beers, Charles	Evergreen Cemetery (Morristown)	7th NJ Vol.	K
Beers, Jabez	Evergreen Cemetery (Morristown)	7th NJ Vol.	K
Beers, William W.	Evergreen Cemetery (Morristown)	15th NJ Vol.	C
Benjamin, Daniel	Greenwood Cemetery (Boonton)	2d DC Vol.	K
Bennett, Sedgwick	Orchard Street Cemetery (Dover)	27th NJ Vol.	A
Benson, Monmouth	Pleasant Hill Cemetery (Chester)	27th NJ Vol.	K
Bentley, James	Evergreen Cemetery (Morristown)	2d NJ Cavalry	C
Berry, Edward P. (Capt.)	Orchard Street Cemetery (Dover)	5th NJ Vol.	I
Berry, Joseph H.	Evergreen Cemetery (Morristown)	11th NJ Vol.	E
Berry, Moses	Hurdtown Methodist Cemetery (Jefferson)	7th NJ Vol.	K
Berry, Titus (1st Lt.)	Orchard Street Cemetery (Dover)	11th NJ Vol.	E
Bigelow, Jonathan	Newfoundland Methodist Church Cemetery (Jefferson)	69th NY Vol.	C
Birmingham, Charles	St. Mary's Cemetery (Wharton)	69th NY Vol.	A
Birney, David	German Valley Rural Cemetery	2d PA Artillery	E
Bishop, Edwin (Capt.)	Boonton Road Cemetery (Boonton)	2d NJ Vol.	H
Black, William	Stanhope Cemetery	5th PA Vol.	B
Blaine, William	First Congregational Church Cemetery (Chester)	27th NJ Vol.	C
Blanchard, George H.	New Vernon First Presbyterian Cemetery	3d NJ Vol.	I
Blanchard, Joseph (1st Lt.)	Evergreen Cemetery (Morristown)	1st NY Mounted Rifles	
Blanchard, Manning	Denville Cemetery	27th NJ Vol.	L
Blanchard, Theodore	Rockaway Presbyterian Church Cemetery	37th NJ Vol.	G
Blanchet, A. D. (Major)	St. Vincent's Cemetery (Madison)	27th NJ Vol.	E
Bloomer, Dennis	Hanover Road Cemetery (Hanover)	106th NY Vol.	B
Boggins, George	United Methodist Church (Montville)	70th NY Vol.	I
Bolden, William	St. Mary's Cemetery (Boonton)	1st NJ Light Artillery	Bat. A
Bond, Herbert T.	Boonton Road Cemetery (Boonton)	Unknown	
Bonnell, William	Mt. Freedom Methodist Cemetery	14th NJ Vol.	G
Bonner, David	Center Grove Methodist Cemetery (Randolph)	2d DC Vol.	K
Bonner, George	Succasunna Presbyterian/Methodist Cemetery	40th NJ Vol.	G
Bonsall, James	Rockaway Presbyterian Church Cemetery	1st NJ Militia	E
Booth, James	Evergreen Cemetery (Morristown)	27th NJ Vol.	I
Booth, Samuel	Orchard Street Cemetery (Dover)	1st NJ Cavalry	G
Boreland, Charles	Evergreen Cemetery (Morristown)	27th NJ Vol.	I
Boss, Jacob	Evergreen Cemetery (Morristown)	2nd NJ Vol.	B
Bostedo, Abner	Bostedo Cemetery (Rockaway Twp.)	27th NJ Vol.	L
Bowman, Joseph	Pleasant Grove Cemetery (Chester Twp.)	27th NJ Vol.	B
Bowman, William B.	Pleasant Grove Cemetery (Chester Twp.)	27th NJ Vol.	B

Name	Cemetery	Regiment	Company
Boyd, Thomas	Orchard Street Cemetery (Dover)	27th NJ Vol.	B
Boyd, William	Millbrook Methodist Church Cemetery (Randolph)	1st NY Vol.	A
Bragg, John	First Congregational Church Cemetery (Chester)	40th NJ Vol.	G
Braint, William	Evergreen Cemetery (Morristown)	7th NJ Vol.	K
Brannin, A. A.	Rockaway Presbyterian Church Cemetery	15th NJ Vol.	C
Brannin, James (Cpl.)	Millbrook Methodist Church Cemetery (Randolph)	11th NJ Vol.	E
Briant, Charles D.	Mt. Freedom Methodist Cemetery	104th PA Vol.	K
Briant, Wellington J.	Orchard Street Cemetery (Dover)	1st NY Engineers	K
Broadwell, Burtis	Orchard Street Cemetery (Dover)	5th NJ Vol.	D
Broadwell, Caleb	Orchard Street Cemetery (Dover)	39th NJ Vol.	K
Broadwell, Manning	Chatham Cemetery	27th NJ Vol.	E
Broadwell, Silas	Rockaway Presbyterian Church Cemetery	1st NJ Light Artillery	Bat. B
Broadwell, Stephen (Sgt.)	Orchard Street Cemetery (Dover)	39th NJ Vol.	K
Broadwell, William B.	Evergreen Cemetery (Morristown)	15th NJ Vol.	B
Brooks, Samuel H.	Center Grove Methodist Cemetery (Randolph)	1st NJ Vol.	A
Brown, Dennis	Boonton Road Cemetery (Boonton)	1st NJ Vol.	K
Brown, George H.	Stanhope Cemetery	27th NJ Vol.	K
Brown, James	Evergreen Cemetery (Morristown)	7th NJ Vol.	K
Brown, Samuel	Evergreen Cemetery (Morristown)	1st NJ Cavalry	D
Brown, Theodore	Evergreen Cemetery (Morristown)	37 NJ Vol.	B
Browning, William J.	Hillside Cemetery (Madison)	10th NJ Vol.	D
Bruen, E. V.	Hillside Cemetery (Madison)	7th NJ Vol.	C
Bruen, Elijah D.	Hillside Cemetery (Madison)	7th NJ Vol.	C
Bruen, James H.	Rockaway Presbyterian Church Cemetery	15th NJ Vol.	C
Bruen, Merritt (Lt.)	Hillside Cemetery (Madison)	7th NJ Vol.	E, K
Bruen, T. N.	Evergreen Cemetery (Morristown)	7th NJ Vol.	K
Buck, Charles W. (Cpl.)	Succasunna Presbyterian/Methodist Cemetery	11th NJ Vol.	H
Budd, Enos G. (1st Sgt.)	Mount Olive Baptist Church Cemetery	15th NJ Vol.	F
Burr, Joseph E.	First Congregational Church Cemetery (Chester)	37th NJ Vol.	E
Burrell, John T.	Orchard Street Cemetery (Dover)	1st NY Engineers	C
Bush, Garrett	Denville Cemetery	7th NJ Vol.	C
Butler, John H. (US Navy)	Orchard Street Cemetery (Dover)		
Callign, James	St. Mary's Cemetery (Wharton)	27th NJ Vol.	C
Carey, Daniel (Cpl.)	St. Mary's Cemetery (Boonton)	10th NJ Vol.	I
Carey, Patrick	Boonton Road Cemetery (Boonton)	1st NJ Vol.	K
Carhuff, Isaac	Succasunna Presbyterian/Methodist Cemetery	1st NJ Light Artillery	Bat. B
Carlisle, John	Pleasant Hill Cemetery (Chester)	15th NJ Vol.	F
Carllough, George (1st Sgt.)	Boonton Road Cemetery (Boonton)	27th NJ Vol.	G
Carman, Stephen	Boonton Road Cemetery (Boonton)	27th NJ Vol.	G
Carmichael, John (Bugler)	Evergreen Cemetery (Morristown)	2d NJ Cavalry	G
Carr, Sylvester	Rockaway Presbyterian Church Cemetery	1st NJ Cavalry	E
Carr, Thomas A.	St. Mary's Cemetery (Wharton)	29th NJ Vol.	I
Carrell, Charles H. (Sgt.)	Mt. Freedom Methodist Cemetery	2d NJ Vol.	B
Carrell, Uriah A.	Greenwood Cemetery (Boonton)	2d NY Cavalry	D
Carter, Elias H.	Hillside Cemetery (Madison)	27th NJ Vol.	E
Case, W. A.	Succasunna Presbyterian/Methodist Cemetery	15th NJ Vol.	I
Castmore, Charles K.	Old Headley Cemetery (Jefferson)	9th NJ Vol.	E
Castmore, Horace B.	Old Headley Cemetery (Jefferson)	2d NJ Cavalry	A
Castmore, Samuel	Old Headley Cemetery (Jefferson)	9th NJ Vol.	E
Chambre, Herbert B. (Assistant Surgeon)	Orchard Street Cemetery (Dover)	14th NJ Vol.	
Chandler, Cornelius W.	First Reformed Church (Pequannock)	47th NY Vol.	E
Cisco, Herman	Parsippany Cemetery	27th NJ Vol.	F
Clark, Isaac (Sgt.)	Mt. Freedom Methodist Cemetery	27th NJ Vol.	B
Clark, Nathaniel (Cpl.)	Center Grove Methodist Cemetery (Randolph)	26th NJ Vol.	H
Clawson, Jacob S.	German Valley Rural Cemetery	11th NJ Vol.	H
Clift, John A.	Evergreen Cemetery (Morristown)	15th NJ Vol.	C
Cole, C. M.	First Congregational Church Cemetery (Chester)	48th NY Vol.	D
Cole, J. C.	Oak Ridge Presbyterian Cemetery (Jefferson)	7th NJ Vol.	C

Name	Cemetery	Regiment	Company
Cole, Simon	Rockaway Presbyterian Church Cemetery	7th NJ Vol.	C
Cole, William	Succasunna Presbyterian/Methodist Cemetery	7th NJ Vol.	E
Collard, James	Union Cemetery (Marcella in Rockaway Twp.)	27th NJ Vol.	L
Condit, Alfred H. (Capt.)	Evergreen Cemetery (Morristown)	27th NJ Vol.	C
Conklin, Charles	Rockaway Valley Methodist Cemetery	2d DC Vol.	K
Conley, Owen J.	St. Mary's Cemetery (Wharton)	27th NJ Vol.	L
Conover, Martin	New Vernon First Presbyterian Cemetery	14th NJ Vol.	E
Conrad, Francis	Orchard Street Cemetery (Dover)	8th NJ Vol.	B
Cook, Asa T.	Rockaway Valley Methodist Cemetery	27th NJ Vol.	G
Cook, Charles Y.	Rockaway Presbyterian Church Cemetery	27th NJ Vol.	B
Cook, Cyrus E. (Sgt.)	Succasunna Presbyterian/Methodist Cemetery	1st NJ Cavalry	F
Cook, Judson	Succasunna Presbyterian/Methodist Cemetery	27th NJ Vol.	C
Cook, Lewis	Evergreen Cemetery (Morristown)	39th NJ Vol.	K
Cook, William H.	Rockaway Valley Methodist Cemetery	1st NJ Cavalry	K
Cool, Harvey S. (Col.)	German Valley Rural Cemetery	1st CT Artillery	E
Coons, Nathan	Evergreen Cemetery (Morristown)	8th NJ Vol.	
Cooper, David E.	Oak Ridge Presbyterian Cemetery (Jefferson)	27th NJ Vol.	B
Cooper, John	Evergreen Cemetery (Morristown)	32d US Colored Troops	D
Cooper, John K.	Locust Hill Cemetery (Dover)	2d NJ Cavalry	A
Cooper, Silas (Hospital Steward)	Evergreen Cemetery (Morristown)	7th NJ Vol.	
Cooper, Stephen A.	United Methodist Church (Montville)	27th NJ Vol.	G
Corbbett, Edward	Evergreen Cemetery (Morristown)	1st NY Engineers	K
Corby, Caleb	Millbrook Methodist Church Cemetery (Randolph)	39th NJ Vol.	K
Cornish, William W. H.	New Vernon First Presbyterian Cemetery	17th NY Vol.	D
Cory, Ira W. (Capt.)	Evergreen Cemetery (Morristown)	11th NJ Vol.	H
Courter, Daniel	Rockaway Presbyterian Church Cemetery	7th NJ Vol.	C
Courter, Henry	Boonton Road Cemetery (Boonton)	5th NJ Vol.	A
Courter, John	Rockaway Presbyterian Church Cemetery	8th NY Cavalry	E
Cox, John B. (Cpl.)	Orchard Street Cemetery (Dover)	2d NJ Vol.	B
Crampton, John	Locust Hill Cemetery (Dover)	26th NJ Vol.	I
Crampton, Joseph	Locust Hill Cemetery (Dover)	15th NJ Vol.	F
Crane, George	Quaker Church Cemetery (Randolph)	39th NJ Vol.	E
Crane, James H.	United Methodist Church (Montville)	1st NJ Vol.	K
Crane, John W. (Musician)	United Methodist Church (Montville)	27th NJ Vol.	G
Crane, L. M.	Chatham Cemetery	14th NJ Vol.	C
Crater, Dennis	Pleasant Hill Cemetery (Chester)	11th NJ Vol.	H
Crater, John P. (Capt.)	Evergreen Cemetery (Morristown)	15th NJ Vol.	K
Crawford, George	Greenwood Cemetery (Boonton)	1st NJ Vol.	K
Crayon, Joseph	Hill Cemetery (Denville)	4th NJ Light Artillery	
Creamer, Milton	Stanhope Cemetery	13th NJ Vol.	F
Crook, Samuel	Rockaway Presbyterian Church Cemetery	83d PA Cavalry	K
Crowell, William B.	Evergreen Cemetery (Morristown)	35th NJ Vol.	D
Culver, Lawrence	First Congregational Church Cemetery (Chester)	31st NJ Vol.	H
Cummings, George B.	United Methodist Church (Montville)	27th NJ Vol.	G
Cummings, Michael	St. Mary's Cemetery (Boonton)	27th NJ Vol.	G
Cyphers, Philip H.	Pleasant Grove Cemetery (Chester Twp.)	1st NJ Cavalry	M
Dabbs, John	Rockaway Presbyterian Church Cemetery	70th NY Vol.	D
Dalrymple, A. P. (Wagoner)	Mt. Freedom Methodist Cemetery	30th NJ Vol.	G
Dalrymple, H. M. (Lt.)	Evergreen Cemetery (Morristown)	1st NY Engineers	K
Darling, James	Evergreen Cemetery (Morristown)	31st US Colored Troops	A
Darragh, John K.	Greenwood Cemetery (Boonton)	27th NJ Vol.	G
Davenport, Charles	Succasunna Presbyterian/Methodist Cemetery	15th NJ Vol.	F
Davenport, Edward	Locust Hill Cemetery (Dover)	39th NJ Vol.	K
Davenport, Hudson	Succasunna Presbyterian/Methodist Cemetery	27th NJ Vol.	G
Davenport, William H.	Succasunna Presbyterian/Methodist Cemetery	1st NJ Cavalry	K
Davis, Charles	Evergreen Cemetery (Morristown)	7th NJ Vol.	K
Davis, Horatio H.	Rockaway Presbyterian Church Cemetery	30th NJ Vol.	H
Davis, Lewis (Cpl.)	Evergreen Cemetery (Morristown)	15th NJ Vol.	C
Davis, Rhinehardt	Berkshire Valley Presbyterian Cemetery (Jefferson)	39th NJ Vol.	K

Name	Cemetery	Regiment	Company
Davis, William	United Methodist Church (Montville)	26th NJ Vol.	D
Davis, William	Succasunna Presbyterian/Methodist Cemetery	27th NJ Vol.	K
Day, Ezra S.	Hilltop Cemetery (Mendham)	30th NJ Vol.	I
De Camp, John	Evergreen Cemetery (Morristown)	2d NJ Cavalry	G
De Camp, John C.	Pleasant Hill Cemetery (Chester)	48th NY Vol.	D
De Forrest, Amidee	John Hancock Cemetery (Florham Park)	9th NJ Vol.	E
De Groot, Edward P.	Evergreen Cemetery (Morristown)	2d NJ Cavalry	B
De Hart, Job	Mt. Freedom Methodist Cemetery	8th NJ Vol.	B
Dearborn, George (Surgeon)	Rockaway Presbyterian Church Cemetery	15th NJ Vol.	
Decamp, Edward T.	Succasunna Presbyterian/Methodist Cemetery	1st NY Engineers	K
Decker, George	St. Vincent's Cemetery (Madison)	8th NJ Vol.	A
Decker, Hudson	Rockaway Valley Methodist Cemetery	1st NJ Cavalry	E
Decker, William	Rockaway Valley Methodist Cemetery	1st NY Mounted Cavalry	K
Dee, John	First Congregational Church Cemetery (Chester)	15th NJ Vol.	F
Demouth, Cyrus	Rockaway Presbyterian Church Cemetery	27th NJ Vol.	L
Denman, John	Evergreen Cemetery (Morristown)	7th NJ Vol.	E
Denton, John L.	Hilltop Cemetery (Mendham)	7th NJ Vol.	K
Depew, Abraham	Evergreen Cemetery (Morristown)	26th NJ Vol.	E
Depoe, James H. (Cpl.)	Boonton Road Cemetery (Boonton)	39th NJ Vol.	K
Dickerson, Joseph	Denville Cemetery	2d NY Cavalry	A
Dilts, George S. (Surgeon)	Pleasant Grove Cemetery (Chester Twp.)	5th NY Heavy Artillery	
Dilts, John	Succasunna Presbyterian/Methodist Cemetery	31th NJ Vol.	C
Dixon, James	Pine Brook Methodist Church Cemetery	13th NJ Vol.	G
Dixon, Marcos	Parsippany Cemetery	13th NJ Vol.	G
Dobbins, Jeremiah	Evergreen Cemetery (Morristown)	1st NJ Light Artillery	Bat. B
Dodd, Willliam H.	United Methodist Church (Montville)	4th NY Cavalry	K
Doe, John	Evergreen Cemetery (Morristown)	1st NJ Light Artillery	E
Doering, John	Succasunna Presbyterian/Methodist Cemetery	38th NY Vol.	D
Dolan, Manning	Succasunna Presbyterian/Methodist Cemetery	65th NY Vol.	F
Doland, John	Quaker Church Cemetery (Randolph)	4th NY Vol.	E
Doland, Peter (Blacksmith)	Oak Ridge Presbyterian Cemetery (Jefferson)	1st NJ Cavalry	M
Dolson, Charles M.	First Reformed Church (Pequannock)	95th NY Vol.	H
Doremus, James H.	Montville Reformed Church Cemetery	27th NJ Vol.	G
Doty, Edwin	Evergreen Cemetery (Morristown)	15th NJ Vol.	C
Doty, Joseph	Evergreen Cemetery (Morristown)	1st NJ Cavalry	K
Douglas, Horace	Evergreen Cemetery (Morristown)	118th US Colored Troops	K
Downey, James W.	Holy Rood Cemetery (Morristown)	58th IN Vol.	F
Drake, George M.	Mt. Freedom Methodist Cemetery	26th NJ Vol.	C
Drennon, William	Old Catholic Cemetery (Boonton)	2d NJ Cavalry	F
Dukins, Charles	Stanhope Cemetery	15th NJ Vol.	H
Duncun, William	Evergreen Cemetery (Morristown)	24th US Colored Troops	C
Dunham, A. S.	Hillside Cemetery (Madison)	1st NJ Cavalry	H
Dunlap, James	Hilltop Cemetery (Mendham)	27th NJ Vol.	F
Dunster, George W.	Evergreen Cemetery (Morristown)	7th NJ Vol.	K
Dupell, David (Musician)	St. Mary's Cemetery (Boonton)	4th NJ Vol.	
Eackley, Lemuel (Cpl.)	Evergreen Cemetery (Morristown)	56 NY Vol.	C
Eagles, David	Millbrook Methodist Church Cemetery (Randolph)	27d NJ Vol.	B
Eagles, Isaac	Quaker Church Cemetery (Randolph)	1st NY Engineers	K
Earles, William	Rockaway Presbyterian Church Cemetery	3d NJ Vol.	D
Easton, Joseph	Rockaway Presbyterian Church Cemetery	US Navy	
Edwards, George W.	Locust Hill Cemetery (Dover)	102d NY Vol.	K
Edwards, John	Oak Ridge Presbyterian Cemetery (Jefferson)	9th NJ Vol.	H
Egan, Frank	Evergreen Cemetery (Morristown)	2d DC Vol.	K
Eldridge, John H.	Hillside Cemetery (Madison)	27th NJ Vol.	E
Ellicks, Samuel	New Vernon First Presbyterian Cemetery	1st NJ Vol.	K
Elmerdorf, Oliver	Orchard Street Cemetery (Dover)	2d NY Cavalry	K
Emery, John (Lt.)	Evergreen Cemetery (Morristown)	15th NJ Vol.	A
Emmel, Hayward C.	Morristown Presbyterian Cemetery	7th NJ Vol.	K
Emmons, William	Evergreen Cemetery (Morristown)	15th NJ Vol., Color Guard	F

Name	Cemetery	Regiment	Company
Emmott, William	Evergreen Cemetery (Morristown)	1st NJ Militia	E
Ennon, William (Com. Clerk)	St. Mary's Cemetery (Boonton)	1st NJ Vol.	K
Erb, Charles H. (Capt.)	St. Mary's Cemetery (Wharton)	9th NJ Vol.	E
Ervy, John N.	Locust Hill Cemetery (Dover)	27th NJ Vol.	K
Estelle, John H.	Parsippany Cemetery	29th NJ Vol.	K
Esten, George S. (1st Lt.)	Boonton Road Cemetery (Boonton)	27th NJ Vol.	G
Estille, Daniel	Parsippany Cemetery	15th NJ Vol.	C
Estille, John W.	Parsippany Cemetery	1st NJ Light Artillery	Bat. E
Etsell, Lewis	Evergreen Cemetery (Morristown)	27th NJ Vol.	E
Evans, James	Orchard Street Cemetery (Dover)	2d District Colored Vol.	
Evans, John D.	Evergreen Cemetery (Morristown)	11th NJ Vol.	C
Evens, George H.	Parsippany Cemetery	39th NJ Vol.	D
Everly, Stephen	Chatham Cemetery	26th NJ Vol.	C
Everman, John	Rockaway Presbyterian Church Cemetery	1st NJ Cavalry	M
Evermen, Hiram	Boonton Road Cemetery (Boonton)	15th NJ Vol.	K
Everts, Thomas	Boonton Road Cemetery (Boonton)	NJ Light Artillery	Bat. B
Fairchild, James	Evergreen Cemetery (Morristown)	13th NJ Vol.	E
Farlow, Thomas	Rockaway Presbyterian Church Cemetery	12th NH Vol.	G
Farr, Stewart A.	Orchard Street Cemetery (Dover)	71st NY Vol.	A
Ferris, J. D. (US Navy)	Hillside Cemetery (Madison)		
Finney, Patrick J.	St. Vincent's Cemetery (Madison)	7th NJ Vol.	K
Fitzgerald, Timothy	Holy Rood Cemetery (Morristown)	12th NJ Vol.	E
Foley, Jeremiah	St. Mary's Cemetery (Wharton)	15th NJ Vol.	F
Forbes, George	First Reformed Church (Pequannock)	27th NJ Vol.	C
Force, Corydon G.	Hillside Cemetery (Madison)	15th NJ Vol.	C
Force, Lewis (Musician)	Succasunna Presbyterian/Methodist Cemetery	27th NJ Vol.	C
Force, S. S.	Pleasant Grove Cemetery (Chester Twp.)	39th NJ Vol.	K
Ford, Amidee E.	Orchard Street Cemetery (Dover)	39th NJ Vol.	K
Ford, John W.	Orchard Street Cemetery (Dover)	11th NJ Militia	E
Ford, Marcus	Orchard Street Cemetery (Dover)	11th NJ Vol.	E
Ford, William F. (Sgt.)	Chatham Cemetery	9th NJ Vol.	K
Foster, Richard	Boonton Road Cemetery (Boonton)	1st NJ Vol.	K
Foster, Samuel	Rockaway Presbyterian Church Cemetery	9th NJ Vol.	A
Frace, Ezekiel A.	German Valley Rural Cemetery	27th NJ Vol.	B
Frederick, Charles	Evergreen Cemetery (Morristown)	15th NJ Vol.	C
Fredericks, George	Rockaway Presbyterian Church Cemetery	2nd NJ Vol.	A
Freedman, Edward	Locust Hill Cemetery (Dover)	2d NJ Cavalry	F
Freeman, Albert J.	Succasunna Presbyterian/Methodist Cemetery	11th NJ Vol.	A
Freeman, Amos G.	Succasunna Presbyterian/Methodist Cemetery	4th NJ Vol.	G
Freeman, Peter	Denville Cemetery	1st NJ Vol.	B
Fuller, James H.	Rockaway Presbyterian Church Cemetery	27th NJ Vol.	L
Gage, George	Orchard Street Cemetery (Dover)	NJ-PA Emergency Militia	E
Gage, Smith C.	Boonton Road Cemetery (Boonton)	15th NJ Vol.	C
Gaines, Stanley	Montville Reformed Church Cemetery	7th NJ Vol.	K
Gale, Robert	Evergreen Cemetery (Morristown)	27th NJ Vol.	E
Gannon, Solomon G.	Evergreen Cemetery (Morristown)	11th NJ Vol.	H
Gardner, David	Greenwood Cemetery (Boonton)	27th NJ Vol.	D
Gardner, Warren	Succasunna Presbyterian/Methodist Cemetery	4th RI Vol.	K
Garland, Preston (US Navy)	Evergreen Cemetery (Morristown)		
Garrabrant, Charles Z.	Rockaway Presbyterian Church Cemetery	28th NJ Vol.	F
Garrabrant, John	Rockaway Presbyterian Church Cemetery	39th NJ Vol.	B
Garrison, J. F.	Hillside Cemetery (Madison)	27th NJ Vol.	E
Garrison, Menzies	Hillside Cemetery (Madison)	9th NJ Vol.	B
Garrison, Theodore	Hillside Cemetery (Madison)	27th NJ Vol.	E
Gaston, Thomas C.	Hilltop Cemetery (Mendham)	15th NJ Vol.	H
Geary, Williams	Greenwood Cemetery (Boonton)	1st NJ Vol.	K
Geddis, George (Cpl.)	First Congregational Church Cemetery (Chester)	15th NJ Vol.	F
Gillen, Leonard V. (Cpl.)	Orchard Street Cemetery (Dover)	11th NJ Vol.	E
Gillespie, Samuel	Mount Olive Baptist Church Cemetery	33d NJ Vol.	K

Name	Cemetery	Regiment	Company
Gillig, George A.	Succasunna Presbyterian/Methodist Cemetery	1st NJ Militia	E
Goarch, William S.	Locust Hill Cemetery (Dover)	11th NJ Vol.	H
Goble, Charles H.	New Vernon Cemetery	1st NJ Light Artillery	Bat. E
Goble, Chilleon	New Vernon First Presbyterian Cemetery	27th NJ Vol.	I
Goble, Nicholas M.	New Vernon First Presbyterian Cemetery	27th NJ Vol.	I
Gordon, Abraham	Boonton Road Cemetery (Boonton)	27th NJ Vol.	C
Gordon, Isaac	Hillside Cemetery (Madison)		
Gordon, Samuel	Greenwood Cemetery (Boonton)	72d NY Infantry	F
Grant, William	Rockaway Presbyterian Church Cemetery	11th NJ Vol.	F
Green, Robert	Boonton Road Cemetery (Boonton)	1st NJ-PA Emergency Militia	E
Greer, Charles	Evergreen Cemetery (Morristown)	32d US Colored Troops	C
Gregory, Lewis	Evergreen Cemetery (Morristown)	15th NJ Vol.	E
Griffith, Ebenezer	Hanover Road Cemetery (Hanover)	10th NJ Vol.	D
Griffith, Nathan R. (1st. Sgt.)	Succasunna Presbyterian/Methodist Cemetery	14th CT Vol.	F
Grill, Moore	Locust Hill Cemetery (Dover)	27th NJ Vol.	F
Grimes, John	Parsippany Cemetery	15th NJ Vol.	C
Gruenwald, Otto	Greenwood Cemetery (Boonton)	68th NY Infantry	D
Guerin, Charles (Sgt.)	Evergreen Cemetery (Morristown)	15th NJ Vol.	C
Guerin, Orland K.	Evergreen Cemetery (Morristown)	7th NJ Vol.	K
Guest, Isaac	Locust Hill Cemetery (Dover)	30th NJ Vol.	A
Guest, Jacob	German Valley Rural Cemetery	15th NJ Vol.	F
Gusick, John	St. Mary's Cemetery (Boonton)	7th NJ Vol.	C
Gustin, John,	Rockaway Presbyterian Church Cemetery	1st NJ Cavalry	E
Haines, Aaron W. (Cpl.)	New Vernon First Presbyterian Cemetery	23th NJ Vol.	E
Haines, William H.	New Vernon First Presbyterian Cemetery	27th NJ Vol.	I
Haler, David	Mount Olive Baptist Church Cemetery	39th NJ Vol.	A
Haley, John H.	New Vernon Cemetery	7th NJ Vol.	K
Haley, Patrick	St. Joseph's Cemetery (Mendham)	1st NJ Vol.	K
Hall, Barnabas K.	Rockaway Presbyterian Church Cemetery	27th NJ Vol.	L
Hall, Edwin (Sgt.)	Locust Hill Cemetery (Dover)	7th NJ Vol.	C
Hall, Enoch W.	Rockaway Presbyterian Church Cemetery	71th NY Vol.	H
Hall, Ephraim F.	Locust Hill Cemetery (Dover)	1st NJ Vol.	K
Hall, George	Rockaway Presbyterian Church Cemetery	15th NJ Vol.	F
Hall, John	Rockaway Presbyterian Church Cemetery	15th NJ Vol.	F
Hall, John H.	Rockaway Presbyterian Church Cemetery	7th NJ Vol.	C
Hall, Stephen D.	Rockaway Valley Methodist Cemetery	7th NJ Vol.	C
Halsey, Andrew C.	Morristown Presbyterian Cemetery	7th NJ Vol.	K
Halsey, Edmund (Adjutant)	Rockaway Presbyterian Church Cemetery	15th NJ Vol.	
Halsey, Thomas J. (Major)	Orchard Street Cemetery (Dover)	11th NJ Vol.	
Halstead, David W.	Newfoundland Methodist Church Cem. (Jefferson)	15th NJ Vol.	K
Halstead, William	Evergreen Cemetery (Morristown)	1st NJ Militia	E
Hamilton, John	Orchard Street Cemetery (Dover)	27th NJ Vol.	L
Hamler, William	Succasunna Presbyterian/Methodist Cemetery	9th NJ Vol.	K
Hamma, Elijah (Cpl.)	Boonton Road Cemetery (Boonton)	27th NJ Vol.	G
Hamms, William	Montville Reformed Church Cemetery	30th NJ Vol.	I
Hand, Charles	St. Vincent's Cemetery (Madison)	18th NY Cavalry	H
Hankinson, James	First Congregational Church Cemetery (Chester)	6th NJ Vol.	B
Hankinson, John	Rockaway Presbyterian Church Cemetery	27th NJ Vol.	D
Hannaka, Augustus	St. Mary's Cemetery (Wharton)	2d NJ Vol.	F
Hannas, Lucius P.	Evergreen Cemetery (Morristown)	27th NJ Vol.	I
Hanville, Alvah W.	New Vernon First Presbyterian Cemetery	1st NY Engineers	K
Harris, Abram	Rockaway Presbyterian Church Cemetery	13th NJ	D
Harris, Abram (Musician)	Rockaway Presbyterian Church Cemetery	30th NJ Vol.	H
Harris, John	Succasunna Presbyterian/Methodist Cemetery	15th NJ Vol.	A
Harrison, Moses	Hanover Presbyterian Church Cemetery	13th NJ Vol.	D
Hart, Ira D.	Hillside Cemetery (Madison)	1st NJ Cavalry	G
Hart, Nicholas	Rockaway Presbyterian Church Cemetery	15th NJ Vol.	G
Hathaway, James H.	New Vernon First Presbyterian Cemetery	15th NJ Vol.	C
Hathaway, William	Evergreen Cemetery (Morristown)	27th NJ Vol.	I

Name	Cemetery	Regiment	Company
Hawkins, Zeno	Rockaway Presbyterian Church Cemetery	15th NJ Vol.	F
Haynes, John	Evergreen Cemetery (Morristown)	7th NJ Vol.	C
Headland, Thomas	Locust Hill Cemetery (Dover)	1st NJ Vol.	B
Headley, J. Boyd	Evergreen Cemetery (Morristown)	3d NJ Cavalry	G
Health, Sylvester	Locust Hill Cemetery (Dover)	8th NJ Vol.	H
Heath, Samuel	Evergreen Cemetery (Morristown)	15th NJ Vol.	B
Hedden, Alonzo	Succasunna Presbyterian/Methodist Cemetery	15th NJ Vol.	F
Helm, James	John Hancock Cemetery (Florham Park)	26th NJ Vol.	C
Heminover, John T.	Union Cemetery (Marcella in Rockaway Twp.)	3d NJ Cavalry	E
Heminover, William	Union Cemetery (Marcella in Rockaway Twp.)	1st NJ Cavalry	G
Hempstead, John C.	Evergreen Cemetery (Morristown)	27th NJ Vol.	I
Henderson, Aaron	Union Cemetery (Marcella in Rockaway Twp.)	8th NJ Vol.	A
Henderson, Matthias	Union Cemetery (Marcella in Rockaway Twp.)	11th NJ Vol.	E
Henderson, Peter	Union Cemetery (Marcella in Rockaway Twp.)	11th NJ Vol.	E
Henderson, Samuel	Union Cemetery (Marcella in Rockaway Twp.)	8th NJ Vol.	A
Henry, John H.	Denville Cemetery	5th NY Veteran Corps.	F
Hessey, George (Musician)	Boonton Road Cemetery (Boonton)	7th NJ Vol.	
Hessey, William (Chief Bugler)	Evergreen Cemetery (Morristown)	2nd NJ Cavalry	
Hewitt, Gideon K.	Quaker Church Cemetery (Randolph)	16th NY Vol.	E
Hiler, Samuel	Rockaway Presbyterian Church Cemetery	1st NJ Cavalry	E
Hill, Henry	Greenwood Cemetery (Boonton)	27th NJ Vol.	G
Hillis, Joshua	Boonton Road Cemetery (Boonton)	27th NJ Vol.	G
Hockenbury, Andrew	Rockaway Presbyterian Church Cemetery	27th NJ Vol.	B
Hodgson, William	Evergreen Cemetery (Morristown)	27th NJ Vol.	I
Hoffman, Abraham H.	Pleasant Grove Cemetery (Chester Twp.)	8th NJ Vol.	H
Hoffman, Frederick	Hanover Road Cemetery (Hanover)	1st NJ Light Artillery	Bat. A
Hoffman, Lemuel H.	Pleasant Grove Cemetery (Chester Twp.)	27th NJ Vol.	B
Holland, James	Evergreen Cemetery (Morristown)	41st US Colored Troops	F
Holley, Joseph W.	Oak Ridge Presbyterian Cemetery (Jefferson)	1st NJ Cavalry	K
Holmes, Franklin (US Navy)	Boonton Road Cemetery (Boonton)		
Holmes, William	Succasunna Presbyterian/Methodist Cemetery	39th NJ Vol.	K
Honeyman, Nevins	New Vernon First Presbyterian Cemetery	3d NJ Cavalry	B
Hopkins, Charles	Greenwood Cemetery (Boonton)	1st NJ Vol.	A
Hopkins, John	Union Cemetery (Marcella in Rockaway Twp.)	27th NJ Vol.	I
Hopler, Alexander	German Valley Rural Cemetery	2d NJ Cavalry	A
Hopler, Alfred B.	Boonton Road Cemetery (Boonton)	15th NJ Vol.	C
Hopper, Abraham P.	Oak Ridge Presbyterian Cemetery (Jefferson)	1st NJ Cavalry	K
Hoppings, Augustus Stiles	Hanover Presbyterian Church Cemetery	15th NJ Vol.	C
Housel, Jacob	Orchard Street Cemetery (Dover)	15th NJ Vol.	H
Howard, James	Pine Brook Methodist Church Cemetery	26th NJ Vol.	H
Howell, Caleb	First Congregational Church Cemetery (Chester)	48th NY Vol.	D
Howell, Caleb H.	Pleasant Hill Cemetery (Chester)	48th NY Vol.	D
Howell, William	Rockaway Presbyterian Church Cemetery	27th NJ Vol.	L
Hugler, William H.	Stanhope Cemetery	27th NJ Vol.	K
Hull, Charles	Rockaway Presbyterian Church Cemetery	5th NJ Vol.	D
Hull, George	Rockaway Presbyterian Church Cemetery	7th NJ Vol.	C
Hulmes, Frederick	Rockaway Presbyterian Church Cemetery	27th NJ Vol.	L
Hurlings, Charles	Hillside Cemetery (Madison)	US Colored Troops	
Hurton, Horrace	Hillside Cemetery (Madison)	1st NY Engineers	E
Husk, William	Montville Reformed Church Cemetery	27th NJ Vol.	G
Hyland, William H. (Cpl.)	St. Vincent's Cemetery (Madison)	27th NJ Vol.	E
Hyler, Richard	Montville Reformed Church Cemetery	27th NJ Vol.	G
Hyler, Thomas	Union Cemetery (Marcella in Rockaway Twp.)	8th NJ Vol.	A
Ike, Albert F.	Stanhope Cemetery	27th NJ Vol.	D
Ingle, James M.	Pleasant Hill Cemetery (Chester)	15th NJ Vol.	F
Jackley, Joseph	Evergreen Cemetery (Morristown)	26th NJ Vol.	D
Jackson, Benjamin B.	Succasunna Presbyterian/Methodist Cemetery	27th NJ Vol.	C
Jackson, John	Montville Reformed Church Cemetery	32d US Colored Troops	C
Jackson, Joseph	Montville Reformed Church Cemetery	32d US Colored Troops	F

Civil War Veteran Grave Sites

Name	Cemetery	Regiment	Company
Jackson, Moses	Evergreen Cemetery (Morristown)	1st US Colored Troops	E
Jackson, Philip (Sgt.)	Montville Reformed Church Cemetery	32d US Colored Troops	H
Jackson, Theodore	Evergreen Cemetery (Morristown)	32d US Colored Troops	E
Jackson, Thomas	Evergreen Cemetery (Morristown)	26th NJ Vol.	D
Jacobus, Abraham R.	United Methodist Church (Montville)	27th NJ Vol.	G
Jacobus, John U.	United Methodist Church (Montville)	27th NJ Vol.	G
Jayne, Joseph	Rockaway Presbyterian Church Cemetery	61st NY Vol.	B
Jennings, John D.	Orchard Street Cemetery (Dover)	9th NJ Vol.	E
Johnson, A. L.	Evergreen Cemetery (Morristown)	15th NJ Vol.	C
Johnson, Charles E.	Rockaway Valley Methodist Cemetery	7th NJ Vol.	K
Johnson, John	Middle Valley Cemetery (Washington Twp.)	27th NJ Vol.	B
Johnson, Manuel	Evergreen Cemetery (Morristown)	15th NJ Vol.	C
Johnson, Pierson	Succasunna Presbyterian/Methodist Cemetery	7th NJ Vol.	B
Johnson, William	Greenwood Cemetery (Boonton)	2d NJ Vol.	I
Jolley, Edward S.	Evergreen Cemetery (Morristown)	27th NJ Vol.	I
Jones, Joseph W.	Succasunna Presbyterian/Methodist Cemetery	27th NJ Vol.	C
Kain, Peter (Sgt.)	Holy Rood Cemetery (Morristown)	7th NJ Vol.	K
Kanouse, Henry	Rockaway Valley Methodist Cemetery	27th NJ Vol.	L
Kayhart, H.	Pine Brook Methodist Church Cemetery	27th NJ Vol.	G
Keeler, George W.	Evergreen Cemetery (Morristown)	3d NJ Vol. (3 months)	H
Keeler, Philip M.	Evergreen Cemetery (Morristown)	3d NJ Cavalry	I
Kemble, Zenas	New Vernon First Presbyterian Cemetery	43d US Colored Troops	G
Kent, John T.	Evergreen Cemetery (Morristown)	7th NJ Vol.; 33d NJ Vol.	K, D
Kiem, John	Stanhope Cemetery	35st NJ Vol.	K
King, George (Capt.)	First Congregational Church Cemetery (Chester)	15th NJ Vol.	F
King, Joseph	Rockaway Presbyterian Church Cemetery	15th NJ Vol.	C
King, Patrick	St. Mary's Cemetery (Wharton)	11th NJ Vol.	H
King, Thomas (Sgt.)	Succasunna Presbyterian/Methodist Cemetery	27th NJ Vol.	C
Kingard, Thomas	Rockaway Valley Methodist Cemetery	214th NY Vol.	K
Kingsland, Abram	Boonton Road Cemetery (Boonton)	2d DC Vol.	K
Kinney, Edward (Sgt.)	Orchard Street Cemetery (Dover)	11th NJ Vol.	E
Kinney, Jacob	Rockaway Presbyterian Church Cemetery	8th NJ Vol.	A
Kinsler, Frederick	Locust Hill Cemetery (Dover)	33th NJ Vol.	H
Kirkpatrick, Samuel	Boonton Road Cemetery (Boonton)	2d NJ Vol.	K
Kitcham, Jacob	Evergreen Cemetery (Morristown)	40th NY Vol.	C
Kitchell, Edward E.	United Methodist Church (Montville)	15th NJ Vol.	H
Kitchell, Samuel	Rockaway Presbyterian Church Cemetery	7th NJ Vol.	K
Kitchell, Warren (1st Lt.)	Evergreen Cemetery (Morristown)	33d NJ Vol.	I
Kitchum, William W.	Mt. Freedom Methodist Cemetery	61st NY Vol.	H
Knapp, Benjamin	Hillside Cemetery (Madison)	27th NJ Vol.	C
Knott, Daniel	Boonton Road Cemetery (Boonton)	1st NJ Vol.	K
Kronmiller, John B.	German Valley Rural Cemetery	27th NJ Vol.	B
Kuth, Anton	Old Catholic Cemetery (Boonton)	2d NJ Vol.	D
Lambert, William H.	Locust Hill Cemetery (Dover)	1st NJ Cavalry	E
Lance, David C.	New Vernon First Presbyterian Cemetery	15th NJ Vol.	F
Lance, George A.	German Valley Rural Cemetery	2d NJ Cavalry	M
Langdon, Foster	Evergreen Cemetery (Morristown)	15th NJ Vol.	B
Larrison, John (Sgt.)	Pleasant Hill Cemetery (Chester)	15th NJ Vol.	F
Lawler, Thomas	Evergreen Cemetery (Morristown)	12th NH Vol.	G
Lawrence, George	Evergreen Cemetery (Morristown)	27th NJ Vol.	B
Lawrence, John	Orchard Street Cemetery (Dover)	1st NJ Cavalry	B
Lawrence, Nathanial C.	Millbrook Methodist Church Cemetery (Randolph)	27d NJ Vol.	B
Layson, Henry	Orchard Street Cemetery (Dover)	2d DC Vol.	K
Leitze, John G.	St. Mary's Cemetery (Wharton)	1st NJ Vol.	I
Lemons, John	Hilltop Cemetery (Mendham)	3d NJ Cavalry	B
Leonard, Silas	Pine Brook Methodist Church Cemetery	15th NJ Vol.	E
Leonard, Silas	Evergreen Cemetery (Morristown)	15th NJ Vol.	E
Leport, George	Succasunna Presbyterian/Methodist Cemetery	27th NJ Vol.	C
Lewis, Charles	Evergreen Cemetery (Morristown)	24 US Colored Troops	B

Name	Cemetery	Regiment	Company
Lewis, Charles M.	Evergreen Cemetery (Morristown)	15th NJ Vol.	C
Lindsley, Ira (Capt.)	Evergreen Cemetery (Morristown)	15th NJ Vol.	C
Lindsley, Philip	New Vernon Cemetery	1st NJ Light Artillery	Bat. B
Lish, John D.	German Valley Rural Cemetery	2d NJ Cavalry	C
List, James	Berkshire Valley Presbyterian Cemetery (Jefferson)	25th NJ Vol.	E
Lockwood, William	Pine Brook Methodist Church Cemetery	27th NJ Vol.	E
Logan, Charles B.	Succasunna Presbyterian/Methodist Cemetery	14th NJ Vol.	H
Logan, Dorastus P. (Capt.)	Succasunna Presbyterian/Methodist Cemetery	11th NJ Vol.	H
Loree, Charles C.	Evergreen Cemetery (Morristown)	27th NJ Vol.	I
Losere, Philip (US Navy)	Greenwood Cemetery (Boonton)		
Losey, George Dallas	Mt. Freedom Methodist Cemetery	27th NJ Vol.	B
Losey, James	Evergreen Cemetery (Morristown)	27th NJ Vol.	B
Lousbury, William (US Navy)	Evergreen Cemetery (Morristown)		
Love, Andrew	Orchard Street Cemetery (Dover)	1st NJ Cavalry	A
Love, George	Orchard Street Cemetery (Dover)	9th NJ Vol.	E
Lowry, Lewis	Rockaway Presbyterian Church Cemetery	11th NJ Vol.	E
Lum, Israel D. (Color Sgt.)	Chatham Cemetery	15th NJ Vol.	C
Lum, William H.	Chatham Cemetery	35th NJ Vol.	A
Lunger, Abraham	First Congregational Church Cemetery (Chester)	7th NJ Vol.	E
Lunger, Isaac	Rockaway Presbyterian Church Cemetery	15th NJ Vol.	H
Lynch, Thomas	St. Mary's Cemetery (Wharton)	33d NJ Vol.	D
Lynn, Sylvester L. (Sgt.)	Hilltop Cemetery (Mendham)	7th NJ Vol.	C
Lyons, Albert	Rockaway Presbyterian Church Cemetery	11th NJ	E
Lyons, William	Evergreen Cemetery (Morristown)	37th NJ Vol.	G
Madden, Patrick	St. Mary's Cemetery (Boonton)	5th NH Vol.	F
Mansfield, David H.	Hillside Cemetery (Madison)	54th NY Vol.	H
Mansfield, John W.	Holy Rood Cemetery (Morristown)	7th NJ Vol.	E
Marsh, Edward	Rockaway Presbyterian Church Cemetery	38th NY Vol.	E
Marsh, Theodore	Rockaway Presbyterian Church Cemetery	1st NJ Light Artillery	Bat. B
Marshall, Henry	Rockaway Valley Methodist Cemetery	60th NY Vol.	D
Martin, Freeman	Greenwood Cemetery (Boonton)	4th NY Cavalry	K
Massacker, John	Parsippany Cemetery	25th NJ Vol.	C
Massaker, A. D.	Quaker Church Cemetery (Randolph)	67th NY Vol.	C
Mast, Frederick	Succasunna Presbyterian/Methodist Cemetery	20th NY Vol.	I
Mattoon, R. D.	Parsippany Cemetery	1st NJ Light Artillery	Bat. B
Mattox, Jacob	Evergreen Cemetery (Morristown)	15th NJ Vol.	C
Mattox, Samuel	Rockaway Presbyterian Church Cemetery	1st NJ Vol.	K
Maxton, James L.	Rockaway Presbyterian Church Cemetery	9th PA Vol.	E
Mc Laughlin, Henry (Lt.)	Rockaway Presbyterian Church Cemetery	27th NJ Vol.	C
Mc Nair, Robert W.	Boonton Road Cemetery (Boonton)	2d NJ Vol.	H
McCartney, Andrew	Montville Reformed Church Cemetery	124th NY Vol.	F
McComb, William	Evergreen Cemetery (Morristown)	2d NJ Cavalry	C
McCormick, William N. (Chaplain)	Locust Hill Cemetery (Dover)	1st NJ Vol.	
McDavitt, James (Sgt.)	Orchard Street Cemetery (Dover)	11th NJ Vol.	E
McDonald, John	Greenwood Cemetery (Boonton)	2d NY Cavalry	A
McDonald, William	First Congregational Church Cemetery (Chester)	4th MI	F
McDougal, Alfred	Succasunna Presbyterian/Methodist Cemetery	40th NJ Vol.	G
McDougal, Wesley	Succasunna Presbyterian/Methodist Cemetery	1st NJ Light Artillery	Bat. B
McDougal, William	Succasunna Presbyterian/Methodist Cemetery	28th NY Vol.	D
McDowell, George	Evergreen Cemetery (Morristown)	27th NJ Vol.	I
McEmore, D. G. (Lt.)	Hillside Cemetery (Madison)	27th NJ Vol.	E
McGee, Samuel	Whippany Cemetery	27th NJ Vol.	E
McGowan, Robert	Evergreen Cemetery (Morristown)	15th NJ Vol.	C
McGrill, John H.	Mount Olive Baptist Church Cemetery	15th NJ Vol.	F
McKain, John R.	Mount Olive Baptist Church Cemetery	15th NJ Vol.	F
McKay, Simon	Parsippany Cemetery	27th NJ Vol.	K
McKee, George C.	Evergreen Cemetery (Morristown)	2d NJ Vol.	B
McKee, William	Evergreen Cemetery (Morristown)	7th NJ Vol.	K

Name	Cemetery	Regiment	Company
McKinney, John (Lt.)	Boonton Road Cemetery (Boonton)	72d NY Vol.	F
McNacy, Henry	Holy Rood Cemetery (Morristown)	5th NJ Vol.	F
McNair, Robert W.	Boonton Road Cemetery (Boonton)	2d NJ Vol.	H
McNair, Samuel	Boonton Road Cemetery (Boonton)	1st NY Engineers	
McPeek, David S.	Succasunna Presbyterian/Methodist Cemetery	7th NJ Vol.	F
McPeek, William J.	Parsippany Cemetery	26th NJ Vol.	D
Meeker, Garnet B. (1st Lt.)	Hanover Road Cemetery (Hanover)	2d NJ Cavalry	G
Meeker, Marcus (Cpl.)	Succasunna Presbyterian/Methodist Cemetery	27th NJ Vol.	C
Meeker, Samuel	Evergreen Cemetery (Morristown)	15th NJ Vol.	F
Merchant, Frank M. (Sgt.)	Mt. Freedom Methodist Cemetery	27th NJ Vol.	B
Merritt, Alonzo M. (2d Lt.)	Rockaway Presbyterian Church Cemetery	11th NJ Vol.	A
Merritt, Edwin	Rockaway Presbyterian Church Cemetery	27th NJ Vol.	B
Meslar, Jonathan (Wagoner)	John Hancock Cemetery (Florham Park)	3d NJ Vol.	I
Messenger, John H.	Orchard Street Cemetery (Dover)	124th NY Vol.	B
Meyers, Charles	Boonton Road Cemetery (Boonton)	8th NJ Vol.	A
Millburn, John W.	Succasunna Presbyterian/Methodist Cemetery	31th NJ Vol.	G
Millburn, Joseph P.	Succasunna Presbyterian/Methodist Cemetery	15th NJ Vol.	E
Millen, George H. (2d Lt.)	Hilltop Cemetery (Mendham)	7th NJ Vol.	K
Miller, Barnabas	Rockaway Presbyterian Church Cemetery	27th NJ Vol.	L
Miller, Cornelius H.	Rockaway Valley Methodist Cemetery	15th NJ Vol.	K
Miller, Garrett	First Reformed Church (Pequannock)	33d NJ Vol.	D
Miller, George	Evergreen Cemetery (Morristown)	33d NJ Vol.	B
Miller, James	Rockaway Presbyterian Church Cemetery	27th NJ Vol.	B
Miller, Orra	Rockaway Presbyterian Church Cemetery	33d NJ Vol.	
Mills, Charles	Orchard Street Cemetery (Dover)	2d DC Vol.	K
Mills, James	Whippany Cemetery	15th NJ Vol.	C
Mills, John	Quaker Church Cemetery (Randolph)	1st NY Engineers	K
Mills, Mahlon T.	First Congregational Church Cemetery (Chester)	39th NJ Vol.	K
Mingo, Charles C. (Sgt.)	Mt. Freedom Methodist Cemetery	27th NJ Vol.	B
Minsterman, Joseph	Millbrook Methodist Church Cemetery (Randolph)	7th NJ Vol.	E
Minton, William	Evergreen Cemetery (Morristown)	11th NJ Vol.	E
Mitchell, David	Locust Hill Cemetery (Dover)	40th NJ Vol.	F
Mitchell, Thomas	Rockaway Presbyterian Church Cemetery	15th NJ Vol.	B
Mitchell, William	Rockaway Presbyterian Church Cemetery	27th NJ Vol.	L
Monice, Stansil O.	Succasunna Presbyterian/Methodist Cemetery	11th NJ Vol.	E
Moore, David	Locust Hill Cemetery (Dover)	15th NJ Vol.	I
Moore, Farrington P.	Quaker Church Cemetery (Randolph)	31th NJ Vol.	B
Moore, James	Pleasant Hill Cemetery (Chester)	27th NJ Vol.	B
Moore, John	Denville Cemetery	39th NJ Vol.	K
Moore, Patrick	Holy Rood Cemetery (Morristown)	2d NJ Cavalry	F
Moore, Peter	Pleasant Grove Cemetery (Chester Twp.)	27th NJ Vol.	K
Moore, Samuel	Evergreen Cemetery (Morristown)	27th NJ Vol.	I
Moore, William	Evergreen Cemetery (Morristown)	27th NJ Vol.	I
Moorehouse, David	Evergreen Cemetery (Morristown)	26th NJ Vol.	D
Mooreland, William H.	Evergreen Cemetery (Morristown)	27th NJ Vol.	I
Morgan, Abraham	Hanover Road Cemetery (Hanover)	15th NJ Vol.	E
Morgan, Amos	Pleasant Grove Cemetery (Chester Twp.)	4th NJ Vol.	H
Morgan, Byrnes	St. Cecilia Cemetery (Rockaway)	1st NY Cavalry	M
Morgan, Daniel	Rockaway Presbyterian Church Cemetery	15th NJ Vol.	F
Morgan, Garreti	Boonton Road Cemetery (Boonton)	1st NJ Light Artillery	Bat. B
Morgan, George	Boonton Road Cemetery (Boonton)	27th NJ Vol.	G
Morgan, John	Boonton Road Cemetery (Boonton)	27th NJ Vol.	G
Morgan, John	Rockaway Presbyterian Church Cemetery	27th NJ Vol.	L
Morgan, Walter	Rockaway Presbyterian Church Cemetery	26th NJ Vol.	A
Morris, Jared	Hilltop Cemetery (Mendham)	27th NJ Vol.	E
Morrison, George	Boonton Road Cemetery (Boonton)	2d NJ Vol.	H
Morrison, John	Locust Hill Cemetery (Dover)	39th NJ Vol.	K
Morse, Abraham	Locust Hill Cemetery (Dover)	2d NJ Cavalry	A
Morse, Samuel	Orchard Street Cemetery (Dover)	11th NJ Vol.	E

Name	Cemetery	Regiment	Company
Moses, William W.	John Hancock Cemetery (Florham Park)	7th NJ Vol.	B
Mott, G. B.	Evergreen Cemetery (Morristown)	7th NJ Vol.	K
Mott, Theodore	Rockaway Presbyterian Church Cemetery	27th NJ Vol.	B
Mount, Theodore	Whippany Cemetery	46th NY Vol.	H
Mount, William	Whippany Cemetery	1st NY Engineers	H
Muchmore, Fred	Evergreen Cemetery (Morristown)	27th NJ Vol.	B
Muir, William (Lt.)	St. Mary's Cemetery (Boonton)	1st NJ Vol.	K
Mulford, Amos	Parsippany Cemetery	27th NJ Vol.	E
Munn, Charles	Boonton Road Cemetery (Boonton)	1st NJ Vol.	K
Munn, Isaac	Pleasant Grove Cemetery (Chester Twp.)	2d NJ Cavalry	E
Murphy, George	Locust Hill Cemetery (Dover)	11th NJ Vol.	H
Murray, Timothy	Succasunna Presbyterian/Methodist Cemetery	38th NY Vol.	D
Naughright, Williams	German Valley Rural Cemetery	31st NJ Vol.	E
Nicholas, Elias B.	Hilltop Cemetery (Mendham)	15th NJ Vol.	B
Nichols, Josiah J.	Orchard Street Cemetery (Dover)	39th NJ Vol.	K
Nix, Calvin	Rockaway Valley Methodist Cemetery	7th NJ Vol.	K
Nix, George	Rockaway Valley Methodist Cemetery	4th NJ Vol.	F
Nixon, Samuel J.	Evergreen Cemetery (Morristown)	1st NJ Vol.	A
Norris, Charles	Boonton Road Cemetery (Boonton)	33d NJ Vol.	C
Norton, Benjamin	Locust Hill Cemetery (Dover)	7th NJ Vol.	K
Nunn, Alfred C.	German Valley Rural Cemetery	27th NJ Vol.	B
Nunn, James	German Valley Rural Cemetery	27th NJ Vol.	B
Nunn, Samuel	German Valley Rural Cemetery	27th NJ Vol.	B
Nunnenmaker, Jacob	Hillside Cemetery (Madison)	15th NY Heavy Artillery	E
Ockobuck, William	Rockaway Valley Methodist Cemetery	27th NJ Vol.	C
O'Donnell, John W.	Holy Rood Cemetery (Morristown)	2d NJ Vol.	B
Olmstead, Silas H.	Millbrook Methodist Church Cemetery (Randolph)	39th NJ Vol.	K
Onderdonk, James B.	First Reformed Church (Pequannock)	1st NJ Light Artillery	Bat. B
Ort, William H.	Pleasant Grove Cemetery (Chester Twp.)	27th NJ Vol.	B
Owens, Bartley	Evergreen Cemetery (Morristown)	11th NJ Vol.	H
Owens, Frederick (Surgeon)	Evergreen Cemetery (Morristown)	38th NY Vol.	
Palmer, Bartholomew	Rockaway Presbyterian Church Cemetery	7th NJ Vol.	F
Palmer, James	Rockaway Presbyterian Church Cemetery	15th NJ Vol.	A
Palmer, William H.	New Vernon First Presbyterian Cemetery	2d NJ Cavalry	B
Parker, John E. (2d Lt.)	Evergreen Cemetery (Morristown)	1st NJ Militia	E
Parker, Obadiah	Locust Hill Cemetery (Dover)	27th NJ Vol.	C
Parks, Robert M.	First Congregational Church Cemetery (Chester)	30th NJ Vol.	I
Parliament, John	Mount Olive Baptist Church Cemetery	15th NJ Vol.	F
Parsons, Charles O.	Millbrook Methodist Church Cemetery (Randolph)	31st NJ Vol.	H
Parsons, Henry	Mt. Freedom Methodist Cemetery	39th NJ Vol.	K
Paul, David	Evergreen Cemetery (Morristown)	27th NJ Vol.	I
Peer, Calvin	John P. Cooks Cemetery (Denville)	27th NJ Vol.	L
Peer, George	John P. Cooks Cemetery (Denville)	7th NJ Vol.	K
Peer, George W.	John P. Cooks Cemetery (Denville)	7th NJ Vol.	K
Peer, Jacob	Greenwood Cemetery (Boonton)	2d DC Vol.	D
Peer, Peter	Denville Cemetery	27th NJ Vol.	C
Peer, Theodore	Denville Cemetery	10th NJ Vol.	A
Pepper, Patrick	Succasunna Presbyterian/Methodist Cemetery	27th NJ Vol.	C
Peterson, George (US Navy)	Boonton Road Cemetery (Boonton)		
Pettinger, A. V.	Stanhope Cemetery	27th NJ Vol.	K
Pettit, Charles (Musician)	Pine Brook Methodist Church Cemetery	33d NJ Vol.	F
Pettit, Sydney (Cpl.)	Pine Brook Methodist Church Cemetery	33d NJ Vol.	F
Pevey, John H.	Boonton Road Cemetery (Boonton)	51st NY Vol.	F
Phelan, John	Holy Rood Cemetery (Morristown)	14th NJ Vol.	K
Philhower, John	Succasunna Presbyterian/Methodist Cemetery	30th NJ Vol.	A
Pier, John	Pine Brook Methodist Church Cemetery	26th NJ Vol.	D
Pierce, William H.	Stanhope Cemetery	27th NJ Vol.	D
Pierson, Allen H.	Evergreen Cemetery (Morristown)	7th NJ Vol.	K
Pierson, George	Mt. Freedom Methodist Cemetery	38th NJ Vol.	F

Name	Cemetery	Regiment	Company
Pierson, Henry W.	John Hancock Cemetery (Florham Park)	14th NJ Vol.	C
Pierson, Mactby G.	Evergreen Cemetery (Morristown)	139th NY Vol.	D
Pierson, Stephen	Locust Hill Cemetery (Dover)	27th NJ Vol.	C
Pierson, Stephen (Adjutant)	Morristown Presbyterian Cemetery	33d NJ Vol.	
Pittenger, John	Boonton Road Cemetery (Boonton)	1st NJ Light Artillery	Bat. B
Pollard, David (2d Lt.)	Parsippany Cemetery	1st NJ Light Artillery	Bat. D
Pollard, Thompson	Parsippany Cemetery	1st NJ Light Artillery	Bat. D
Post, George	Union Cemetery (Marcella in Rockaway Twp.)	12th NJ Vol.	C
Post, Horace W.	Oak Ridge Presbyterian Cemetery (Jefferson)	7th NJ Vol.	C
Potts, John G.	Center Grove Methodist Cemetery (Randolph)	84th NY Vol.	B
Potts, William	New Vernon First Presbyterian Cemetery	11th NJ Vol.	H
Powers, Sopher (Sgt.)	Succasunna Presbyterian/Methodist Cemetery	7th NJ Vol.	B
Powers, Thomas	Locust Hill Cemetery (Dover)	33th NJ Vol.	E
Powers, William	Greenwood Cemetery (Boonton)	31th NJ Vol.	D
Price, George	Orchard Street Cemetery (Dover)	30th NJ Vol.	A
Price, Joseph	Evergreen Cemetery (Morristown)	9th NJ Vol.	E
Proudfit, Robert (Chaplain)	Evergreen Cemetery (Morristown)	10th NJ Vol.	
Pruden, Amos	Evergreen Cemetery (Morristown)	27th NJ Vol.	I
Pruden, Charles H.	Succasunna Presbyterian/Methodist Cemetery	27th NJ Vol.	C
Pruden, Edmund W.	Evergreen Cemetery (Morristown)	27th NJ Vol.	I
Pruden, Isaac	Center Grove Methodist Cemetery (Randolph)	7th NJ Vol.	K
Pruden, Timothy K.	Evergreen Cemetery (Morristown)	11th NJ Vol.	H
Pursell, Peter	Montville Reformed Church Cemetery	31th NJ Vol.	C
Quacko, John	Evergreen Cemetery (Morristown)	25th US Colored Troops	G
Ramsey, Allen H. (Musician)	Boonton Road Cemetery (Boonton)	33d NJ Vol.	G
Rareck, William H.	Succasunna Presbyterian/Methodist Cemetery	15th NJ Vol.	F
Ray, George	Evergreen Cemetery (Morristown)	27th NJ Vol.	B
Recario, John	Evergreen Cemetery (Morristown)	7th NJ Vol.	C,K
Reed, Jacob B.	Mt. Freedom Methodist Cemetery	2d NJ Cavalry	
Reed, John T.	Mt. Freedom Methodist Cemetery	5th NY Artillery	C
Reed, William	Parsippany Cemetery	31th NJ Vol.	A
Reger, Edwin H.	Succasunna Presbyterian/Methodist Cemetery	15th NJ Vol.	C
Reger, Elisha E.	Succasunna Presbyterian/Methodist Cemetery	27th NJ Vol.	C
Reid, George R.	First Congregational Church Cemetery (Chester)	15th NJ Vol.	F
Reil, Nicholas W.	Hilltop Cemetery (Mendham)	30th NJ Vol.	I
Renkel, William	Pleasant Hill Cemetery (Chester)	27th NJ Vol.	K
Revere, Joseph Warren (Brig. Gen.)	Holy Rood Cemetery (Morristown)	NY Excelsior Brigade	
Rickley, Edward (Cook)	Evergreen Cemetery (Morristown)	23d US Infantry	
Rickley, William	Evergreen Cemetery (Morristown)	27th NJ Vol.	E
Ridge, John J.	Evergreen Cemetery (Morristown)	5th NJ Vol.	D
Rigby, John (1st Lt.)	Montville Reformed Church Cemetery	51st NY Vol.	C
Rigby, Matthew C.	Montville Reformed Church Cemetery	70th NY Vol.	D
Rigey, Evan	Boonton Road Cemetery (Boonton)	1st NJ Light Artillery	Bat. B
Riker, Lewis B.	Boonton Road Cemetery (Boonton)	23d MI Vol.	B
Riley, Andrew	Pleasant Grove Cemetery (Chester Twp.)	31st NJ Vol.	B
Riley, Bernard	St. Mary's Cemetery (Boonton)	1st NJ Vol.	K
Roach, Jacob	Parsippany Cemetery	5th NJ Vol.	A
Robare, Joseph	Old Catholic Cemetery (Boonton)	11th NJ Vol.	H
Robare, Louis	Old Catholic Cemetery (Boonton)	27th NJ Vol.	G
Rockwell, Edgar	Rockaway Presbyterian Church Cemetery	33d NJ Vol.	C
Rodgers, Daniel	Rockaway Presbyterian Church Cemetery	1st NJ Cavalry	K
Roff, Elias	Center Grove Methodist Cemetery (Randolph)	35th NJ Vol.	E
Roff, Elias	Evergreen Cemetery (Morristown)	35th NJ Vol.	E
Rogers, Peter F. (Capt.)	Hanover Road Cemetery (Hanover)	39th NJ Vol.	E
Rolph, Aaron	Pleasant Grove Cemetery (Chester Twp.)	27th NJ Vol.	I
Romine, Richard	Berkshire Valley Presbyterian Cemetery (Jefferson)	15th NY Cavalry	L
Rood, Edson W. (1st Lt.)	Hilltop Cemetery (Mendham)	30th NJ Vol.	K
Rose, John	Rockaway Presbyterian Church Cemetery	27th NJ Vol.	K

Name	Cemetery	Regiment	Company
Ross, Francis (US Navy)	Hillside Cemetery (Madison)		
Ryan, James	St. Vincent's Cemetery (Madison)	37th NY Cavalry	D
Salmon, Andrew F.	Mount Olive Baptist Church Cemetery	15th NJ Vol.	F
Salmon, Augustus W.	Mount Olive Baptist Church Cemetery	27th NJ Vol.	C
Salmon, Henry	Greenwood Cemetery (Boonton)	27th NJ Vol.	C
Sands, Hiram (Musician)	Berkshire Valley Presbyterian Cemetery (Jefferson)	15th NJ Vol.	B
Sawyer, Abraham	Old Catholic Cemetery (Boonton)	15th NJ Vol.	C
Schaaf, Michael	Old Catholic Cemetery (Boonton)	27th NJ Vol.	E
Schaff, Michael	Locust Grove Cemetery (Dover)	27th NJ Vol.	E
Schofield, Edward	Evergreen Cemetery (Morristown)	9th NJ Vol.	H
Scofield, Erastus H. (Cpl.)	First Reformed Church (Pequannock)	33d NJ Vol.	F
Scribner, William	Zeek Cemetery (Marcella in Rockaway Twp.)	27th NJ Vol.	L
Scudder, Joseph (Wagoner)	Millbrook Methodist Church Cemetery (Randolph)	9th NJ Vol.	F
Scudder, Theodore	First Congregational Church Cemetery (Chester)	48th NY Vol.	D
Scudder, Thomas	Stanhope Cemetery	27th NJ Vol.	I
Seals, Zacheriah	Evergreen Cemetery (Morristown)	15th NJ Vol.	B
Searing, Alonzo B.	Millbrook Methodist Church Cemetery (Randolph)	11th NJ Vol.	E
Searing, W. H.	Orchard Street Cemetery (Dover)	27th NJ Vol.	K
Seatz, Ferdinand	Evergreen Cemetery (Morristown)	4th NJ Vol.	D
Sequine, James	Pleasant Grove Cemetery (Chester Twp.)	27th NJ Vol.	B
Sharp, Elijah	Center Grove Methodist Cemetery (Randolph)	3d NJ Vol.	D
Sharp, Samuel	Locust Hill Cemetery (Dover)	39th NJ Vol.	K
Shaw, James	Union Cemetery (Marcella in Rockaway Twp.)	27th NJ Vol.	L
Shaw, John	Boonton Road Cemetery (Boonton)	56th NY Vol.	D
Shawger, Abraham	Rockaway Presbyterian Church Cemetery	8th NJ Vol.	A
Shawger, Columbus	Union Cemetery (Marcella in Rockaway Twp.)	11th NJ Vol.	E
Shawger, John	Rockaway Presbyterian Church Cemetery	27th NJ Vol.	B
Shawger, Lewis	Union Cemetery (Marcella in Rockaway Twp.)	51st NY Vol.	F
Sheeran, James (Chaplain, CSA)	Holy Rood Cemetery (Morristown)	14th LA (Confederate)	
Sheridan, Michael	Locust Grove Cemetery (Dover)	27th NJ Vol.	E
Sheridan, Patrick	Old Catholic Cemetery (Boonton)	27th NJ Vol.	E
Sherkee, E. S.	Hillside Cemetery (Madison)	27th NJ Vol.	E
Shoenheitt, Louis R.	German Valley Rural Cemetery	5th NJ Vol.	H
Shupe, William	Succasunna Presbyterian/Methodist Cemetery	1st NJ Light Artillery	Bat. A
Sickle, Mahlon T.	Rockaway Presbyterian Church Cemetery	1st NJ Light Artillery	Bat. B
Silsee, Thompson	Succasunna Presbyterian/Methodist Cemetery	1st NY Engineers	K
Simpson, James H. (Capt.)	Orchard Street Cemetery (Dover)	15th NJ Vol.	I
Skellinger, E. L.	First Congregational Church Cemetery (Chester)	26th NJ Vol.	B
Skellinger, Phineas (Sgt.)	First Congregational Church Cemetery (Chester)	15th NJ Vol.	F
Skillhorn, George W.	Mt. Freedom Methodist Cemetery	1st NY Engineers	K
Skinner, Abraham	Succasunna Presbyterian/Methodist Cemetery	27th NJ Vol.	C
Slockbower, George	Stanhope Cemetery	33d NJ Vol.	C
Smith, Andrew R.	Stanhope Cemetery	3d NJ Cavalry	B
Smith, Elijah	Boonton Road Cemetery (Boonton)	1st NJ Light Artillery	Bat. B
Smith, Henry	Old Walnut Grove Baptist Cemetery (Randolph)	7th NY Vol.	K
Smith, Hudson	Union Cemetery (Marcella in Rockaway Twp.)	1st NJ Cavalry	E
Smith, James	Rockaway Presbyterian Church Cemetery	11th NJ	E
Smith, John R.	Holy Rood Cemetery (Morristown)	11th NJ Vol.	E
Smith, Joseph	Denville Cemetery	2d DC Vol.	
Smith, Mahlon	Rockaway Presbyterian Church Cemetery	35th NJ Vol.	A
Smith, Peter (Capt.)	Evergreen Cemetery (Morristown)	144 NY Vol.	H
Smith, Samuel	German Valley Rural Cemetery	27th NJ Vol.	B
Smith, Stephen	Greenwood Cemetery (Boonton)	1st NJ Vol.	G
Smith, Theodore	Evergreen Cemetery (Morristown)	7th NJ Vol.	K
Smith, Thomas	Rockaway Presbyterian Church Cemetery	27th NJ Vol.	F
Smith, William F.	St. Mary's Cemetery (Wharton)	5th NJ Vol.	E
Snyder, George	Succasunna Presbyterian/Methodist Cemetery	34th NJ Vol.	G
Snyder, George	Evergreen Cemetery (Morristown)	1st NJ Light Artillery	Bat. B
Sowers, Abraham	Mount Olive Baptist Church Cemetery	2d NJ Vol.	F

Name	Cemetery	Regiment	Company
Spear, George	John P. Cooks Cemetery (Denville)	34th NJ Vol.	E
Speer, John	John P. Cooks Cemetery (Denville)	27th NJ Vol.	L
Spencer, Charles	Stanhope Cemetery	27th NJ Vol.	K
Spenser, William	Succasunna Presbyterian/Methodist Cemetery	10th US Infantry	K
Sperry, Zaddock	Hurdtown Methodist Cemetery (Jefferson)	11th NJ Vol.	E
Springer, Augustus	Evergreen Cemetery (Morristown)	2d NY Vol.	D
Springstein, Charles	Whippany Cemetery	14th NJ Vol.	G
Squier, Charles	Hanover Road Cemetery (Hanover)	1st NJ Light Artillery	Bat. B
Stackhouse, Frank	Rockaway Presbyterian Church Cemetery	3d NJ Cavalry	A
Stage, John H.	Locust Hill Cemetery (Dover)	48th NY Vol.	E
Stalter, John	Union Cemetery (Marcella in Rockaway Twp.)	11th NJ Vol.	H
Starr, Frederick	Rockaway Presbyterian Church Cemetery	15th NJ Vol.	F
Steelman, Isaac	Center Grove Methodist Cemetery (Randolph)	7th NJ Vol.	K
Stephens, Amos	Mount Olive Baptist Church Cemetery	27th NJ Vol.	G
Stephens, Charles	Mount Olive Baptist Church Cemetery	27th NJ Vol.	C
Stevens, Charles	Evergreen Cemetery (Morristown)	2d NJ Vol.	B
Stevenson, Albert	Boonton Road Cemetery (Boonton)	1st NJ Light Artillery	Bat. B
Stevenson, Alonzo	Boonton Road Cemetery (Boonton)	5th NY Artillery	
Stevenson, Joseph	Boonton Road Cemetery (Boonton)	1st NJ Light Artillery	Bat. B
Stickle, Abraham	Rockaway Presbyterian Church Cemetery	11th NJ	D
Stickle, Daniel T.	Chatham Cemetery	1st NJ Vol.	H
Stickle, James	Rockaway Presbyterian Church Cemetery	33d NJ Vol.	F
Stickle, John	Rockaway Presbyterian Church Cemetery	2nd NJ Vol.	B
Stickle, Mahlon	Rockaway Presbyterian Church Cemetery	1st NJ Light Artillery	Bat. B
Stites, Lemuel	Locust Hill Cemetery (Dover)	35th NJ Vol.	H
Stone, Charles	Center Grove Methodist Cemetery (Randolph)	10th NJ Vol.	I
Stone, Charles (1st Lt.)	Rockaway Presbyterian Church Cemetery	10th NJ Vol.	I
Stork, John	Mount Olive Baptist Church Cemetery	15th NJ Vol.	F
Storms, William	United Methodist Church (Montville)	15th NJ Vol.	C
Straway, William H.	Locust Hill Cemetery (Dover)	11th NJ Vol.	H
Struble, Elias	Locust Hill Cemetery (Dover)	2d NJ Cavalry	F
Struble, Horace R.	Stanhope Cemetery	3d NJ Vol.	D
Struble, Peter	Evergreen Cemetery (Morristown)	27th NJ Vol.	D
Struble, William H.	Evergreen Cemetery (Morristown)	2d NY Heavy Artillery	C
Stuart, Peter	Succasunna Presbyterian/Methodist Cemetery	27th NJ Vol.	C
Sturdevant, Epithalet (Sgt.)	Rockaway Presbyterian Church Cemetery	11th NJ	E
Sturges, H. T.	Hillside Cemetery (Madison)	90th NY Vol.	H
Sturtevant, Henry	Rockaway Presbyterian Church Cemetery	84th OH Vol.	A
Sullivan, Cornelius	Old Catholic Cemetery (Boonton)	5th MD Vol.	F
Sutton, Aaron W.	Pleasant Grove Cemetery (Chester Twp.)	11th NJ Vol.	B
Sweazey, Wesley	German Valley Rural Cemetery	2d NJ Cavalry	B
Sweeney, James	Holy Rood Cemetery (Morristown)	11th NJ Vol.	H
Sweeney, John	Succasunna Presbyterian/Methodist Cemetery	7th NJ Vol.	H
Sweet, George	Rockaway Presbyterian Church Cemetery	7th NJ Vol.	C
Tallman, Jacob J.	Oak Ridge Presbyterian Cemetery (Jefferson)	27th NJ Vol.	B
Talmadge, Absolom	Rockaway Presbyterian Church Cemetery	11th NJ Vol.	E
Talmadge, Cyrus	Rockaway Presbyterian Church Cemetery	11th NJ	E
Talmadge, George H.	Hillside Cemetery (Madison)	40th NY Vol.	D
Tappen, A. T. (Cpl.)	Hanover Road Cemetery (Hanover)	27th NJ Vol.	I
Taylor, Henry	Greenwood Cemetery (Boonton)	67th NY Vol.	G
Taylor, William	Greenwood Cemetery (Boonton)	1st NJ Vol.	A
Teets, Joseph	Pleasant Hill Cemetery (Chester)	1st NJ Cavalry	D
Teneyck, John	Rockaway Presbyterian Church Cemetery	27th NJ Vol.	L
Thompson, Chilleon	John P. Cooks Cemetery (Denville)	7th NJ Vol.	C
Thompson, John	Rockaway Presbyterian Church Cemetery	1st NJ Cavalry	E
Thompson, John G.	Evergreen Cemetery (Morristown)	15th NJ Vol.	C
Thompson, Robert R. (Chaplain)	Oak Ridge Presbyterian Cemetery (Jefferson)	5th NY Cavalry	
Thompson, William	Rockaway Presbyterian Church Cemetery	7th NJ Vol.	K
Thorpe, Philip (Cpl.)	Succasunna Presbyterian/Methodist Cemetery	31th NJ Vol.	A

Name	Cemetery	Regiment	Company
Tiballs, George (Musician)	Greenwood Cemetery (Boonton)	4th NJ Vol.	G
Tichenor, Moses	Parsippany Cemetery	1st NJ Light Artillery	Bat. B
Till, William	John P. Cooks Cemetery (Denville)	7th NJ Vol.	K
Tobin, James (Cpl.)	Locust Hill Cemetery (Dover)	10th NJ Vol.	C
Todd, Silas (Sgt.)	Greenwood Cemetery (Boonton)	11th NJ Vol.	H
Toombs, Edward C.	John Hancock Cemetery (Florham Park)	2d IA Vol.	D
Topping, William (US Navy)	Rockaway Presbyterian Church Cemetery		
Totten, David	Hillside Cemetery (Madison)	27th NJ Vol.	B
Totten, Stephen Y.	New Vernon First Presbyterian Cemetery	11th NJ Vol.	A
Townsend, John J.	Mount Olive Baptist Church Cemetery	3d NJ Cavalry	B
Trelease, Elitah	Parsippany Cemetery	1st NJ Vol.	B
Trelease, George W.	Parsippany Cemetery	15th NJ Vol.	C
Trimmer, Asa	Middle Valley Cemetery (Washington Twp.)	2d NJ Cavalry	C
Trimmer, George S.	Pleasant Grove Cemetery (Chester Twp.)	27th NJ Vol.	C
Trowbridge, David	Mt. Freedom Methodist Cemetery	27th NJ Vol.	B
Trowbridge, Edward Y.	Millbrook Methodist Church Cemetery (Randolph)	39th NJ Vol.	E
Trowbridge, Ferdinand	Evergreen Cemetery (Morristown)	15th NJ Vol.	H
Troxell, Eugene	Evergreen Cemetery (Morristown)	26th NJ Vol.	H
Truax, James	Evergreen Cemetery (Morristown)	52d US Colored Troops	H
Tucker, Charles	Rockaway Valley Methodist Cemetery	7th NJ Vol.	K
Tucker, Elias	Rockaway Valley Methodist Cemetery	1st NJ Light Artillery	Bat. B
Tucker, John	Demouth Cemetery (Boonton Twp.)	1st NJ Vol.	K
Tuers, Andrew	Rockaway Presbyterian Church Cemetery	27th NJ Vol.	L
Tuesh, William L. (Musician)	Boonton Road Cemetery (Boonton)	4th NJ Vol.	
Tull, Jonathan K. (Carpenter's Mate, US Navy)	New Vernon First Presbyterian Cemetery		
Tunis, Nehemia (Brevet Major)	Evergreen Cemetery (Morristown)	15th NJ Vol.	D
Tuttle, Daniel D.	Millbrook Methodist Church Cemetery (Randolph)	27d NJ Vol.	B
Tuttle, William	Rockaway Presbyterian Church Cemetery	11th NJ Vol.	H
Valentine, William E.	Evergreen Cemetery (Morristown)	7th NJ Vol.	C
Van Burskirk, John	Greenwood Cemetery (Boonton)	33d NJ Vol.	D
Van Doran, Isaac	New Vernon First Presbyterian Cemetery	4th NJ Vol.	D
Van Duyne, Eliah	Rockaway Valley Methodist Cemetery	2d NJ Vol.	H
Van Dyke, Joseph M.	Mount Olive Baptist Church Cemetery	2d NJ Vol.	C
Van Dyne, Henry G.	United Methodist Church (Montville)	27th NJ Vol.	G
Van Fleet, Conrad (Wagoner)	John Hancock Cemetery (Florham Park)	8th NJ Vol.	A
Van Houton, George	Evergreen Cemetery (Morristown)	1st NJ Militia	E
Van Orden, Anthony	Rockaway Presbyterian Church Cemetery	27th NJ Vol.	L
Van Orden, David	Hurdtown Methodist Cemetery (Jefferson)	25th NJ Vol.	K
Van Orden, Ira	Denville Cemetery	7th NJ Vol.	C
Van Orden, Peter	Cuff Cemetery (Newfoundland in Jefferson)	25th NJ Vol.	E
Van Winkle, Jacob	Rockaway Presbyterian Church Cemetery	27th NJ Vol.	L
Vanderbilt, John	Rockaway Presbyterian Church Cemetery	27th NJ Vol.	L
Vanderhoof, David	John P. Cooks Cemetery (Denville)	7th NJ Vol.	C
Vanderhoof, Garrett	Locust Hill Cemetery (Dover)	27th NJ Vol.	F
Vanderhoof, George	Rockaway Valley Methodist Cemetery	7th NJ Vol.	C
Vanderhoof, George	Locust Hill Cemetery (Dover)	1st NY Engineers	K
Vanderhoof, Richard	Rockaway Presbyterian Church Cemetery	11th NY Cavalry	A
Vandonia, Alexandria (Musician)	John Hancock Cemetery (Florham Park)	27th NJ Vol.	E
Vanness, Henry (Cpl.)	First Reformed Church (Pequannock)	27th NJ Vol.	C
Vanness, John	Rockaway Presbyterian Church Cemetery	1st NJ Light Artillery	Bat. B
Vaughn, James	United Methodist Church (Montville)	1st NJ Light Artillery	B
Vaughn, John	United Methodist Church (Montville)	1st NJ Light Artillery	B
Vincent, George	Evergreen Cemetery (Morristown)	26th NJ Vol.	H
Voorhees, Edward	Evergreen Cemetery (Morristown)	1st NJ Militia	E
Voorhees, Edward	Evergreen Cemetery (Morristown)	39th NJ Vol.	G
Voorhees, George	Evergreen Cemetery (Morristown)	29th US Colored Troops	F

Name	Cemetery	Regiment	Company
Vreeland, Cornelius	United Methodist Church (Montville)	22d NJ Vol.	C
Vreeland, Joseph	Pine Brook Methodist Church Cemetery	27th NJ Vol.	E
Waddell, Andrew C.	Parsippany Cemetery	14th IL Vol. Cavalry	M
Waer, Amzi	Rockaway Presbyterian Church Cemetery	1st NJ Cavalry	E
Waer, Wallace J.	Locust Hill Cemetery (Dover)	7th NJ Vol.	B
Waer, William	Rockaway Presbyterian Church Cemetery	39th NJ Vol.	E
Walker, Henry (Maj. Gen., CSA)	Evergreen Cemetery (Morristown)	40th VA (Confederate)	
Walsh, James	St. Vincent's Cemetery (Madison)	27th NJ Vol.	E
Walsh, John	St. Vincent's Cemetery (Madison)	27th NJ Vol.	E
Ward, A. S.	Stanhope Cemetery	27th NJ Vol.	K
Ward, John	Stanhope Cemetery	27th NJ Vol.	K
Ward, Lewis	Rockaway Presbyterian Church Cemetery	27th NJ Vol.	L
Ward, Marcus	Millbrook Methodist Church Cemetery (Randolph)	US Colored Troops	
Ward, Richard	Chatham Cemetery	13th NJ Vol.	D
Ward, Stephen (Drummer)	Rockaway Presbyterian Church Cemetery	22d NY Vol.	H
Wardell, George	Greenwood Cemetery (Boonton)	1st NJ Vol.	C
Waters, John	Hillside Cemetery (Madison)	14th NJ Vol.	C
Watkins, Joseph S. (Cpl.)	Hilltop Cemetery (Mendham)	7th NJ Vol.	K
Wear, Lyman M.	Orchard Street Cemetery (Dover)	30th NJ Vol.	C
Weaver, Henry	Rockaway Presbyterian Church Cemetery	8th NJ Vol.	A
Weir, Wilmot	Evergreen Cemetery (Morristown)	27th NJ Vol.	I
Weise, Lawrence	German Valley Rural Cemetery	15th NJ Vol.	F
Wemarse, Edward	Rockaway Valley Methodist Cemetery	11th CT Vol.	C
West, Jacob	Evergreen Cemetery (Morristown)	24th US Colored Troops	C
Wheeler, Emory A.	Mt. Freedom Methodist Cemetery	3d NJ Vol.	D
Wheeler, G. F.	Stanhope Cemetery	31st NJ Vol.	C
Whighton, Robert	Orchard Street Cemetery (Dover)	NJ-PA Emergency Militia	E
Whitehead, Francis L.	Morristown Presbyterian Cemetery	2d NJ Cavalry	H
Whitehead, Henry	Rockaway Presbyterian Church Cemetery	39th NJ Vol.	K
Whitehead, John	Berkshire Valley Presbyterian Cemetery (Jefferson)	7th NJ Vol.	F
Whitenlock, Haliman	New Vernon First Presbyterian Cemetery	27th NJ Vol.	I
Whitenlock, Peter W.	New Vernon First Presbyterian Cemetery	27th NJ Vol.	I
Whitenlock, Samuel E.	New Vernon First Presbyterian Cemetery	27th NJ Vol.	I
Whitham, Robert	Rockaway Presbyterian Church Cemetery	15th NJ Vol.	C
Whitmore, Jacob	Succasunna Presbyterian/Methodist Cemetery	9th NJ Vol.	E
Whitmore, William	Succasunna Presbyterian/Methodist Cemetery	27th NJ Vol.	K
Whitten, William	Pine Brook Methodist Church Cemetery	27th NJ Vol.	G
Williams, Lyman	Hillside Cemetery (Madison)	1st NJ Light Artillery	Bat B
Williams, Nichols	Orchard Street Cemetery (Dover)	5th OH Cavalry	M
Williamson, John	Mount Olive Baptist Church Cemetery	15th NJ Vol.	F
Williamson, Martin	Succasunna Presbyterian/Methodist Cemetery	27th NJ Vol.	C
Willson, John L.	Hillside Cemetery (Madison)	50th PA Vol.	E
Wilson, Henry	Orchard Street Cemetery (Dover)	30th NJ Vol.	A
Wilson, John	Rockaway Presbyterian Church Cemetery	11th NJ	E
Winart, Peter L.	Orchard Street Cemetery (Dover)	29th PA Vol.	D
Winget, Charles	Rockaway Presbyterian Church Cemetery	27th NJ Vol.	L
Wintermute, John W.	Succasunna Presbyterian/Methodist Cemetery	31th NJ Vol.	G
Winters, Jacob	Newfoundland Methodist Church Cem. (Jefferson)	1st NJ Cavalry	M
Wise, Andrew	German Valley Rural Cemetery	4th Calif.	F
Wolfe, Ferninand	Succasunna Presbyterian/Methodist Cemetery	27th NJ Vol.	K
Wolfe, George H.	Mt. Freedom Methodist Cemetery	27th NJ Vol.	B
Wolfe, John B.	Evergreen Cemetery (Morristown)	30th NJ Vol.	B
Wolfe, Theodore E.	Succasunna Presbyterian/Methodist Cemetery	11th NJ Vol.	H
Wood, L. C.	Hillside Cemetery (Madison)	27th NJ Vol.	E
Woodruff, George S.	Hilltop Cemetery (Mendham)	30th NJ Vol.	A
Woodruff, Henry C.	Hilltop Cemetery (Mendham)	11th NJ Vol.	H
Woodruff, James H.	Hilltop Cemetery (Mendham)	11th NJ Vol.	H
Woodruff, William	Stanhope Cemetery	15th NJ Vol.	I

Name	Cemetery	Regiment	Company
Voorhees, Jacob G. (Commissary Sgt.)	Parsippany Cemetery	3d NJ Vol.	E
Woods, Hiram	Locust Hill Cemetery (Dover)	39th NJ Vol.	K
Wright, Clark A.	German Valley Rural Cemetery	2d NY Cavalry	A
Wright, George A.	Succasunna Presbyterian/Methodist Cemetery	28th NJ Vol.	F
Wright, George A.	Succasunna Presbyterian/Methodist Cemetery	7th NJ Vol.	F
Wright, James O.	Center Grove Methodist Cemetery (Randolph)	39th NJ Vol.	K
Wright, John	Old Walnut Grove Baptist Cemetery (Randolph)	11th NJ Vol.	H
Wright, John	Center Grove Methodist Cemetery (Randolph)	1st NY Engineers	K
Yatman, John N.	Mt. Freedom Methodist Cemetery	27th NJ Vol.	G
Youmans, James	Rockaway Presbyterian Church Cemetery	11th NJ	E
Young, David (1st Sgt.)	Orchard Street Cemetery (Dover)	170th NY Vol.	E
Young, Ira W.	Mt. Freedom Methodist Cemetery	27th NJ Vol.	B
Young, John N. (Sgt.)	Succasunna Presbyterian/Methodist Cemetery	39th NJ Vol.	K
Youngblood, Charles	Evergreen Cemetery (Morristown)	27th NJ Vol.	E
Youngblood, James	Evergreen Cemetery (Morristown)	1st NJ Militia	E
Zeek, Edwin	Rockaway Presbyterian Church Cemetery	1st NJ Cavalry	E
Zeek, Gilbert	Rockaway Presbyterian Church Cemetery	27th NJ Vol.	L
Zeek, Thomas A.	Stanhope Cemetery	1st NJ Cavalry	E
Zellers, George W.	Pleasant Grove Cemetery (Chester Twp.)	38th NY Heavy Artillery	H
Zindle, Joseph	Rockaway Presbyterian Church Cemetery	11th NJ	E

Select Bibliography

General History

Foote, Shelby. *The Civil War: A Narrative*. New York: Vintage Books, 1986.

McPherson, James. *Battle Cry of Freedom*. New York: Ballantine Books, 1988.

Nevins, Allan. *The War For the Union*. 4 vols. New York: Charles Scribner & Sons, 1971.

The Mexican War

Johannsen, Robert W. *To the Halls of Montezumas: The Mexican War in the American Imagination*. New York: Oxford University Press, 1985.

Weems, John Edward. *To Conquer a Peace: The War Between the United States and Mexico*. College Station: Texas A&M University Press, 1974.

New Jersey and the Civil War

Bilby, Joseph C. *Forgotten Warriors: New Jersey's African American Soldiers in the Civil War*. Hightstone, N.J.: Longstreet House, 1993.

_____. *Three Rousing Cheers: A History of the Fifteenth New Jersey from Flemington to Appomattox*. Hightstown, N.J.: Longstreet House, 1993.

Chadwick, Bruce. *Brother Against Brother: The Lost Civil War Diary of Edmund D. Halsey*. New York: Carol Publishing Group, 1997.

Durkin, Joseph T., ed. *Confederate Chaplain, A War Journal*, [diary of the Rev. James Sheeran, a Catholic chaplain in the Confederate Army who later pastored the Church of the Assumption in Morristown, N.J.] Milwaukee: Bruce Publishing Company, 1960.

Gillette, William. *Jersey Blue: Civil War Politics in New Jersey, 1854-1865*. New Brunswick, N.J.: Rutgers University Press, 1995.

Haines, Alanson A. *History of the Fifteenth Regiment, New Jersey Volunteers*. New York: Jenkins & Thomas, 1883. Reprint. Gaithersburg, Md.: Butternut Press, 1987.

Knapp, Charles M. *New Jersey Politics During the Period of the Civil War and Reconstruction*. Geneva, N.Y.: W. F. Humphrey, 1924.

Marbaker, Thomas B. *History of the Eleventh New Jersey Volunteers*. Trenton, N.J.: MacCrellish & Quigley Book and Job Printers, 1898. Reprint. Introduction by John W. Kuhl. Hightstown, N.J.: Longstreet House, 1990.

Miers, Earl Schenck. *New Jersey and the Civil War*, Vol. 2, New Jersey Historical Series. Princeton: Van Nostrand, 1965.

Siegel, Alan A., *For the Glory of the Union: Myth, Reality and the Media in Civil War New Jersey*. Rutherford, N.J.: Fairleigh Dickinson University Press, 1984.

Sinclair, Donald A., comp. *A Bibliography: New Jersey and the Civil War*, [a list of over 1,300 works including many published during the nineteenth century]. New

Brunswick, N.J.: Friends of the Rutgers University Library, 1968.

Styple, William B. and Fitzpatrick, John J., eds. *The Andersonville Diary and Memoirs of Charles Hopkins, 1st New Jersey Infantry*. Kearny, N.J.: Belle Grove Publishing Co., 1988.

Wright, William C. *The Secession Movement in the Middle Atlantic States*. Rutherford, N.J.: Fairleigh Dickinson University Press, 1973.

Memorializing the War

Piehler, G. Kurt. "The Divided Legacy of the Civil War." In *Remembering War the American Way, 1783-1993*. Washington. D.C.: Smithsonian Institution Press, 1995.

Index of Names

Green, Lewis O., 58
Grimes, Ann Elizabeth, 92
Grimes, Eliza Ann (Lizzy), 94, 99, 105, 100, 108
Grimes, James, 23
Grimes, John, 8-10, 22, 23, 24, 35, 92
Grimes, Josiah Quincy, 8, 92-112
Grimes, William (Willy), 95
Grimes, William H., 92
Guerin, Charles H., 96
Guerin, Silas, 96
Gunderman, Peter, 172

H. C. Pitney, 38
Haines, Alanson, 136, 142, 173, 174
Halet, 144
Hall, Charles, 172, 173
Halsey, Edmund D., 29, 135-174
Halsey, Joseph, 135, 141, 146
Halsey, S. S., 38
Halsey, Sam, 137
Halsey, Samuel Beach, 29, 135
Halsey, Thomas J., 186
Hamilton, Ellis, 158
Harrison, William Henry, 21n
Hart, O. H., 128
Hatfield, S. O., 31
Hathaway, James, 96
Headley, 79
Headley, S. F., 43
Hedges, Henry, 8
Henry, William, 160
Hicks, David E., 150
Hiler, James, 108
Hill, A. P., 125
Hill, John, 22, 23, 35, 41, 43, 83-87, 90
Hoagland, Mahlon, 29
Hooker, Joseph, 51, 58, 99, 105, 119-122, 133, 147, 148
Hopkins, Charles F., 8, 10, 22, 23, 175-181
Hopkins, Nathan, 8, 22, 23
Houston, Sam, 4
Howell, Virgil, 96, 145
Hunter, Alexander, 14
Husted, David, 166
Hutchinson, Henry, 106

Irving, D., 41

Jackson, Andrew, 4
Jackson, Claiborne Fox, 48n
Jackson, John W., 29
Jackson, Stephen J., 29
Jackson, Thomas J., (Stonewall), 57n, 106, 120, 126
Jenkins, George, 35
Jewett, David, 155
Johnson, Andrew, 183
Johnson, Edward, 160
Jones, 79
Justice, George C., 161

Kearny, Philip, 188
Keep, Henry, 20
Kelsey, William, 153
King, 35
Kitchell, Charles H., 31

Lathrop, Francis Stebbins, 8
Lathrop, William G., 22, 23
Layton, Hugh H., 96

Lee, Fitzhugh, 105
Lee, George W., 29
Lee, Robert E., 57n, 105, 106, 109, 120, 126, 148, 163
Lincoln, Abraham, 2, 32n, 39, 48n, 61, 66, 77, 97n, 105, 121, 143
Lindsley, Ira, 92, 108, 141, 150
Little, Theodore, 41, 43
Logan, Durastus B., 58
Logan, John A., 154, 183, 184
Longstreet, James, 141, 154
Lyon, Nathaniel, 48n, 49n
Lyons, Robert, 108

Mackenzie, 79
Mackenzie, Sandy, 118
McDavitt, John, 186
McMills, Condit James, 96
McCarty, Charles A., 29, 31
McCarty, John M., 29
McClellan, George B., 2, 54, 55, 57n, 71n, 77, 97, 97n, 99, 100, 140, 143, 145
McClusky, John, 57, 58
McFarland, Henry, 60
McGrath, Thomas B., 29
McPeak, Joan B., 57
Meade, George G., 147, 152, 154, 167
Meagher, T. F., 185
Meiss, John R., 170
Miller, 35
Miller, R. K., 58
Mills, Alfred, 38, 41
Milner, 87
Minie, Claude Etienne, 152
Mott, Gershom, 127
Mott, John, 29
Mott, John G., 29
Mott, N., 29
Mouder, John, 170
Mullery, Michael, 55
Myers, 87

Nichols, Ed, 58
Norris, Alex, 29
Norris, Charles B., 22, 23
Norris, D. C., 24

Ocobec, William, 58
Odell, Thomas, 58
Olden, Charles S., 47, 61, 119
Oliver, William, 96
Olmstead, 79
O'Neil, James, 57

Page, George Shepard, 185
Parker, Joel, 61, 62
Parrish, William F., 108
Paul, Charles R., 157, 171
Peer, Francis, 29
Peer, George Wesley, 56
Peer, Jacob, 56
Peer, Ralston, 57
Penrose, William, 156-158, 160, 170, 171
Perrine, 85
Pettigrew, Wilson, 57
Piatt, Abraham S., 149
Pickett, George E., 152
Pierce, Franklin, 14n
Pierpoint, Francis Harrison, 72, 74

Morris County Board of Chosen Freeholders, 1998

Frank J. Druetzler,
  Director
Douglas R. Cabana,
  Deputy Director
Joan Bramhall
John Eckert
John M. Fox
Cecilia G. Laureys
John J. Murphy

Morris County Heritage Commission

P.O. Box 900, Morristown, NJ
07963-0900
(Office in the Morris County
Cultural Center,
300 Mendham Road,
Morris Township)
Tel: (973) 829-8117, 829-8114

Nancy B. Knapp, Chairman
Maria W. Fenton, Vice-Chairman
Marie L. Moore, Secretary
David R. Stivers, Treasurer
Frances D. Pingeon, County Historian
Margaret J. Cushing
Arline F. Dempsey
Ruth R. Silberman
Richard C. Simon
Mary L. Chalfant, Honorary Member